Madeleine Deese grew up figure skating and the culmination of her career was traveling and touring with a well-known skating organization on five continents for a decade. She then went on to become a nurse and eventually a nurse anesthetist. She has been published in poetry and is currently living in NC.

Dedicated to my father and fellow writer, Nelson Blish; my mother, Debra Blish, for all the early morning training sessions and editing assistance; and my patient husband, Ken Deese.

Madeleine Deese

LIFE ON ICE

AUSTIN MACAULEY PUBLISHERS

LONDON * CAMBRIDGE * NEW YORK * SHARJAH

Ordering Information
Quantity sales: Special discounts are available on quantity purchases by corporations, associations, and others. For details, contact the publisher at the address below.

Publisher's Cataloging-in-Publication data
Deese, Madeleine
Life on Ice

ISBN 9781685629151 (Paperback)
ISBN 9781685629175 (ePub e-book)
ISBN 9781685629168 (Audiobook)

Library of Congress Control Number: 2023917668

www.austinmacauley.com/us

First Published 2024
Austin Macauley Publishers LLC
40 Wall Street, 33rd Floor, Suite 3302
New York, NY 10005
USA

mail-usa@austinmacauley.com
+1 (646) 5125767

Table of Contents

Foreword

This novel is based on true events as I remember them. The names of people, places, and businesses have been changed. These are my thoughts and memories and may not align with anyone else's. With the gossip I give, dear readers, please remember my life is not without fault. However, she who writes history, makes history, and I write my tale in rose-tinted glasses as I see fit.

Tour Years

Toys on Ice: 2001–2004

Under Water Fantasy on Ice: 2004–2009

Holiday Celebrations on Ice: 2009–2011

Prologue

There seems to be so many dramatic, exciting, unusual, and sometimes upsetting memories, that many of my most intriguing flashbacks are just a blur as I speed by, making new recollections. I know I am not alone, there are others who have shared this lifestyle and have equally great past exploits filling their lives. I have jotted down some of my experiences before they disappear in the review mirror of forgetfulness.

My parents moved to Houston, TX, when I was five years old. We went to the Galleria. It was three enormous buildings, that took up several city blocks of upscale shopping and each building was three stories tall. In the center of it all, on the ground level, was an ice rink. As I looked down, I saw skaters jumping and spinning. I grabbed at my mom's coat and tugged, "Mommy, I want to do that."

She replied, as mothers often do, "That's nice, dear." We went home, and she hoped I would forget about it. A futile wish! I followed her around the house saying I wanted to skate until she finally took me to the ice rink to start private lessons.

Skating, I was frequently reminded, is the second most expensive sport in America; first is horseback riding. I marched, and marched, and marched on the ice. I refused to glide, which is the logical progression, and continued marching for a year. Yes, obviously I was a protégé; I continued to walk on the ice for a whole year.

Mom said, "If you don't glide, we're going to quit!" So, I glided. After that, my progress escalated at a staggering rate until puberty and a growth spurt of eight inches in two years.

My two favorite things about skating were jumping and exhibitions. My coaches could never get me to work on spins or posture. The more my mom tried to correct my posture, the worse it got. Defiance? Possibly. The Galleria was the perfect place to learn to perform with its unique setup of three stories of shoppers watching you. Every hour during public sessions, there was a sign-up to skate after the ice cut for anyone who wanted to perform. Most shoppers would stop what they were doing and watch. That was my favorite time.

I never was one for the judges, I am sure they are fine people, but for me it was the audience. If my friends were there or we had a large crowd, I was always at my best.

When I was about ten, I was interviewed on TV after a competition. They asked what my goals were in skating; did I want to go to the Olympics? Almost any child says they want to skate in the Olympics, but not me. I told them I wanted to perform at the Summit. The Summit was a new arena that had just opened, and the Houston hockey team played there. The higher-level skaters were sometimes selected to skate an exhibition for the hockey game's intermission. I did not want to go to the Olympics; I wanted to perform for the crowd; which should have been a sign.

I achieved that goal at thirteen. I skated a Christmas time themed performance to Mannheim Steamroller. The crowd went nuts and people were screaming my name. When I joined my parents in the stands, people waved, said hello, and whispered about me as I went by. It was an intoxicating high. I was lucky enough to return and perform at the original scene of inspiration in a professional capacity my first year on tour in 2021 before the Summit was converted to a church.

I continued as an amateur skater, fighting on, for many more years until I was twenty. But I always skated my best when friends watched. I would ignore the judges and wink at my friends, which they told me was disturbing and I should stop. More than once, I was told by the judges that my choreography, music choice, or style was just too different or strange. I thought I was cutting edge, but what did I know? I was a wild card, I wasn't consistent, and neither was my confidence.

At my last amateur competition, North Atlantics Regionals, there was a last-minute buy-in, the automatic promotion of a competitor to the next round. This means that because of the skater's international competition status, he or she was guaranteed a position at Mid Atlantics, which was the next level of competition. Since they took the top five instead of just the top four, I was able to compete. I skated my best with two triples and came in sixth. The girl in fifth did no triples. This was before the Olympic scandal and changes in the judging system, which I believe has created other problems and hasn't fixed much.

I looked around at all the girls that had now moved up to senior ladies, all my friends my age were gone, and I was the geriatric senior lady. I smiled, no tears this time as I left saying, "I'm going pro, see yah!"

Everyone laughed at the twenty-year-old veteran and said they would see me next year; I just shook my head and said my goodbyes. I was not sorry to leave behind the toils of training and simultaneously going to college. My family and friends who had supported a lifetime of ice skating encouraged my decision to move on. The next day, I landed my one and only triple Lutz, and that was it. Six months later, I graduated from community college and Family Fun on Ice called me back.

Chapter 1
The Audition

This chapter should actually be called Auditions, plural. The first time I auditioned for Family Fun on Ice was with the Snow Princess show in Rochester, NY. There were about seven nervous girls at the Blue Cross Arena. We started off showing basic skills by doing exercises together demonstrating our ability to follow choreography and work with one another and finally we skated on our own to show off our jumping and spinning capability.

Afterward, the performance director, or PD, took us aside one by one and spoke about what we could improve on for future auditions. When it was my turn, she sat me down and said, "At first, I didn't think you could skate. Your basic skills are terrible. But then, we let you free skate and you blew me away!" She also told me to work on stopping on the left foot. I thought, do they really need to stop on their left foot? Later I found out why.

At the time, I was teaching learn to skate on the weekends and attending Monroe Community College. I figured since I had to learn to stop on my left, all my little recruits, I mean, students would learn to stop on both feet too. I think it helped all of us.

One day, I went to skate between college classes because performers for the ice show Jocks & Dolls were skating at my ice rink. I was excited to skate with other performers but what really made me cut classes was skating with a former men's Olympian who asked me if it was always this cold. My home arena is one of the coldest ice surfaces I've ever glided on. I took down the contact information for the show and followed it to Buffalo, NY, to audition. I still couldn't stop on my left foot, but there were several skaters that stayed to watch and cheer me on.

The winter of 1999, I went to the Lake Placid NY State games. I was competing with long-time skating rivals who were also friends about my age.

They stopped me before my warmup and each of them demonstrated all the different left foot stops, perfectly. Apparently, word got around. Well, maybe I couldn't stop on my left foot, but I became NY State Women's Champion!

During this time, I regularly emailed and checked in with my contact at Family Fun on Ice. My last audition was with A Magical Adventure on ice. I was warming up and a woman called me over to the side. I thought it was the performance director. She introduced herself and after staring blankly at her, she explained, "I'm the person you are always emailing." Oops, one more way for me to leave a lasting impression.

It was the usual audition process, but this time I was able to demonstrate stops on my left foot. Clearly, I was winning. Toward the end of the audition, we were told to skate around in a circle and act out different things. The first was to act like a dog. I was quite embarrassed to act like a dog, but it wasn't too difficult. Another was to be a princess. My first thoughts of a princess were of snotty little girls, being waited on hand and foot. So, I proceeded to do this and looked around to see everyone else's versions of a princess, which happened to be dignified and beautiful, a typical storybook princess. This made me think I had it all wrong, so I changed my MO to pretty princess. To be honest, the whole thing made me feel very self-conscious and silly. Afterward, my email pen pal told me congratulations on stopping on my left foot, finally some recognition.

For the record, in my first show, we had a left foot stop every show at the end of a flying pinwheel. For the first year and a half, I stopped on my right, until I got caught.

The skating community can be an exceedingly small world, and it gets tinier when you join a skating company like Family Fun on Ice. The men's line captain on A Magical Adventure on Ice was Bart. I recognized him from when I trained one summer in Indianapolis. When I got home, I found an old picture of all of us from that summer of 1994. I sent it to my email pal and asked if she would pass the photo on to Bart. It still makes me smile and yet cringe to think how microscopic the skating world is.

I never heard back from Bart. I chalked it up to being written off as stalker material. Bart and I met up years later after I was hired into the Family Fun on Ice (spoiler alert, I finally got in). We reminisced about training away from home in the nineties and stalker status changed to coworker. I tend to be a shy person by nature until I am familiar with my surroundings and the people who populate them. I also have an irrational phone phobia. I just don't like to talk on the phone. I am working on getting over this phobia, but sometimes I am on the phone with an acquaintance and my brain goes on the fritz, and I can't think of anything to say. Embarrassingly, I should be talking, but am at a loss for words. Cue awkward silence. Thank goodness for the rise of texting.

Out of character, but fueled by desire, I emailed, called, and snail mailed the Director of Talent, who oversees hiring. I did this about once a month, every month for a year and a half, new resumes, new videos, and new photos. The video was like a game of add on. I'd attach my latest competition, program, or holiday show to the video, so it just kept getting longer. In the end, I think I might have been hired just to stop the avalanche of mail they received. That and they needed a 5'6" girl. Unless you have a particular look or special talent, besides ice skating, you are a cog in a wheel; one of a hundred, replaceable, moving parts. It's a lot like filling out an order request for chorus skaters. We need three five-footers and one five-sixer.

Chapter 2
The In-Between

When I was finally hired for Family Fun on Ice, the Director of Talent told me I was going to Toys on Ice, which would be the new show and would tour East Coast, USA. I emailed back and asked if I could start overseas. My audacity was amazing; a new hire, having no ideas about seniority or show mannerisms, and already asking for favors, especially considering how long it had taken me to get hired. She responded that for a new hire, they thought it was best to start in the States. What I wanted more than anything when I joined this company was to travel abroad. Instead, I spent the next five touring seasons in the USA. But I was still not done asking for favors.

Having won the NY state games at the beginning of 2001, I qualified to go to the first ever American State Games. The problem was it overlapped when I would be starting Family Fun on Ice. I incorrectly assumed you could just ask for leave of absence. Barely hired and before I had even left for the tour, I asked the Director of Talent if I could leave for a competition. She said I couldn't miss work time, but there might be a later starting show she could put me with. I saw my precious opportunity to join the company, after multiple auditions and countless dollars lost in VHS tapes and shipping, slipping away so I said that's okay and joined Toys on Ice.

The guidance counselors at my college changed every time I walked through the rotating door. They helped me select classes each semester. I had a conference halfway through my last semester to see about graduating with a Liberal Arts associate degree. I wanted to tie up loose ends as I had already accepted my job with Family Fun on Ice and would be starting at the end of June. My counselor surprised me saying I couldn't graduate as I was one class short, about 3 credits. Obviously, I was upset. I wanted to leave with the tour, and I wanted my associate degree. My fear was that by the time I returned to college, my collection of credits would not be accepted, or the college of my choosing would go shopping through my credits and keep what they wanted. A two-year degree is a package deal, take it or leave it.

Never one to take no for an answer, I discovered you could take a test for certain classes and if you passed, you received credit for that class. There weren't many appealing choices. My Dad was an attorney and I had questioned being an attorney. His significant other taught Business Law 2 at another college. I signed up and set my test date in May for Business Law 2. I decided law was not for me; the language alone ran you in circles and tied itself in knots. The night before the test, I went online to take some pretest Questions: 6 out of 12 questions were on Business Law 1. I tried to cram, but it was futile. I checked the next available test date, and it was after I'd be gone. It was a pass or fail exam and I passed by one question. I'm sure there was a puddle of sweat in my testing chair when I exited the building. This graduation was certainly different than high school, we all hit a beach ball around while the important speeches went on. I graduated with a 3.9 average, cursing my one A minus. And then finally, it was off to the ice show!

But how does one pack for ten months of differing weather, and only two suitcases at 70lbs each and two carry-ons? I needed at least one suitcase for shoes; what's a girl to do? If I could not accessorize, they, whoever they are, might cancel my extra X-chromosome.

Chapter 3
Packing

I thought 70 lbs. per bag was tough. But like everything else, 70 pounds per checked bag became a luxury when it went down to 50 lbs. Sometimes the company had to make other arrangements to ship our bags, or we would hide them in the trailers.

I began the packing process by picking out all my favorite clothes, which is an arduous task for any woman, but an even bigger challenge for me as I had two rooms full of clothes. Next, I divided the pile into winter and summer. The pile was getting a bit smaller, but I still had to take out all the clothes I didn't need, like a fuzzy shag carpet top that went with a slinky skirt and could only be worn during in between seasons like fall and I'm not sure what occasion would call for this particular combination. There was a surprising amount of these unnecessary clothes, followed by removal of all the 'maybe' piles.

I had to make sure it all fit. For suitcase one I had all the expendables unzipped, and I was sitting on my suitcase, so, of course, it fit. Next, I brought the scale up to my room, weighed myself, and then weighed again attempting to hold my 70-pound bag by the strap. Eventually, I wised up and invested in a luggage weigher; not a muscle-bound big guy to carry my bag, just a digital scale. On my welcome letter, it had said something about the dimensions of the bag, so I found measuring tape and measured. Two days later, suitcase one was done.

Suitcase two was filled with shoes, sandals, sneakers, boots, walking shoes, dressy shoes, casual dressy shoes, and one extra pair of impractical shoes that I did not think I could live without. Toiletries comprised a huge part of suitcase two, also the jewelry, perfume, make-up, vitamins, any sort of medicine I'd need, and hair products. I lucked out on this one since, with a pixie cut my hair was only about three inches long.

Needless to say, after packing all the female accessories and unmentionables, I was annoyed with men. All they had in their suitcase were a few pairs of socks, jocks, and some t-shirts, almost nothing to pack.

Next were electronic cords, their devices, books, this was prekindle days, and miscellaneous things to keep me entertained. The old 8 lb. laptop was saved for my back. Any room left in suitcase two was devoted to the impractical. I like to play the piano and know that sometimes in a hidden corner of a hotel, there is a piano, so I brought six big piano books with me. How do I know about hidden pianos? Well, I have gotten in trouble a time or two for playing piano after hours in a hotel bar or during a movie shoot in Rochester.

On the set of an independent film in Rochester, NY, I found an old, abandoned piano tucked behind the stairwell. When you see a piano, you must play the piano. I did not think about me as the stand in for the leading lady, and I sat down and started playing The Entertainer, the song that is heard from every ice cream truck throughout childhood memory. That was not the mood they were looking for on the production set and I was severely shushed. Some scenes were at an old church, and I crawled up in the bell tower and rang the bells. I am surprised I kept my job that summer.

What you actually need to live out of your suitcase is quite different than what you'd like to have in your suitcase. My carry on was another strategy session. Remember the short-lived phenomena of mini disks? I couldn't travel with a giant case of CDs so, I spent hundreds of dollars and thousands of hours recording all my must-have music from CDs to mini disks to travel with. Later I ended up travelling with a giant CD case because I could not live without my entire DVD collection.

Digital media developed over the course of my touring career, making things much smaller and lighter in weight. Looking back now I don't know how I got a full winter and summer wardrobe into my suitcase. Having a larger suitcase does not help. When you see any empty space you just need to fill it. In Las Vegas, my second year on tour, we found "big green", it was a suitcase big enough to put a full-grown man inside and wheel around. When "big green" was filled, it could weigh anywhere from 120–200 lbs. So, size didn't really help matters.

On tour, I learned we could have trunks. It was an early 8 am on our only day off and I called Pete and Carrie who oversaw the trunks. I woke them up and asked what the dimensions were for a trunk. I wasn't given specific dimensions and was standing in front of a wall of Tupperware trunks. I'm a girl in her twenties who likes clothes, what can I say, I went for the biggest, back breaking one.

The company allows one trunk on state tours and travels the container on the trucks. The trunk is available every four weeks, and you can put whatever you want in it. At the end of your career with Family Fun on Ice, the company will mail your trunk home for you. This is a one-time offer. If you quit and come back and have used the trunk mail home credit you don't get another one. So, I stuffed all my cold weather clothes, shoes, and coats into my trunk and forgot about it until winter. This prompted me to immediately go out and buy more summer clothes, I'm pretty sure, I have a clothing addiction; Dad's medical diagnosis is "indumentis proclivitas" or a clothing shop acholic.

We spent the first six weeks of a new show's life, in Lakeland, FL doing rehearsals and opening performances. Our hotel had a microwave and a small fridge. Many hotels do not have these things. Actually, I found cheaper hotels have more kitchen utilities, which is better for our road way of life. I went to the grocery store and stared with new eyes. I have grocery shopped before, but never solely for myself. And what was I to cook with? Or eat on? Or eat with? It had never occurred to me when packing that I also needed to pack an entire kitchen. How do you fit an entire kitchen into an already full, suitcase? And where do you cook in a small hotel room? Build a fire in the waste basket?

Chapter 4
The Problem with Eating

At Walgreen's, I bought my first electric burner with low, medium, and high settings. I 'borrowed' a fork, knife, and spoon from our first hotel. I traveled with salt and pepper, so no room for anything fancy. At Wally World, I bought one plastic plate, a bowl, and a pot. After all, a good home-cooked meal is priceless.

My mother, trying to help matters, sent recipes and a huge bag full of every spice a cook, with a full kitchen, could ever need. I appreciated the sentiment, but half the written labels rubbed off, and I could not identify anything but paprika. Airport security always looked suspicious and most recipes required an oven, which definitely does not fit in my suitcase.

Traveling between the US and Canada, the border patrol would make us remove our luggage and x-ray it. My Japanese friend traveled with many foreign spices that can't be found in the States. They took my friend's spice bag out and wanted to know the exact contents. She spoke English quite well but couldn't name her spices. She could give them full detail in Japanese, so they made her throw away her imported cooking spices.

Where to pack cooking stuff? Suitcase two got a makeover. A nice burner always seemed to weigh at least 5lbs, that's a lot of extra poundage. I also quickly learned that I needed a sharp knife for cutting tough food. I just threw it in the zip lock with the rest of my utensils. Bad idea. It knifed through the bag, jabbed holes in anything it could find, and attempted to mutilate my suitcase. I had to buy an expensive knife cover just to muzzle it. I realized I had no use for regular knives; a sharp one spreads butter and cuts. So out with all the old knives.

You would think that with a burner and pot there would be endless cooking possibilities, right? There could have been, but many hotels had no refrigerator.

That was a difficult lesson. I filled up garbage cans with ice and put small, refrigerated items in them. They became waterlogged and sank to the bottom. Okay so I need zip lock baggies; which would keep them afloat like little ships on the surface until I could change the ice. It was usually just lunch meat, cheese and a few other things that had to be kept cold and as long as they remained cool, they were usually okay. I certainly didn't want to give anyone dysentery, especially me.

Sometimes I ran into the problem of out of order ice machines or the kind that limited the amount of ice. Then the makeshift garbage fridge is just a garbage can full of groceries. The most annoying lesson with my little waste basket fridge was that the house keepers saw my refrigerator as a garbage can and threw my groceries away. Or did they? Maids gotta eat too. Then I got clever and started taping notes over the garbage can, Groceries, DO NOT THROW AWAY! Sometimes this worked, but not often.

The easiest option was to eat out; it is also the most costly. The first-year salary, on probation, minus hotel and NY tax doesn't leave much cash flow. Fast food was always an easy solution, but it was more expensive than buying groceries and not as healthy. Often, we stayed downtown in the touring city. This is wonderful, except city centers close down by five or six at night. Typically, we would eat after the show, at nine or ten. Without a fridge, this left little option but to order pizza or room service.

Everyone eats on the road differently. I eat; breakfast around noon, depending how late I was out the night before, lunch at three-ish and dinner at ten, not your typical standard of living, but it worked for me.

After solving the fridge dilemma, where do you cook in your room with two beds and four enormous suitcases? Few hotels had kitchenettes; this left the desk, eating spaghetti or sloppy-joes right next to your expensive laptops, or the bathroom. People often cringe when I tell them I cooked in the bathroom; it's not like I cooked while sitting on the toilet, but I'm sure that was the image they concocted. Sometimes there was a large area adjacent to the sink suitable for cooking. This also meant that in tight quarters you cleaned up your mess immediately after you are done.

Being a neat roommate was priceless when selecting your roommate from a broader group. Rooming rotations were made several months in advance. If not, you were left with the reject roommate that no one wanted, it could make that week one of torture. The roommate reject could be smelly and bad socks are the worst, they infect the entire room. After a week your sense of smell dies, and you stink by association. Other times a roommate might be messy or encroach on your increasingly small territory. Or they might like to borrow your stuff, eat your food, and drink your beer. This bothered me the most when they looked better than I did in my clothes.

Often there was the odd man out. The show could not make men and women room together unless they chose to. So, some ran the risk of playing the odds for last man standing and a private room. The risk with putting your name up with no one next to it, is that an undesirable might sign next to you and then you're stuck.

Once Edward and I started dating we roomed together almost exclusively. Occasionally, it was fun to room with a girlfriend. On one of the rotations Edward ended up with Blake. A nice enough fellow but he could not spell hygienic, let alone practice it. Bathing was not Blake's favorite activity.

Blake often smelled of ass and cinnamon. The cinnamon came from a tiny candle he lit in the room hoping to eradicate all the funky smells. He loved to partake in our drinking excursions, but this usually impaired his aim when he arrived back at the hotel. You would think a target the size of a toilet would be hard to miss, but not for Blake. His favorite drunk game after wearing the contents of the missed toilet was to chase people down and hug them! Any room coupled with men's sweaty shoes and socks has a unique smell all its own, but Edward and Blake's room took that funk to a whole new level. I went to see Edward; I knocked on the door but refused to enter. I was bowled over by the disgusting smell that greeted me standing in the hallway. That was the last time we roomed with other people.

When I arrived, Toys on Ice was the new show and we had six weeks of rehearsals. The days were long, starting at eight or nine and going until five or later. This sounds like an average workday, but when it requires standing and skating on ice skates all day, it's a painful experience. We had an hour and fifteen minutes for lunch and our hotel was right next door. I had more energy than I knew what to do with, so I ran back to the hotel, inhaled my favorite quick meal of ramen noodles with butter and salt, and then ran back to the building to skate for thirty minutes. However, this wasn't the full extent of my day. I would skate during lunch, and after our workday I would jog a mile to the gym, work out, come back to the arena, skate some more, and stay up until all hours partying only to rise, rinse and repeat.

It was no wonder I lost so much weight during rehearsals. Now, the mere thought of such a day makes me want to take a nap. I had always been a set 120 pounds at 5'6". During our six weeks of putting the show together I dropped to 114lbs. The running joke when I turned sideways was, "Where's Maddie?"

There are standards that must be observed. We had to wear tight spandex costumes and appeal to an audience. No one wants to see a fat fish in spandex. The Performance Director (PD) weighed each of us every other week on Saturdays before the first show. After observing our first three weigh-ins, she set an eight-pound range. I was still at 114 lbs., and she told me I looked fine but that I shouldn't lose any more weight and my range was 114 to 122. I settled into tour life, gained back my normal weight plus a little extra drinking weight and was now 125lbs. The PD took me aside while was I was eating a bagel dripping with butter and told me, "You look healthy; I'm going to change your range to, 120–128." This was all right by me. Mexico, tequila, stress, relationship blues, and Montezuma's revenge or the threat of it, dropped me back down to 116 pounds. I didn't like being this thin and the PD was concerned. When we got to the West Coast, I bounced back to normal weight and stayed there for about two years.

Weight problems followed me to a new show two years later. Aerialist training, using silks like cirque-du-soleil to wind myself up and drop down the silks thirty feet, gave me upper body strength I'd never had. When I went to Underwater Fantasy on Ice, I gained five pounds in newly acquired muscle and went up one t-shirt size.

The PD for Under Water Fantasy was new to his job. Right before Christmas break, he put a dozen names in yellow marker on the board. As these performers went to see him, their names were crossed off. Everyone quickly realized that these names were having weight talks. I was pulled into his office, and he showed me a chart of all my weigh-ins. He had my range as 119–127. I had pretty consistently been around 129. I told him that I had new muscles from aerial training. He told me he just wanted me to be aware of it since we were going on Holiday break and there would be lots of goodies to eat at home. I promptly left his office and ate a piece of pizza that the promoters had given us, "No guilt trip here."

My friends were shocked when I told them I'd had a weight talk. Even at that weight and height, I was still slim and trim. I dropped some weight six months later because I was back in Mexico. The weight yo-yoed back up, another talk, moved my range up to 128, and I started to jump rope. I did about twelve shows a week, yoga every day, and climbing silk but now I must jump rope to lose some weight?

One easy way to avoid eating was at company meals. If it was a three-show day, the company fed you one dinner meal between the second and third show. Sounds great, but the chicken was always dry and the pasta sauce always bland. There was not enough salt to fix that pasta sauce. The joke was: What's for company meal? It was always three show chicken and pasta. There was usually a secondary dish that was different but equally bland and a bit of sad salad on the side. I don't know how each city communicated the menu and blandness to each other, but they always did. The one light at the end of the tunnel was that there were always cookies. Not so good for my weigh-ins but they made a fine dinner.

When I finally made it to Japan, the performance director pulled me aside again and told me, "You look good, so I'm going to move your range up to 129." That's nice but at that time, I was repeatedly weighing in at 130 pounds. The line up for biweekly weigh-ins on Saturday was amusing, all the girls had on as little as possible, and the guys had weights in their pockets!

Weight ranges and weigh-ins are there to keep us healthy and they fulfill a role even though I don't like them. I have heard show tales about old school performance directors when things were stricter. They lived by the adage you are this tall so you must weigh this much. God help you if you were on that show. The cabbage soup diet for you, plus an eating disorder free of charge. I saw one girl from such a show sniffing a chocolate wrapper. Luckily, a healthy guilt trip about food, body image issues, and OCD about exercise are all that I came away with.

Chapter 5
The Lonely Hour

I remember being awakened at 4am each morning by Mom. I think this ritual started about age six or seven. Freezing cold I'd jump in the shower. Drag my little brother out of bed to shower with me. He didn't have to be up for another two hours but, because I was cold, I wanted to share my misery. All I had time for was a 5-minute shower. Brush the teeth before breakfast because I could eat in the car to save time. By 4:15 in the car and flying through empty Houston streets, catching air off the railroad tracks as Mom drove. Every morning I got a five alive fruit juice. The name on the box amused me because it was almost five, but I was not alive yet. And on some special mornings I got McDonald's breakfasts. Skates on and skating by 05:00 am.

After skating practice, I would change in the car as my coach drove me to school. Trying to avoid a Houston traffic spotting as I put on my school uniform. Once or maybe twice I forgot my uniform. The first time the school receptionist took pity on me and gave me lost and found uniform pieces, a patch work myriad, to get me through the day. The last time I forgot my uniform I was forced to wear my hot pink and purple, spandex skating dress and tights all day while all the other Catholic school girls made fun of me. As I said, that was the last time, I forgot my uniform.

Luckily, these nuns would not smack my knuckles with rulers. In fact, with both parents working, I would be the last kid standing on the playground. I loved it, all the extra play time. Sometimes the nuns would take me into their home on school campus and I had to stop playing and do homework.

I changed schools for middle school and was much closer to the skating rink. As if skating before school was not enough, now I would walk almost a mile back to the rink after school to skate some more. It was either that or get trapped at the YMCA until Mom or Dad could pick us up, I left my brother to this happy fate where he and his friends would get to play video games. I would do homework on the car ride home and at the dinner table, to bed by eight, and up before dawn the next day. This was the norm for me.

When I moved to Rochester, NY, I practiced mostly in the evenings. However, there were some Sunday early morning sessions to be had if five days a week wasn't enough. I both loved and hated these sessions. I remember leaving a friend's sleep over, where unlike the name implied, I'd had little sleep as I drove through the frosty, deserted roads of Upstate NY. The world was still asleep, the roads abandoned, and the eerie lights lining the highway looked like a runway to nowhere. I loved this lonely feeling. What I did not love was showing up to be locked out of the ice rink. No coach as promised showing up. Having to climb a snowy hill and pray that the window was unlocked. Wide awake and freezing my butt off I wasn't going to turn back now. My reward an ice rink all to myself.

There was always ice available at the college campus rink. Four sheets of ice begging to be skated on and yet empty. That lovely alone feeling in a freezing cold rink would creep into my bones. The arena wanted to charge me for ice time when no one else wanted it in the abandoned rink. I found a way to pry the back door open and had my own skating time. Then they started turning off half the lights, maybe to deter me? I just skated in the half darkness. Free ice time is free ice time. But that cold alone feeling always followed.

I liked my lonely hours.

Chapter 6
The Time of Your Life

I think I came on the road at the right time and the right age. For Toys on Ice, there were about seven new girls, but everyone else on the 36-skater cast were seasoned veterans. The veterans varied from 20 to 30 years of age. Added to the skaters were about 15 crew guys, 5 office staff, and 56 concessions vendors who sold all the toys, cotton candy, and accoutrement. The office staff consisted of a company manager, a tour business manager that took care of the budget, and a tour coordinator that booked travel arrangements and hotels along with other responsibilities. The fifteen or so crew members on most shows generally had two people for the wardrobe, two or three in the props department, two or three carpenters, two in charge of sound and about six electricians. That is a pretty big group to tote around the country. I was twenty, going on the big 21 when I joined the tour. They were pretty loose about "ID checks" in the local bars during rehearsals and I often got away by just being herded in with the group. I was extremely quiet, and people thought I was a little older.

I was more interested in sightseeing than in bar-hopping my first few years on the road. It became difficult to keep up with all the partying. Luckily, two weeks after rehearsals and Providence, RI solved that problem for me. Happy 21st Birthday at an overpriced Dave & Busters.

An understudy is a performer that plays a principle's role when needed. I was scheduled to go into my big understudy role the day after my 21st celebration. I talked to the performance director and asked if I could go in earlier that week. Her reply was, "Yes, but as an understudy, you must be prepared to go in at all times."

I felt like everyone's little kid sister as I was given advice on how to survive my big birthday night: lots of water, stick to one kind of drink, it is okay to say no to a drink, make them take the shot with you. I listened intently, but I have a hard time saying "no".

Despite all the good advice, light weight that I was I had seven different shots in twenty minutes. I signed my name on a paper after every shot. There was no difference in my signature because the alcohol had not been processed yet. A few moments after my seventh shot, all that booze ganged up on me. I was cut off from the bar as I loudly proclaimed Waverly as my best friend for bringing me bread and water. Security followed me around, and my body was like a 3D version of a slip and slide. Saying I had to be propped up in my chair would be understating the spectacle. I took quick sprints to the bathroom to throw up. Then I would cry while Jenny rubbed my back, and I would transform from a manic depressive to chipper and cheery until the next wave hit. Then it was rise and repeat. My signature next to the water I had to drink at the end of seven shots was illegible. Good thing we start with 100 billion brain cells because I killed a few that night.

Dad *called* me at 7 am the next morning, "Are you alive? Did you survive?"

That following day we had a schedule of three shows. Red eyed and feeling like I was wearing my skin inside out, I read the board when I got to the arena and I was in my big understudy again. Hard life lessons; always be prepared.

At intermission, I stood in the makeup room, hoping for a less painful, faster way to die than the one I had brought on myself. Later, when I was given my notes on my performance, they were surprisingly good. My first thought was, *now I am a real pro.*

Did I learn my lesson about drinking? Nope.

Note, any of you who think you recognize this family-oriented company remember the Company I was working for does not promote drinking or coming to work even with a slight hang over. However, we were basically a collage bus on wheels full of young people, and for many the first time away from home, so life happens. The consequence of being caught drunk was termination, not the CIA rubric, 'termination with extreme prejudice', but the end of a skating career none the less.

Chapter 7
Airborne

When I was a little girl, there was a local skating competition where I competed with another local girl. I was from the warm and sunny Galleria; she was from the frozen tundra of Sharpstown Ice Arena, where the competition was held. Coming out of the frozen tundra you were slapped in the face by the hot, humidity of Houston. In the wasteland that was a parking lot, there was only one tree behind the building. This poor excuse for a tree was kicked and stripped bare of all leaves and branches save one. Was this tree tortured into shape by angry little brothers trapped at the ice rink? This broken-off branch was smooth, worn and perfect for swinging from.

I had just won the competition; my local rival and I were swinging from the tree while our mothers became fast friends over margaritas. She complimented me on how big and high my jumps were. I arrogantly told her, "Some people say I was airborne." I didn't even fully understand the joke myself. I quickly got over myself when she won the next competition, and we were ever more best friends. She has no problem reminding me of that time.

Airborne or not, there is nothing so tiring as travel. It makes no sense that sitting on our butts for endless hours is exhausting. It is a little more understandable in tour life when we travel every week on one of our only days off. If we travel by bus, we leave Sunday night after the last show, usually between eight or nine at night. Earlier that morning we checked out of our rooms and put all our luggage into a Luggage Room.

These rooms were usually located anywhere but the ground floor, meaning we all had to stand in line and fight for the perpetually slow elevators both to load our suitcases into the luggage room and after, to take them to the lobby and then to the bus. With the weight, size, and amount of luggage we had, two people were lucky to fit on one elevator and the stairs were obviously not an option. Multiply by a 100 people on tour and timing is tricky.

The luggage was loaded into a tiny room. The order in which you brought down your belongings was reminiscent of a disorganized cattle call. The crew had to stash their suitcases in the luggage room first. This was because the crew had to load out after the show was done and the audience had left. They would be the last to leave the hotel. Next the concessions vendors would load their suitcases and extras into the room and finally all the skaters.

It was amazing the amount we could get into that room. Good luck that evening locating your luggage. Some never follow directions, which would mess up the sardine order of things. Then the late-to-arrive luggage would have to be removed so the rest of us could claim our suitcases and then return the extricated suitcases to the luggage room. The ever-present sense of urgency to load the bus was due in part to ensuring you had a drink and some food before the exceedingly long road trips.

Life on tour has made us deeply resentful of airport travel. The weight restriction on airlines changed a lot for us and led to major inconvenience. When I first joined tour, airline weight restriction allowed two checked suitcases at 70lbs per suitcase. One personal item, which includes a backpack, purse, or laptop bag, and a carry on. As you can imagine we all had a smaller rolling suitcase and a backpack, to travel with as much as possible. We would be ushered to stand in line at the ticket counter for what seemed like an eternity; being moved from one clerk to another because we were 'a group' but had to be checked in individually. About one hundred people all stood in a line for one clerk who meticulously weighed our lives stuffed into a suitcase while those in line would stand and stare.

We would take out our coats and wear them through the airport in summer just so our luggage was underweight. Because of the single file line, we had to arrive at the airport excessively early. We enviously watched normal passengers pass us by with the assistance of five customer service people while we had the one employee who was unhappy with her life and not afraid to let us know. We often got ugly stares from other travelers at our two huge suitcases, how badly I wanted to ask: Do you have to live out of your suitcase for ten months? Cooking equipment included? All your seasonal clothes? But instead, I behaved and just shook my head.

We all traveled together unless choosing to drive your own vehicle or the few caravan gypsies that had their own RVs. The company does not pay for the expense of traveling in your own car or trailer. Toys on Ice was the only show that I was on that had their own caravan. There were three trailers that circled up behind the building and we spent a lot of time there with a drink by a fire, true gypsy style. Many of the truck drivers would join us out back of the arena. Once they had pulled in the show trailers, there wasn't much to do until they hauled their trailers to the next city.

Seventy pounds still isn't as much as it sounds. Some of us were always over the limit. This would hold up the line while you unzipped the overburdened beast and tried to pick out the heaviest objects that could be crammed into back packs. The other option was trying to stuff it into someone else's lighter suitcase. This was followed by having to sit on the bag to close it again. Travel days were so tiring.

One airline day, I was told that I had an extra carry on, my backpack, my laptop and they said Trampy was an extra carry on. Trampy is a pillow sized ladybug, that I use to lay on during flights. She is also notorious for 'sleeping around' on travel days, hence her name. As I tried to stuff her into my suitcase, I notice that Brittany was allowed her two carry-ons and her Scooby-Doo pillow, but my gate keeper would hear no protests. Trampy almost got dissected once when an old man at the X-ray monitor thought the scissors in my backpack were inside Trampy. I made them send it through again before surgery.

Poor Trampy has been through a lot. She has been re-stuffed at least once and she takes a monthly shower in the washer and dryer. Right after the re-stuffing operation, she was bug-napped by a plotting little crew man who stuffed her into a triangle box for a week. When she came out, she was lumpy and so stretched so that the new stuffing was loose. When lent as a pillow on a travel day, I caught our French-Canadian drooling on her in his slumber. At a house party she went to, she tried to comfort my friend who was throwing up and she got puked on for her troubles. Whenever Trampy is out in any social capacity, if she likes you, and she likes everyone, she humps you in greeting. Adults stare at my travel companion and children gravitate toward it.

My third year on tour the airlines lowered the luggage weight to 50lbs. per suitcase and the company said, we do not expect you to live like this. The company tried to strike a deal with the airlines but to no avail. Sometimes the company had to make other arrangements to ship our bags, or we would hide them in trailers like stowaways; cramming for space and vying for favors to get them on board. So, for one year the company rented a truck when we had flights and our two faithful luggage guys would load up all the suitcases the day before the flight and our bags would greet us at the door of the next hotel. What a nice set up we all thought, no more checking bag issues, our lazy bags could gain a few un-noticed pounds. The only downside was when our bags got there after us, we would lose a whole day waiting for them to show up. The bags couldn't arrive and be left sitting alone outside for the curious.

The contract for fourth year I read and re-read the luggage part thinking that maybe we only had a 50 pounds luggage restriction for arrival and departure of tour. No. With a new contract, apparently, we would be asked to live with fifty pounds a bag. My clothes for all seasons weighed that much without toiletries, pots, pans, shoes, and everything else. I am amazed by our veteran friends, who have one big suitcase each, and one rather large backpack. Although it is easier to carry one pot and pan between two people. Amy, one of the one suitcase wonders, says she packs about a month before tour and looks through the stuff every other day asking herself if she will really wear that, and then removing it.

Initially we were required to travel with our skates on the bus with us. There have been multiple occasions when they have been left on the top shelf of the bus as it drives off to its next destination. Luggage guy, Edward, always did an idiot check and usually caught any tour goof ups. Thank goodness for luggage guys. Once we got wise many of us would squeeze our skates into our overflowing lock boxes that went on the trucks or beg a crew guy to store them in their crate. Our lock boxes were the size of half a gym locker and would travel with the trucks. These little lockers would usually hold our show make up, mirrors, and robes. On airport trips, since we could not carry our skates onto the planes, they were put into two trunks that went on the trailers with the rest of the show equipment and were driven to the next city. I'm always thankful that the guys and girls' skates were separated. The boys had stinky feet and it was a dank and dark environment perfect for spreading foot fungus.

Chapter 8
Travel Drunks

Our work environment is alcohol and drug-free. At least that's what the fine print says. What we do outside of work is our own prerogative unless you end up in the news for drunken misconduct and the company identified. Then you are confined to your room like a child and your garbage cans are checked for liquor bottles and drugs. This brings up some legal questions. We have random drug tests and if tested positive, you will be fired. This also extends to company transportation and PRs, where we interact with the media on the company's behalf.

All hundred or so of us usually travel together. Sometimes the concessions and the skater/crew/office staff are separated, but we're a big group and half the time people are wearing Family Fun on Ice memorabilia, identifying us to the world. We are supposed to uphold a wholesome, marketable image.

To add to the many, many complications of travel days are the travel day drunks. I don't mean the homeless, bums, but the ones that belong to us. Our lifestyle leads to very different schedules and habits. Many people on a morning flight would go to the bar, the only thing open, and start our morning off with a screwdriver, mimosa, or the even healthier Bloody-Mary.

Here, however, we slip into the gray areas. In between rest stops on the bus, we might have a beer, or grab a brew at the bar before we board the plane. So, for a drink or two, administration will just look the other way, or in some cases, join you. But it's those that go beyond a "few" or are still drunk from the night before and get out of control. Then we all get in trouble.

When I was in college, for nursing, I learned about the CAGE questionnaire. Ever felt the need to cut down? Yes. Has anyone annoyed you by criticizing your drinking? No, they're all drinking too. Have you ever felt guilty about drinking? Well not until this questionnaire. Ever had an eye-opener first thing in the morning? According to this questionnaire I might have a problem. If I have a problem, do I need to go to meetings?

One such airport travel day found a Russian skater sauced on our flight. He was being loud and unruly. He annoyed the businessmen in front of him who asked who he worked for. Unfortunately, he told them, and they wrote a complaint. That was the last we saw of that Russian skater. It was not his first offence. Public image, when related to Family Fun on Ice is top priority.

The same flight saw two crew guys yelling across the whole plane at the top of their lungs, using profanities, about the last night's events and a girl. Both were called into the office opening night and put on suspension for a week with no pay. The suspension held them in suspense as they waited a week to learn if they would lose their jobs. One gave his two weeks' notice and they both came back to work on Sunday.

I do have to thank one of our drunk Russians on our exodus from Mexico. After a long load out for the crew and a long night of celebrating, Edward and I missed our alarm clock going off. We woke up to the maid opening our door. I'm running around in a naked panic throwing stuff in a suitcase. We managed to pull it together and get ourselves into a cab. We no longer had any pesos since we had exchanged or spent them the night before and at this time Mexican taxis did not take credit cards.

A quick stop at the ATM and we were off to the airport. I was close to tears, and Edward was coming up with plans B, C, and D to get out of the country. He strategized that we could take a bus to the border that was not far from our next performing city. Luckily, we jetted through check in and security. We only made our flight because, a drunk and disorderly Russian had delayed take off. Thank you drunk Russian!

Once a plane was delayed because of an anaphylactic peanut allergy. Since one of our skaters was deathly allergic to peanuts, they had to discard all the killer snacks and circulate the air to make sure there was no trace of the menacing nuts.

In another incident, a French Canadian had passed out on the airport floor after a late night of partying. In 2011, on our first flight post 9–11, many flights had been transferred, changed, delayed, or rerouted. He was sleeping on someone's new coat and the owner was not happy about him christening the coat with drool. So, she whipped out her handy permanent marker (never travel without one) and proceeded to draw a penis on his face. Then she strategically placed French fries all over him. He was not happy when his wake-up call came.

Frenchie had many travel issues. One travel day we had a two-hour bus trip to LAX and then a flight. The bus had to leave on time, and no one ever wants to pay for a two-hour taxi ride. The night before Frenchie had consumed so much that he passed out in the elevators where the hotel staff found him. They called an ambulance because they could not find a pulse. He woke up in the early morning hours still drunk and escaped the hospital. He crashed in the tour coordinator's (TC) room, hospital dressing gown and all. The next morning the TC went out of her way and loosely packed his belongings, and had the luggage held behind the front desk. We were all on the bus ready to leave and there was no Frenchie. Edward and Martin ran back to the hotel, called his room multiple times, went up and banged on the door. There was no response, and the alarm clock could be heard going off inside. They begged the hotel for a room key.

Meanwhile, I was on the bus panicking because the TC was ready to leave anyone not on the bus behind, which included my boyfriend, one of the nice guys trying to find Frenchie. They finally got into his room to find him passed out, naked on the bed. They must have dressed him, and then fireman carried him to the bus. We gave him feeble applause as he got on the bus.

One drunken night, Frenchie knocked on what he thought was a hotel door, turns out it was a government building, and he broke a window. He used his one phone call for Edward, "Dude, I'm in jail!" Unfortunately, that was last call for our French Canadian, he had overslept and overstepped one to many times.

Some of the more tragic gray areas happen by accident. A friend on the crew had too much to drink one night out. He had an early morning publicity and was not sober. He was called into the office, his alcohol level was tested, and he was gone.

One back flip too many found a pro with a mild head injury, but the EMTs smelled alcohol. This resulted in no more back flips for our company. This pro went on to work for a more liberal European skating company that served drinks at the backstage coffee stand during intermission of the show.

The company policy of no drinking on company transportation also applied to the buses. When I first joined Family Fun on Ice, the rule was loosely overlooked with ease, and the skaters at the back of the bus partied it up, and sometimes played music or cards. At the beginning of my tour career, there was the unspoken bus designations of loud bus and quiet bus. The quiet bus was usually the first bus, self-explanatory. The loud bus would often have beverages disguised in water bottles, games, movies, and in the early days a boom box in the back. Because of complaints from both drivers and cast the company became stricter on enforcing the no alcohol rules.

One night on a long bus trip, one bus broke down. They piled everyone onto the remaining bus at two am and continued our trip to the hotel in the next city. The driver and one of the lucky luggage guys had to stay behind until the bus was repaired. Edward was the lucky winner and went above and beyond by staying with the bus driver and the extra luggage on the broken-down bus. His nap attempts were thwarted when the bus driver asked him to stay awake and keep him company so he could continue driving all night. He was not very reassuring as he told Edward he was worried about falling asleep. So red eye and dutifully, Edward complied.

We had two guys, usually skaters that got a pittance of extra money to load the luggage room and the suitcases underneath the bus. Some skaters paid them to take their luggage to their room. They were also in charge of retrieving trunks once a month. The extra pay for luggage delivery was worth the money and judgmental looks when there were only two slow elevators and a line of fifty cranky people waiting. No one ever said thanks, but the luggage guys were very vital to our travel day survival.

After many tours of loading the bus, the luggage guys knew the best way to stack all the suitcases so that we get everything under the bus. When they were done, a sardine could not be jammed in. Sometimes we ran into trouble when a bus driver insisted on helping. Good as his intentions might have been, he just added more work. The luggage guys had to remove and rearrange the suitcases.

The worst was the rare bus driver on a power trip. These drivers would not let our guys touch or organize the luggage. They would then insist that it didn't all fit, at which point the luggage guys would swoop in and save the day. Sometimes Edward, when he was one of the luggage guys, would sneak over to the other side of the bus and start re-organizing the luggage, under the bus driver's nose. But if the power hungry bus driver insisted that nothing else could go below, then the isles were littered with giant suitcases.

Half the cast has travel size coolers, but that is a misnomer. The coolers were the size of a small doghouse and just as awkward to carry. The bonus to these large coolers was you could plug it in. No more *garbage can* refrigerator. My fridge was the size of a picnic cooler.

Halfway through a drive, the floor would be covered with bodies as people stretched out under the seats and across the isles. Going to the bathroom or exiting the bus for our brief breaks improved my gymnastics and mountain climbing abilities greatly.

When corporate is not trying to cut back, we get two seats. The most athletic feat was sleeping stretched across the aisle, with your feet up on the window, or on someone else's arm rest. If you were able to get over the thought of the dirty bus floor, it was a more comfortable option. Sometimes there was the dreaded sunken aisle. Where the aisle is lower than the seat floor. To most skating people they didn't care, but when trying to sleep, it became an irritating nuisance subjecting us to great bouts of grumpiness. Edward was laughed at for packing his pool floaty, but he became the envy of everyone once he was comfortable sleeping beneath the seats.

Another deterrent to the floor option is that it is hot down there!

Then there's the all coveted back seat, which is three seats in a row and is great for sleeping. It loses part of its appeal as its back rests are immovable, and it is located in the area of the toilet. The three-seat back row is also the noisy section of the bus, usually where party people aren't supposed to consume their contraband alcohol.

After budget cuts, the second bus was usually shared with concessions, it leaves about two hours later than the first bus to accommodate concession vendor's load out. The third bus to leave has the rest of concessions people, and they do not have luggage guys to help load. What a scary thought. Who does battle with the power tripping bus driver? And the crew are the last ones to load up and leave after taking the show apart at midnight.

With all the stops and the drivers getting lost at least once, it always seemed like we would roll into our new hotel home between two or four in the morning. The luggage guys would immediately start unloading, while we all waited for our room keys in a cranky half-conscious state. There was always a traffic jam of suitcases crowding the street curb outside of the hotel lobby. We would get organized into a line and fight with our bags to stay hooked together and onto the elevator. The random sneaky guest, not with our group, believed they could cut the line. Nope! Take the stairs.

There is no written rule about the exact number of miles for flying or busing. The deciding factor was money. If it's under 600 miles, then we bus, if it's over, then we fly. One luxury the crew had that we did not was that if the trip was over 360 miles, they got a sleeper bus. This meant there was a curtain partition and a single bed to lay down in. I have a thing about curtains because no one ever washes curtains, and they retain smells. I remember spending an eternity on a bus crammed into a ball trying to sleep. I was so cramped and hobbled that I would have taken the curtains smell and all.

I would invest in pool floaties like Edward, to sleep on the floor of the bus between seats. I shudder to think of the gross things under there and we would fight for the piss-smelling last row. There was an art to getting the last row. I mastered this art by getting out of my costume and skates and already having my makeup packed up so that I was one of the first on the bus to mark my territory.

One Monday morning we had a particularly long trek from Tucson, Arizona, to Lubbock, Texas. I purposely got up early to grab the back three seats and was yelled at by a grumpy crew guy who informed me it wasn't fair and I should give up the seat to him. I told him the early bird gets the worm, but he did not appreciate my sage advice.

The seats turned out to be a dud. There was something wrong with the bathroom and the whole twelve-hour bus ride stank like pee. With my prime location, the smell was the strongest. What is worse than the smell of pee? The smell of old pee with odor neutralizer added in! So, people more gracious than I moved over, and we doubled up and tried to get away from the bathroom. We suspect that the driver illegally dumped at McDonalds because for the last four hours of the trip the smell was slightly better. But still, recycled air for more than two hours made me ill.

We would watch the same six VHS videos over and over on different bus trips. The bus only had a VHS player and we only had a few videos. I still have trouble watching Cast Away because I felt brain washed after ten years of bus trip viewings.

At one point, when corporate was trying to cut expenses, they took away one of the skater buses. Besides all of us having to share seats for the whole drive, it was impossible to get two buses worth of luggage onto one bus. We ended up with luggage in the isle and below our feet. Eventually they worked out the kinks and we shared a second bus with concessions but there were some uncomfortable trips until it was sorted. I feel corporate should have to ride the buses after making some of their changes.

Most of the buses had bathrooms the quality of which was questionable and housed a variety of odors. There is such a thing as bus etiquette. There are movements we do not do on the bus unless it is an emergency if you catch my whiff. When those were out of order, it was like a horror movie in slow motion for me. I have a bladder the size of a pea, and early skating travel days with mom where we didn't have time to stop have made not being able to use a bathroom or the threat of it is a trigger. So, I need to go every five minutes.

There is a travel decorum that is learned early on, you do not cut the line. When exiting the bus, the rear of the bus exits last. The seats on a bus are designed so that the chairs across from you are slightly in front of, or behind you. You wait until those in front of you get their stuff and get off before making your own exit. If you were lucky enough to get your three seats, then you have to wait for every other sleepy head to get up and find all their belongings that they lost over a 12-hour bus ride before you can exit. This means that you will be last to get your room key and last waiting for the elevators with your luggage but, that is the trade off on the coveted rear three seats. So, you had to weigh your options. Is this a long bus trip where I need the extra room or do I feel the need to jettison off the bus and get to my room as fast as possible?

A new crew guy attempted to jump the line and was held back and yelled at by all the veterans. He was then made to get off last every time until the crew felt that the lesson had been sufficiently learned. It would be nice if the general public followed these simple rules. I have memories that still make me angry of a little old woman on a plane ramming my legs with her carry on when there is a line that is not moving, in front of me.

43

Chapter 9
The Politics of an Ice Show

There are politics in every sport and every career. You may not call them politics, but the polite social banter or blatant butt kissing, never ceases to do wonders to the elevation of any position. I thought when my amateur career was over, that the politics would be over, I thought wrong.

As I've stated before, I'm a rather shy person. I can hide it, but my MO is usually to watch from the sidelines before I join the dialogue. My teachers in school would send home progress notes at the beginning of school that said, "does not participate but does well in school". Those reports were the polar opposite during the second half of the year when I came out of my social cocoon and began to interact. When I first came on the road I would watch for a long, quiet time. I was respectful to, if not intimidated by, the people higher up. I did notice how the female principal Lucy and her new best friend Bethany looked a lot alike, both blonde with pale skin, both from the same central northern part of the US. I had to wonder later when understudies were picked, and I was overlooked, whether it was the similarities they saw between the women, or their close friendship? Unfortunately, this relationship came to a bad turn of events in Mexico when Bethany chose her fiancée over Lucy and her cult. I don't know all the details, but I know that girls can be cruel.

My third year on Toys on Ice, I auditioned for the female lead again. For the past two years, I had been sharing the second understudy position. There were far too many understudies, six all told: two first, two second, and two third, for the same spot. There were not enough shows a week to rotate all those people through, and it was too much money to pay everyone. It always came down to money. During third year they cut the understudies to three. Confidently, I assumed they would keep me since I was one of the seconds, and one of the firsts had left. After my first-year audition, one of the compliments I had been praised for was 'really feeling' my solo.

All of those auditioning for the position were called in to speak with the performance director about the final decision. After two years of being a second understudy, I was suddenly no longer *any* understudy. The girl who had become third understudy halfway through the previous year, and the BFF of the principal Lucy, had taken the third and final understudy spot. One of the critique's I was given was I did not emotionally feel the solo. Well, that's confusing since I had previously been praised for that very part of my performance.

I shed a few tears over the decision, but it worked out well in the long run. I ended up doing other things that year; I was a second understudy for one of the male action toys, a backup for the comedy team, and stand in for several of the large costume characters. I kept busy. After a physically busy day, I would flop on the bed, and Edward would look at me with disbelief and ask if I had climbed a tree yet that day. I have to wonder if maybe it was part of the company's plan, because they knew there were better things for me. Or maybe I'm giving them too much credit to make myself feel better.

The female lead for Toys on Ice was one of the most difficult understudies I did in any show. One of the contributing factors was the costume! Originally, the pants didn't stretch, so just about every show doing the Russian splits cause the crotch to be ripped out. Eventually this was fixed, but it was through the trickledown effect. The principle got the new stretch pants, and when she got a new pair, the understudies got the older ones. Not that I minded this, it makes sense, the principle must do every show. What I minded was the non-stretch pants I had to wear. Added to this, were heavy chaps and fat padding, so that we looked like a doll. And to top it off a big round head that seemed to weigh five pounds, giving us limited air supply and vision.

If it sounds like a torture device, it's because it was, I was the woman in the iron mask. I would come off after a show with bruise marks on my cheeks. I had to shove pads in the head gear to keep it so tight that it wouldn't move. I couldn't risk having the mask move and being unable to see. The face had painted mesh so that you could see. That is, if your cheeks weren't pushed up into your eyeballs and the spotlight wasn't blinding you. Since you were the lead, the spotlight was always on you, so you were ice blind all the time. With the padding in place you were locked in and your hair was glued to your face.

I did not think I was claustrophobic until I could not get out of the head by myself. It was a fight of sheer will power at the end of every Act 1. All the extra weight of the costume, plus being top heavy with that head, took some getting used to for jumping and spinning in my two solos. By the end of act one, it felt as if I were lifting pounds of wet blankets with rubber arms.

Jumping and spinning were amusing in those costumes. Sometimes I would take off on a jump I considered easy, have no idea where I was and land splat on my stomach. Spinning when you are top-heavy turns into a teeter-totter that slowly unravels your spins into wide drunken circles.

The costume was so bad originally that the principles had to have cooling packs added. And other than my 21st birthday, if I knew I was in the principal show track the next day, I didn't go out the night before. I may not be the smartest person in the world, but I was fairly sure of what would happen to me if I tried an axel with a five-pound head piece and a hangover.

The problems with the men's lead costume were similar. One of the understudies weighed in before and after the show and he had lost five pounds in sweat. The male lead hated his costume so much at first that he drop-kicked the head across backstage. I hated skating in the costumes, too; but did he stop to think how much money just the head costs? He received a fine for his troubles and a stern talking to.

For the show Underwater Fantasy on Ice during its first year, everyone did auditions. I was asked after long rehearsal days to stay and watch the female principle. This gave me hope that I was being considered for an understudy position. We were told at a group announcement, after auditions that tentatively the three understudies for the fabulous female fish with legs were Conner, Bambie, and I. Conner was phenomenal, but he looked uber masculine in the costume and spandex can only hide so much. Instead of bumping me up, Bambie, who had a close relationship with the female principle, and close family ties from the old ice show days, became first understudy. She was a great understudy; however, she was also new to the company, and I often wonder how much of the selection process is political and how much was talent? I did not mind too much, as I was once again splitting second, which was a nice, although small, bump up to the paycheck.

The principal character, fabulous female fish with legs, was a silly character and I had fun whenever I went in. The swimming motion was something I never seemed to get right. Keeping the legs together supposedly gave the illusion of no legs, but I had a wide leg stance from my Blowfish character and previous years as an understudy male action toy. The big fish tail behind me, which was part of the costume, not part of the anatomy, was another learning experience. It hindered split jumps and hitch kicks. It always amazed the crowds (and me) when a fish, fin and all did a back flip!

While choreographing Underwater Fantasy on Ice, management had the two lead fish, with some of the biggest tails in the show, doing side by side double jumps. With the whip lash of the tail, it took me over a month to land the jump. After I finally got it, they took it out of the show. Go figure. The leading female fish had the largest and widest tail, like a giant wind sail. The tail was attached to the head on a cap that fastened under the neck and at the buttocks by a G-string. A shiny blue body suit was worn under it with Hermes ankle wings. The eyeballs of the fish were strategically placed at chest level and attracted their fair amount of attention. A man with his family in tow chauvinistically commented, "Nice eyes!" I shouldn't complain, most men never make eye contact.

The show was sent on its merry way with no one the wiser on how to fix broken fish tails. After several months, the fragile metal bones that held the fish tails together snapped. Wardrobe got creative and soldered everything back together. Over the years, new tails were ordered for the principles and the old, lead weighted tails passed down to understudies.

The more times the tail was soldered the less flexible and the heavier it became. Imagine a heavy object pulling on your neck and head for two hours as you swim-skate around the ice. It couldn't get worse, and then it did. Once the tail broke at the beginning of Act 1. This was one sad female fish, out on the ice for an hour of dialogue that could not be missed, wearing a saggy metal tail that looked like someone had pooped in her pants.

Second year of this fishy show, I figured I had a shot at first understudy since Bambie was leaving. No, the fourth understudy jumped in and took first. While she deserved it, she was also friendly with the performance director. Coincidence?

A friend of ours on Underwater Fantasy on Ice, Sid, knew things were not run to the best of their operating abilities, and not getting better. Early in our third year, he was involved in an incident that got him demoted from his line captain position. There are men and women line captains who oversee the girl and guy performers. They relay the performance director's notes for each show, teach new skaters the show numbers, keep up the mark sheets and books, all for the menial pay of an extra $50 a week.

The mark sheets tell everyone where to be on the ice. This is done by counting headers, which are the side lights that decorate the border of the ice. The books have every skater's placement and pattern during group numbers. So, if you are sparing, (our term for filling in someone else's spot), you can look up their pattern. Not only do you have to know your own show track, but you also need to know your understudy characters, and any other potential spots in the show. Basically, know the entire show!

I think the men's line captain was always trying to make things right, but once he was on the performance director and company manager's hit list, he had to dig his way out of quicksand. He fell getting on the ice because he had left his guards on, plastic protectors worn over our skates. This made him late for the number, and he was fined. Anyone else who fell for the same reason would have received sympathy or laughter, not a fine.

There was confusion about the timing of a downstage entrance for two of the skaters, one of which was Sid. They left on the cue they were given and were late entering the ice. The girl went in to talk to the performance director and company manager who were very polite with her and probably would have let her off the hook until Sid walked in. Then the air became menacingly chilly, Sid was cut off in mid-sentence and they were both given a fine. Politics. It just goes to show that the way to get ahead is to kiss ass and don't piss off the boss. This creates a challenge if you are trying to make change and cannot speak to management.

In a work environment like this, where everyone is so close, it's hard to expunge personal feelings. Once a year we are given the 'Leave your personal life at the door' speech. I suppose this makes sense; you can't skate with a scowl on your face. Perhaps it's not just the skaters that need to remember this.

I took a turn as an assistant line captain. Second year of Underwater Fantasy. Our ladies line captain moved on with her life and we received another line captain. She was an experienced line captain but did not know our show. We had several skaters who were new to our show in Mexico City. The schedule was made more difficult by rehearsals, early mornings, and late-night teaching and for menial pay. Adding to this stress I knew our show, steps, and timing better than the new line captain who had studied videos in preparation. I was told, "No you are wrong." in front of new recruits, and heaven forbid when I corrected her. I was told that I was undermining her authority, so I just let her teach it wrong. I ended up making most of the step books for that show, because the new line captain did not wish to do them. Again, a thankless job.

Chapter 10
Coast to Coast to Coast

The first tour year with Toys on Ice covered major cities on the East Coast, US. We did 32 cities in 10 months. We performed in a different city every week, with a few exceptions; Chicago, Boston, and Cleveland, where we stayed for two or three weeks.

Each tour schedule has positives and negatives. On a brand-new show, East Coast tour, you have the difficult training, exhausting six-week rehearsal period with long, cold on-ice hours. No one ever knows the show as well as when you are part of that creation. And it's a bonding experience for all the departments. Not to mention your face is in the program for the rest of that tour's life span. Benefits of a United States tour means you speak the language, you know what foods are edible since packaging is in English and you have your favorite restaurant chains.

The hardest I ever remember working was my first year when the new show Toys on Ice, opened. We would start rehearsals at eight every morning with warm up class. During this class we worked together in small groups doing footwork. This was harder than it should have been for new people like me. I had always skated solo, so trying to match four other skating styles was like being schizophrenic.

For the next nine hours, we would learn or rehearse show numbers. Even if a skater wasn't in that number, they were required to learn it, just in case they had to spare. If you were learning any number, you couldn't watch from the sidelines, you had to stand on the ice. Eight hours of standing was painful to my legs and especially my poor feet that were crammed into my skates. Besides all the pain I subjected my body to, these were also the best times.

I would get to know the other cast and crew and sometimes ran out to have snowball fights during rehearsals. We not only threw the ice that we'd scraped up, but shoved it down people's pants and shirts rubbing it in. Most of the old pros would poke fun at me for taking the time to jump and spin, but a few appreciated my technical abilities. Two of the guys remarked that 'someone still thinks they're an amateur' and I also heard, 'doesn't she know that she doesn't need all that fancy skatin' here?' I did not listen to them.

Every night during rehearsals there was always somewhere to go and someone to go with. You always knew where the party group would be. Monday was laundry day, Tuesday was the pool hall, Wednesday karaoke, Thursday party by the trailers, Friday the Irish bar Mollys, Saturday company bar-be-que behind the building, and Sunday party all day by the pool. Sunday was our only day off during rehearsals. For the new show, we had six weeks of rehearsals in Lakeland FL. It was the last semblance of routine as we set out on tour.

Last week was especially long because once the costumes were made, we had dress rehearsals and show run throughs late into the night. Then we would spend hours standing in freshly flooded ice to have our pictures taken for the program with water damaging our boots and our skates becoming slimy and moldy. The work hours became longer, and the only compensation was that the company promised meals. One long day standing in my cowgirl costume, which consisted of metal spurs, an accordion, cowgirl hat, fringe, and yellow foam hair, the photographer yells at the squeeze box (me) to move over to the left. No. His Left, not my left. Then I am not moving, and he says I moved, I snapped, and he told Squeeze Box to 'simmer down'.

To downplay my own problems, during all this, the purple cowboy is holding the orange cowgirl over his head in a lift. Her armpits have gone numb, and his arms are shaking. The photographer wants to know if the lift can be higher and do it again, and again. Ever since the photo shoot I have signed the programs next to the accordion player as 'Squeeze Box'. To this day Edward can be heard saying simmer down squeeze box!

The best picture take had to be the Beach dolls. Try to get 16 girls of different heights to kick at the same time and the same height. Well after about an hour of kicking, it still was not working. Now the photographer and his assistant are grumpy and trying to produce alternatives. In the process, girly giggles were not appreciated, and one girl was told 'this isn't Molly's Bar, suck in your gut!'

Rehearsals are the honeymoon phase when we worked, we partied harder, and you still loved everyone. The stress and long tour months hadn't worn away our patience. This was the time when the cast and crew became one family.

A new show also means heavy schedules and worst of all early morning publicity duties. Doing live or taped interviews, while skating production numbers are going on in the background at 5 am, makes anyone cranky. Then there's the overabundance of kiddy shows. Kiddy shows are usually at 10:30 am and schools' bus their children to the show. We arrived an hour before the show. So, we are up at about 8 am, done by 12:30 pm, the next show is at 7:30 pm.

Sometimes rehearsals are scheduled in between the kiddy show and the evening show. After the morning show we sat around the arena, which seemed to be located in a sparsely populated area with an abundance of nothing to do. So, you sat and waited for the next show. Going to the hotel after a kiddy show, left you with just enough time to do nothing.

Getting up at 8 am may not seem early but remember our schedule is set up for night owls. One positive for a new show is that the crew usually makes max money, not that this money affects the skaters. The US cities we toured for a new show were the bigger and more interesting cities.

May was the end of my first year on tour. Most tour years' work like school years, starting in the late summer/early fall and going until the beginning of summer. I was excited to go home after almost a year away from family and friends, but sad to leave my new boyfriend behind. After six weeks unpaid vacation at home, we had six weeks in Mexico; another two weeks off and then the show started the West Coast America tour.

The beginning of West Coast I like to call the dust bowl, tumble weed tour. It's small, dusty, mostly, cow towns; Amarillo, Tucson, El Paso, Bakersfield, OK City, Tulsa, and Lubbock. Remember happiness was Lubbock Texas in the rearview mirror. I have nothing against these cities, but I have seen actual tumble weeds that stared me down as we had a standoff to cross the road.

We played the state fairs with the fragrance of cow paddies wafting through the air. At the Oklahoma City State Fair, we watched a tornado during a three-show day and then a rainstorm that almost collapsed the old arena roof with us inside. Who said there is no excitement at the state fair? In late October, when you head north to Washington State, you're in the clear. The tour cities get better, and you are on the real west coast.

Right before we hit this jack pot of big tour cities, the company dropped a bomb on us, and it was a dud. They told us the Japanese company that buys the show to take to Japan, did not want Toys on Ice. I had already been waiting for two years to go overseas. The normal circuit, until this point had been, East Coast US; Mexico and West Coast US; Japan, S.E. Asia, and Australia; the frozen forgotten states; and Europe.

Not all shows died after this typical rotation, some kept mutating and changing. This means that a show could live forever and travel to many places it had been before. Variety shows versus single story shows were more likely to live forever.

So, no Japan, no S.E. Asia, and no Australia, but there was a small light at the end of the tunnel. We were tentatively to play small city US, followed by Puerto Rico and South America. As its name implied a 'South American' tour by the Company traveled to several South America countries. As time wore on, the South American tour became more of a Central America tour. Edward and I discussed and decided to stay on Toys on Ice another year, meaning a total of three years in the states.

Since the show circuit was thrown out of whack by our show not going overseas, this left a gaping non-paying hole of break time for our show. We had a four-month break between West Coast and our next tour. It is nice to have time off, but this was too long. For US skaters, money is taken out of their paycheck and put into unemployment. If we don't use it, the government gets it, but on our time off we have access to unemployment benefits. After four months, the supply was almost exhausted. Getting a job that pays as much as my weekly benefits and would hire me for the short stints I was home was often a difficult task.

At the end of my third tour with Toys on Ice, we did play Puerto Rico, but Central America had been given to another show that had already played South America. This old classic was revamped and due to go around the globe again. The dream of Central or South America that I had been holding out for, floated off to another show.

Halfway through our third year, Edward got an offer to go to Underwater Fantasy on Ice with a promotion to head carpenter. We said yes and began the repeat circuit that we had just spent three years on. East Coast, only three weeks off, nine weeks in Mexico, straight into eleven months on West Coast with no Christmas break, six weeks off and then finally the light at the end of the tunnel Japan. After five years in the US and seven for Edward, we were finally getting out of the country.

Breaks are funny things with this company. It's an entertainment business so holidays lost a lot of the family touch for me. We performed on Thanksgiving, but they usually provided us with a nice meal. I have done shows on Christmas nine out of ten years. Infrequently we would get a Christmas break and have enough time to go home. When we did get a holiday break, it is not on Christmas it's about a week before, but any time is better than no time. And to stimulate a timely return, we get a holiday bonus if we perform in the last show before break and the first show after. Like luggage weight and promoter parties the holiday return bonus disappeared a few years into tour life; budget cuts.

Chapter 11
Sense of the Ridiculous

Sometimes it's easy to lose your sense of the ridiculous. After the show is done at 9:30 pm, you go to the hotel, make dinner in the bathroom in your one pot wonder and let that digest while watching TV in a vegetative state. Not always having the same TV stations, it's hard to get hooked on any TV series. By this time, it's midnight and by 1 am you're ready to go to sleep. This is a slow night, often practiced, but not religiously, before the dreaded three-show day. The only difference is that pizza is a lot easier to deal with on Friday nights.

On a rotational basis, we take turns doing the early morning publicities, usually between Tuesday and Friday most weeks. This is where we get up at 4 am, after three hours of beauty sleep, and half-awake put on our whore make-up and costumes while smiling manically at the empty seats and waving to the camera as if there is a full show audience in attendance (who knew we were practicing more than a decade early for the 2020 pandemic).

Several different TV stations arrive and take turns taping. We do several takes for them and since each TV station comes at a different time, we do this over and over until 8 or 10 am. Some unfortunates, while holding coffee and acting awake give live interviews. My mastery of such morning skills was not so good, and I was only on live TV twice. My first interview was a few months after I joined Toys on Ice. I went live with another performer who was also a new hire. She was very good on TV, so I slunk to the background and let her do the work. TV and radio frightened me a little bit, much like the dreaded telephone as an adolescent.

I had another chance two years later with the same show when we played close to my hometown. I was alone this time and thought I did better, but the company didn't air me again, so I'm not sure how to take that. Edward got out of it by accidentally swearing live on TV. Good publicity for a family friendly company.

Our treat for these early morning performances was usually stale doughnuts and coffee. First come first served, if you didn't move fast, you often missed even the crumbs. Sometimes we were treated to a full array of goodies, fruit, muffins, juices and once we even got McDonalds.

For these publicities, we usually did abbreviated versions of the shows' chorus scenes. For the rotation schedule to work, some people had to skate in spots they didn't normally do in the show. Add to this an alternative, abbreviated show number, and lack of sleep and you have a few lost beach dolls and confused soldiers, trying to run over the lead characters. A notorious doll company threatened to get legal with us if we didn't stop using the beach doll show scene on these TV promotions, because thousands of little girls would point and call us by that toy company's favorite doll. I thought it was pretty obvious we were the Dollar Store mockups.

There was just enough blend of sleep and no sleep to make us feel a little sick to our stomachs. This lovely feeling is termed 'Gut Rot'. It threw off the sleep schedule for a day or two and just when your body has forgotten the memories required for these early morning performances, it's your turn for early morning week rotation.

Chapter 12
Rules, Rules, Rules

There are so many protocols, procedure, prohibitions, and rules it was difficult to keep them all straight. Being new you were given a rule book and expected to know it by heart. As tour years collected under my belt it seemed the new hires were getting younger each year and management pampered them, treating them like they were at a high school retreat and that is how they acted, not that I was any better my first year.

My least favorite rule:

"Your feet are your livelihood. Wear shoes at all times." Seems like a reasonable request. But I do not like shoes, especially if I have been drinking. At opening night party my first year, I got tired of my nice dancing shoes and kicked them off in a corner. No one said anything but Lizzy hid them in the plants. During rehearsals, if you found a pair of shoes in your room, guaranteed they were mine. Hampton VA's arena had a little peninsula out back with a flock of resident geese. I couldn't run very well in my sandals and the geese were asking to be chased. I kicked off my shoes, unfortunately in front of the men's line captain, and went running after the birds. I had a little talking to that changed nothing. Years later in Europe near Stonehenge I almost got us kicked out for chasing sheep.

My infractions were small for the most part. Wardrobe regulations seem to be the most daunting, so many directives it was hard to remember, especially when rushing to put on your costumes. In the written ordinance, all these things seem simple enough, but when you have a quick change and can barely get out of your robot costume, hang it up correctly while keeping it off the ground seems a nearly impossible challenge. This feat of costume changes requires greater courage, skill, and strength and as much precision as the on-ice performance. Hang your costume; tits to the left, ass to the right; in the order that you use them; zip them up to stay on the hanger. Gators which are skate boot covers, go in the bottom of the bag. No make-up in the costume room, no costumes in the make-up room.

As if the written rubric wasn't enough, there was always someone in authority around to remind you: "Turn your costumes in for repair, preferably when the problems are small. These costumes have to last six years, maybe longer."

"A big problem is harder to fix."

"Pick your costumes up from repair by half hour." Never ever sit or eat in costume. Unless, you are a character, characters can sit in costume. Usually, characters are large costumes that are hard to put on and take off, therefore on short breaks they may stay in costume and sit down for a respite. These giant character costumes look like a toy grave yard hanging from meat hooks and pieces littering the crate floors after hours. You are not allowed in the character room unless you are a character. "No, Maddie, you may not visit your friends in the character room!"

One year on Under Water Fantasy on Ice we had an auction to raise money for a stellar end of the year party. This awesome party was a masquerade at an old home, out in the countryside of Louisiana, complete with shuttling to and from the event like real celebrities. The biggest money maker on the auction table was a show with no wardrobe regulations. I took full advantage of this rule breaking and sat in my puffer fish costume, in the make-up room, eating Haagen-Dazs ice cream. There may be pictures to prove this once in a lifetime opportunity.

Each performer can have different types of show laundry, under their costumes. On Toys on Ice, almost everyone wore flesh colored spandex shorts, grey sports bra for the girls, and white tee-shirts. The girls also got 'booby bras' for the beach doll number. They took one look at me during costume fittings and put shoulder pads in my bra and fitted the rest of my costumes to those pads. Unfortunately, they issued three bras and only two of them had extra cleavage inserted. So, on a three-show day, by the last show, I had reverse indentations, not my most attractive look.

Girls had to wear thongs and guys wore dance belts, the male equivalent of a thong. The guys were given three company issued dance belts. Like 'army standard issue', one size does not fit all. Usually, the men weren't given very many of these articles of underclothes and considering how close they lived to the black hole of your existence, they needed to be washed frequently.

'Company issued' consisted of an uncomfortable, two-inch cheek separator that can be quite painful. After standard laundry detergent with hot water and lack of softener, the apparatus shrank and became skin irritating. The solution was that many of the guys went out and bought their own. On Underwater Fantasy on Ice, the women's show laundry consisted of a strappy leotard thong and we were still required to wear our own thong underwear it was double duty. As thongs shrank, you can image where the impact was felt.

On Underwater Fantasy on Ice, one of the new hires, Slapstick, his nickname, not his real name, continued to forget his dance belts and wardrobe had a soft spot for him. Just like high school homework, he would concoct wild tales (although no self-respecting dog would ever eat that thing) and his dance belt would always be washed and forgotten back at the hotel, and with a 'pretty please' he got away with murder. He ended up with 20 'company issued' dance belts. The size of men's dance belt was not dependent on male ego. Nobody is ever a small and hardly a medium. The most comfortable I'm told is large, but year after year, there was an abundant surplus of smalls and mediums. Why do they continue to order these sizes? Maybe it's a painful joke?

One amusing memory was of a new boy who did not want to wear a dance belt and wore his boxer shorts under his spandex costume with his dance belt on top. No surprise which underwear choice he'd made…the whole audience could see it. I know guys and gals are different but how does one make that outfit choice mentally okay? Avoid mirrors I suppose. And that sounds painful all wadded up in spandex. Maybe this wardrobe choice is okay because many heterosexual ice skaters have a decent amount of self-esteem, I assume. They have already been through hazing at a young age for their sport choice and wearing crushed velvet spandex skating outfits. On the plus side, however, there is half the competition for female attention which, probably, increases their self-confidence and batting average. But does this confidence then lead to the ability to wear bunched up boxer shorts under spandex in front of a large audience? I wish I had that sort of confidence or ambivalence.

Thongs were a new experience for me when I joined the road. I suppose it makes sense, no one wants bunchy panty lines in spandex. While my experience was limited to special occasions, one of my friends wanted to fight thongs the whole way. Thongs can be a painful transition. As I have found with many experiences in life, you can get used to almost anything. Now I have trouble wearing normal underwear and have an unhealthy concern about panty lines.

Show laundry is a very sanitary idea, in concept. One year on Underwater Fantasy on Ice I had to share my beloved role of the puffer fish. As the show's years rolled on and new shows rolled out, the number of shows opening increased, they ran out of performers that had the ability to jump and spin. So, I took a pay cut to play a background role that no one else could fill. *If the jumping chorus role is so difficult to fill*, perhaps that role should receive extra character pay. The company had a 5'6" guy perform act one puffer fish and I would play the puffer fish in act two.

We did not have similar build and I often wonder if the audience sitting in the first row noticed that the fat fish became more feminine. Or maybe my giant unibrow caught most of the attention. Act One male puffer fish would sweat profusely, which would not have been so bad, but he would sweat through his show laundry and saturate the spandex body suit which we shared. These were not cheap costumes so often there was only one of each, especially large or special characters. For Act Two, I would silently gag as I put on the soggy unitard. Especially the piece that fit snuggly around my face. I still dry heave thinking about it.

Wardrobe rules are only the beginning. There are many public relation regulations. You can tell someone what you do in the show, if your face is showing, then you parrot that you are 'portraying the character'. On Toys on Ice, I was part of the ensemble, and I portrayed a band girl in The Cowboy number, a car driver one year, and a Beach doll. What I was not supposed to reveal was that I was an evil robot that was chased and destroyed by the superhero toy, a head light, and an eight-foot purple hairbrush. This rule is a big one for the company Family Fun on Ice and I guess it makes sense, keep up the magic.

The Mouse is always Mr. Mouse, certainly not played by a short 5"–5'3" female or an effeminate Thai boy. We were always given the Santa Clause metaphor. You don't want to be the one that ruins that image for the child, this was usually followed on the slide show by a picture of a wailing child. Personally, that was enough for me, no thank you on screaming children; except when portraying an evil villainess. Then I took secret delight in scaring the pants off the little ones. While that rule makes sense, I didn't think I would ruin anyone's Christmas by revealing I was an evil robot, with a giant wok on my head, or a purple brush with feet sticking out below it.

While we used the company name, we were not actually owned by Family Fun. We were owned by the circus! So technically I am a traveling circus performer! At any given time during my tour life, there were about seven or eight ice shows out touring the world. In 2006, the company also opened a few stage shows. Since we used the company name, there were often company big wigs in to check and make sure the show was behaving, at least while in the United States.

Why didn't the company run their own ice show? There is much speculation about this. An expensive endeavor? Or perhaps they did not know how to travel it? Maybe they were not able to make their own portable ice in arenas that did not have that capability. Add to this the wise businessman who had exclusive ice show contracts with many arenas, that leaves little room for competition.

Can you say monopoly? For years Family Fun on Ice had contractual agreements with arenas that stipulated an ice show could not be in the arena for so many months before or after Family Fun on Ice. So, the company would make sure it strategically had an ice show in that arena on a rotating basis so no one else could book it. Another factor as mentioned earlier was the ability of the company to make and travel its own ice floor in arenas that did not have the capability to make their own ice. At least these were the reasons drifting down to the peon level, seeing as no one of importance discusses such matters with the help. After I left the road, these exclusive contracts expired, and I began to see more traveling ice shows across the US.

Once or twice a year you would be pulled out of the show to watch with the performance director (PD). Unless you were a principal, then you got to watch the show at least once a week when your understudies went in. On one of these occasions, the PD and I sat in front of the sound and electric board. Right before show start, the sound guy leaned over the electric board and said, "Hey, Maddie, can you push that button?" Fast as lightning I pushed that button. The color drained from his face and his mouth hung slack. I had just hit the stop button for the entire show and it would take at least five minutes to reboot. The "show is starting" announcements had already rolled. I later learned that the owner of the entire company had made an unannounced visit to watch the show that now started late. When later asked about his choice of practical joke he said, "I didn't think she would really hit it and she moved so fast!" After that there was a new rule. When watching the show, you are not allowed to sit in front of the sound or electric board.

If a Handbook full of rules was not enough, then there are all the unspoken rules that live in the gray areas. We were told, "You are upholding an image." This one comes down to behaving in public. Don't scream out your employer's name at a bar, don't wear company memorabilia while getting wasted. Don't use a fake ID underage, get arrested, lie about your citizenship, get threaten with deportation and use the company name to bail you out. Don't get a whole cast and crew drunkenly kicked out of a bar with a newspaper photo while you are wearing a company logo shirt at the local bar. But what happens when you are done with the company, no one is there to remind you to behave with your company jacket on then?

Chapter 13
Belle of the Ball

At five, my mom took me for my first haircut; it was memorable. I was so angry at having any one of the hairs on my head cut that I came home, hid behind the chair, took half my hair in one hand and scissors in the other and hacked at my hair. Instead of revenge, I got a bowl on my head and a Dorothy Hamill haircut; but I was no Dorothy. And so started a lifecycle of alternating short and long hairstyles.

When I was about eight years old, a lady stopped me going into the women's restroom and said, "Little boy, the men's room is next door" – I'm not a boy! Another example of being mistaken for a boy occurred at age twelve when sitting next to an elderly gentleman on an airplane. I talked the whole flight about ice skating. I was sporting a pink t-shirt with my name written in puff paint, pink dangly earrings, and jeans with roses on them. At the end of our conversation, he leaned over to his son and said, "Isn't that cute, the little boy is an ice skater." Those were not ambiguous times; it was, after all, the nineties. Now, in the twenty-first century, my androgynous look is all the rage.

I'm not what you would have called a conventional beauty in high school with my pixy haircut, wafer thin body, and non-existent curves. My high school boyfriend took a vote with his bros on whether I was attractive enough to get the respect he desired for his choice of woman. Apparently, this was not something he could solve for himself and needed their approval.

The vote was a big negative on attractive and my boyfriend thought that this was knowledge that needed imparting to his girlfriend: a genius he was not. He also informed me that he cast his vote in agreement with the majority. If there was such a thing as negative IQ, he may have had it. That certainly did not stop him from sleeping with me, so his vote, and judgment, are suspect.

On tour, I would go out to the gay bar and get hit on by gay guys, straight men and women. That was confusing for me and them, and amusing for my friends.

Needless to say, I had little confidence in my looks. When I came to tour, where the libations flowed freely and I had what seemed like many suitors interested in me, I could hardly believe it. I was also a bit naive, and apparently very innocent looking. Not all of them were the cream of the crop and I seem to attract the strangest of strange.

One crew guy that I thought was gay and was about 20 years older than me became quite creepy rather quickly. He had a larger shoe collection than mine and ordered expensive wine delivered to his door at the next stop on tour. This was not yet the age of Amazon and it was quite impressive to have anything delivered to your hotel door. I realized that he was not batting for the other team when we were drinking wine in his room alone and he made a move. I made my move and dashed for the door. He switched shows and got out while the getting was good.

Then there was devil child, who wore creepy contacts and occasionally dressed up like a vampire, said weird things, and followed me around, like a possessed puppy. There was also the incident of the alleged phone sex conversation. That crew guy thought he was having a sexy conversation with me but when he brought it up later, I stared blankly at him, and he realized he had no idea who he had been talking to!

Shortly into my arrival at rehearsals in Lakeland, FL the skaters and crew had a BBQ. All it took was two glasses of wine and one beer, and I was barefoot dancing behind the arena. Somewhere in that haze, there was dancing in shoes on the ice to the annoyance of the lighting designers and I had a make out session in an elevator. Turns out that skater had a serious, long-time girlfriend on tour with him. She politely pulled me aside the next day and explained the real-world situation. There was no anger in her voice, it was a very matter-of-fact conversation, and she didn't appear to be jealous, only mildly annoyed. I was very impressed with her confidence and simultaneously embarrassed by my drunken behavior.

I kissed a lot of frogs before I found my prince, but sometimes you have to jump in the water to find out if your man is royal or amphibian.

Chapter 14
Road Romance

I need to preface this chapter with some history. The summer before I came on the road, I mutually ended a two-year relationship. I then engaged in a quick rebound before I joined the road. In Lakeland, my roommate would get confused with who was on the phone for me because both of their names started with the same letter and she would shout, "One of them is on the phone."

Usually, home boyfriends do not last long when a girl joins tour. It is just two different lifestyles. Long distance is hard when you're young and there are so many sharks in the ice water. I kept in regular contact with my two-year ex. We were both lonely, but we made no promises. I suppose that is not fair, as there may have been unspoken promises. About a month before Christmas break, I started dating Edward, who was on the ice show with me. I chickened out and didn't tell Mr. Two-Year.

Mr. Two-Year, who had never been spontaneous, surprised me by driving up to Albany, NY to see the show, with my parents. Albany was our last city before Christmas break and my parents were going to drive me back to Rochester. I pulled my dad aside after the show and said, "Please walk Mr. Two-Year out to the car, I have to say goodbye to Edward." I didn't want to say a loving goodbye in front of the ex. Mr. Two-Year wouldn't do as instructed and watched me kiss my new boyfriend goodbye. It was a long, silent, three-hour ride home. I took Mr. Two-Year back to his dorm and tried to apologize. He said he'd need time and no contact for a while.

Six months later, on a six-week summer break, he requested the use of our piano at the house. I didn't mind, thinking everything was fine and we were friends now. I can be so naïve. He asked if I was still dating Edward, and then things got weird. Sometimes he'd play the piano and most of the time he'd just sit and stare at me. I don't deal well with confrontation, I'm more of the avoidance type. So I'd leave the house if he was over and stopped answering the phone if he showed up on caller ID. I ended up having to call him for a favor when everyone was out of town and my brother, and I needed a ride to the airport. Just call me the Queen of Awkward.

That was the last time I spoke to Mr. Two-Year for several years. I returned to Chicago with Underwater Fantasy on Ice, and he came to have a drink and catch up in the hotel bar. I told Edward I was going to have a drink with my ex and he was welcome to come along. He said, "No thanks." Conversation was the normal chit chat for a few hours. I was pleased that everything seemed to be friendly and normal and was making the time to go gestures when Mr. Two-Year said, "There's somethings I need to tell you." He paused. "Do you want me to tell you?"

"Well, it seems you want to say something." Feelings of dread washed over me. Everything was going so normally; I didn't want it to go back to awkward. I held my breath, "Maddie, I love you, I'm not in love with you, but I loved you and I never told you that while we were together." Okay that wasn't too bad, a bit of a surprise since in college he listed his top ten priorities. I was number six and pot was number one. My response was, "I had just come out of a rocky high school relationship where we used 'I love you' too much. I didn't need or want to hear I love you, so it's okay." But he wasn't done, "I'm also pretty sure that I didn't tell you I was a virgin before you." Whoa, talk about dropping a bomb. What do you say to that?

"Well, you had me fooled!" We parted on amicable terms, and I went upstairs to bed, Edward asked how it went and the look I gave him made him laugh.

Chapter 15
Cowboy Crunchies

It was in Lakeland FL that I met Edward for the second time. I was skating around before class with my white skates which stood out like homing beacons proclaiming, "I'm a new girl, come and get me." I was skating backward in my knit pants of multiple shades of gray and white, and I said, "I know you, your last name starts with a D and your first name is…" It was almost there when he said, "Edward."

That evening I walked from the Amerisuites to practice. It was late at night, so the building was locked. I had to walk around the back. Edward caught up and, even though it was a short distance to the arena, he said it wasn't the safest neighborhood. He also said that if I was coming to skate, I should call him so that I didn't walk alone. I liked the invitation but didn't really believe his politeness. Who realistically wants to be bothered every night because the new girl is still a die-hard competitive skater? My irrational phone phobia and the fact that I thought he was cute didn't help either.

Later that week some mutual friends introduced us again. And Edward said something about knowing me from Houston. I looked at him quizzically and said, "I don't remember you from Houston, I remember you from Detroit."

He said, "Really? I competed in Detroit, but you and I skated at the Galleria together for several years in the nineties." I wracked my brain and couldn't come up with the memory of a guy fitting his description who had skated with us. To jog my memory, he said, "We all hung out at La Madeleine's and played cards in the evenings. We ate the free bread and drank the water because we didn't have any money." When that failed, he did add, "I remember you, I was really impressed with how you kept to yourself and worked hard, you didn't fool around." I liked the flattery, and we dropped the fact that I could not remember skating with him for two years.

I'd never been a big partier before tour. I was still 20, one more month and a half and I'd be legal. That didn't stop me! Wherever I thought Edward and the gang was going to be, I'd be. I am not an aficionado with a pool cue, I just went to watch him bend over the table in his tight jeans. Rica would laugh at me, as I got distracted from shooting pool. He wore his big belt buckle, boots, and cowboy hat. I was a city girl and had never fancied a cowboy before. He'd come over to socialize and I couldn't shoot with him watching, nor could I talk, or do anything else normal. So, he'd stand there and ask, 'You gonna shoot?' And he'd continue to stand there until I was red in the face.

Once I went to karaoke night and he asked me to dance. Then he asked me if I ever sang, and I replied that I do not sing in public. This was due to my mom playing a recording of me at age eleven, singing memories from cats. This rendition of what sounded like brawling street cats was debuted at my sixteenth birthday.

That evening after getting sauced up I convinced all the girls to sing 'It's Raining Men' with me. We get up there, and no one knew the words. Since it was my idea, I grabbed the mike and went full force, slur and all. There are pictures buried somewhere, to prove it.

All the boys took this as their cue to get up and strip for us below the stage. Belts went flying, shirts came off, and we even saw some drawers and butts. In what they thought was a favor, they sang a Beach Boys tune which was being used in our show. Of course, we practiced our show steps, which ran mercilessly through our heads' day and night. I still cannot listen to the Beach Boys without my body twitching and trying to reenact the choreography.

There was a part in Toys on Ice, where the principle toys watch an old TV version of themselves and then become part of that TV show. The announcement at the beginning of the TV show says something like, 'Cowboy Crunchies Cereal, sugar coated and dipped in chocolate'. Well Edward was a Cowboy if I ever saw one and he looked yummy to me, so my girlfriends and I nicknamed him Cowboy Crunchies. We thought we were so clever, and would giggle about it thinking we were safe in our nickname usage.

Little did I know until much later, that Edward knew what his nickname was. But he did not think of it as a compliment. He sharpened the skates for us, and they gave off a black powder that gets everywhere, particularly in your nose. One of his old bosses used to call the nose build up 'crunchies'. The obvious question is how did his boss know they were crunchy? Edward thought we were making fun of him for his black powdered nose. I personally never noticed any nose crunchies.

My roommate teased me all the time. She went up to him, without my knowledge, and told him she knew someone who liked him, but he wouldn't play the guessing game, so she gave up. Finally, at an arena bar-be-que, where I was fed mostly vodka with a twist of OJ, that Edward could smell a folding chair away, he came up to me.

"You don't like me, do you?" Well, that was blunt. My verbal communication skills were at a loss, but my courage higher and I was trying to explain that he made me nervous, but I couldn't tell him why. It was on the tip of my tongue to say it was because I liked him and my resolve as well as my stomach failed me. I may have lived away from home by age 12, but I was slow to socially mature.

At one of our final dress rehearsals, he forgot his robe and was dressed in a self-made robe out of a towel that barely covered him. That evening when we were all dressed to the hilt for opening night party, I casually said in passing, "I liked you in your robe better." And his reply was a muffled, "Don't tell me things like that!"

Girls will be girls. At the end of rehearsals, I told Catty, who was part of my close girl quartet, that I liked Edward. That very same evening she feigned drunkenness and snuggled up next to him. New to the road and the guiles of some women I thought, *Well I guess that's meant to be. I'll leave it alone* and continued with our girl friendship. With that, I resolved to giving up a chase I never really ran. Things never progressed between Catty and Edward, and she started to get bored with him. Apparently, there was not enough drama. Her interest was only reignited when she thought he was interested in one of his close gal friends, Gigi. Then whenever Gigi wanted to hang out with Edward, Catty was there. I started to see a trend: she only wanted what someone else found attractive.

There was an unspoken connection between Edward and I. We were both loners in certain ways. At the Hampton bar-be-que outside the arena, we were both sitting in the back of the truck having a genuine conversation about nothing. Those are the best kind of conversations where you connect at a core level with someone. That silent connection is never something you can put your finger on, state as fact, but it is there, two people who understand each other. The world continued to spin around us with drunken dancing around the bonfire, but time had slowed to a nice stop for us. Catty must have gotten a whiff of this quiet truce because she came bumbling over and said, "Edward…Edward!" in a drunken he-ha sort of bray. "Edward, I want to do pair lifts." Edward told her he would be a minute. But the donkey kept braying, so he apologized and left to do lifts with her. She wanted to do drunken pair lifts and was wearing a jean skirt, so he did a platter for all to see her thong.

As the tour year progressed there were other moments. In Hershey, PA, we all rented a giant house together across from the hotel. The house said it could sleep up to 22 people. That might be true if 22 people do not wish to be comfortable. The living room pull out had about three people. My European double bed, more like a plush single slept two of us. There were people spilling out into the hallway. Some left for another house that was available, but I stayed for a few days. We took turns cooking on the rare novelty of a real kitchen stove and oven in the house. One night I cooked Mom's lasagna for everyone, and it was a hit.

The house was too crowded for me, so after a night or two I called up an old NY friend of mine and begged to stay with her. As I waited for my ride to her house, Edward and I had another one of those close conversations about nothing and I was hesitant to leave the overly crowded situation.

That's when things became really pregnant at the house. To my trained eye it still looked like Gigi and Catty were at odds over Edward. By now, it was the end of October and we had a pumpkin carving party and dinner party. After I left the house, I missed Edward's supper of Dill Chicken, which I wouldn't taste until four years later. I also missed Catty walking in on what she thought was Gigi and Edward about to kiss. Edward later told me this wasn't the case, it was the moment when it would have happened, but didn't. He felt more like an older, protective big brother to Gigi. Catty didn't see it that way and thought she had a claim on Edward, so the crap hit the fan. I'm glad I missed the drama.

I gave up on Edward for a couple of months, but always watched him out of the corner of my eye. I would still go out to a bar if I thought he was going to be there. The last Sunday in November, we were in East Rutherford, NJ. After a rainy trip into NYC, a group of us went to Applebees. It closed at midnight and we were not ready to call it quits, so the group divided and some of us went to a little hole in the wall bar called Yesterdays. I had Frenchie on one side telling me he had never liked a girl with short hair, Blake drowning in his alcohol and Edward teasing me about the way I licked salt off my margaritas.

Finally, the bar kicked us out at two and we all headed home. Edward left at racing speed and I was stuck stumbling home with the rest of the guys. We all sat by the elevators, had a few more drinks as we talked and shot bottle caps at each other. Eventually everyone had disappeared except Edward and me. He walked me to my hotel door and was massaging my shoulders. I kept thinking, "I should turn around and kiss him, I should turn around…" At the same time Edward was thinking, "I should turn her around and kiss her…" Finally, we both moved at the same time, and Edward kissed me.

After the kiss, I said, "The reason I couldn't talk to you in Lakeland was because I liked you." Master of finesse, I know.

The next day was travel day and I didn't know how to behave so I ignored him, and we didn't talk to each other. I think he was going off my actions. We flew into Indianapolis, and I was staying with a friend. We had no contact for a few days. He wrote me a beautiful letter admitting how he had always admired me. He asked me if I wanted to date, and my response was that we should take it slowly. Then we went on our official first date.

Since we weren't sure what this was, we didn't tell anyone else about our feelings for each other. You can imagine the surprise among the group when, two months later, we signed up to room together, in the same bed. No one but our closest friends knew we were dating. Edward had his butt chewed out in Luggage (the number in Toys on Ice where all the giant suitcases meander around the ice) by his luggage mate, who viewed Luggage as their personal confessional time. He told her we had not told anyone until we were sure we were dating and that this wasn't a passing fling.

And so, I found my prince charming and finally saw the end of the frog era. And for the record, the hole in the wall bar Yesterdays is still around twenty years later.

Chapter 16
Homecoming

I was born in Richmond, VA and I lived there for five years. Then we moved to Houston, TX for ten years. At the age of twelve, I followed a coach to Las Vegas, NV and lived with another skating family for a year. Then when my family moved to Rochester, NY, in 1995, I moved to Indianapolis, IN to train for a year. At fifteen years old, I lived away from home for the second time. After which, I followed my family to upstate NY for my high school years. My mother told me I was a traveling gypsy. She said that I was so independent, that as soon as I learned to walk, I was out the door.

Living away from home at a young age, especially during the awkward teenage years was difficult, but in my estimate, worth it to progress in figure skating. When I initially moved to Las Vegas, my best friend and I lived with my coach for the summer until she could find families to take us in. She did not have room for us, so we slept on the floor under her dining room table. Her awful yip dog would eat the crotch out of our skating tights and attack our feet first thing in the morning. Skating tights, like everything else in the sport were expensive. This annoying dog turned out to be the least of my worries while I stayed with our coach.

I was a big fan of recording everything in my diary. Living and training in proximity with my best friend was at first awesome for a twelve-year-old. Then you realize that living together is not the same as hanging out. All the little things that annoyed me went in my journal. My German coach found my journal, by found I mean she dug it out of my suitcase. She took red pen and corrected my journal. Then she gave the diary to my best friend with highlighted passages. The book-marked sections were what I had written about my best friend when I was angry. That went over well. Who does that? But time healed our adolescent wounds and so did different living arrangements.

The family I ended up living with for a year in Las Vegas were genuinely nice, but I had to share my bedroom with their ten-year-old daughter. Two years age difference did not seem like a lot except when one is a preteen. I did not want to share my friends let alone my living space with a 'child'. We would fight like full on sisters and she would attempt to blame me for everything to try and get me kicked out. During the summer I would check out six books from the library and hide in the bushes to read alone as she circled the apartment complex trying to hunt me down.

I grew four inches that year. This led to knee problems, and I could not train. Not training led to a lot of time to think about how homesick I was. My parents paid this family to take care of me, and they did a good job. But how do you feed an exercising preteen with a growth spurt. It is much like trying to feed a teenage boy. There was not enough food in the house. I would come home from practice and make buttered toast with cinnamon and sugar as pregame for dinner. When I went home over Christmas break, my mother's mouth dropped open at the sight of her skin and bones daughter. This led to some swear words, phone calls, and more money for food to the family I lived with.

The second time I lived away from home was in Indianapolis, I had my own bedroom and bathroom on the third floor of a downtown house. The family I lived with had a daughter who was a senior in high school and living away from home to train. I had adjusted to my living arrangements and my place with my fellow ice skaters when the daughter unexpectedly moved home. I was booted from the nice private third floor room to a shared bathroom on the second floor with her parents. I have seen way too much of her father trapsing naked from the bathroom at night.

Even though most of the skaters were in high school or just graduated, there was a separation between the older skaters and the younger ones (I was a younger one at 15). The daughter took me out with the older skaters one night. That ended with vomiting bud light and Doritos. And that was the last time she allowed me out with the cool kids. Plus, her parents heard me puking in the shared bathroom and this got me a phone call to my parents and a curfew. My dad's bewildered response to questions about what my curfew was must have been apparent because she said, "When my daughter was her age, her curfew was midnight" My parents had never needed to give me a curfew.

After having attended small private schools, my downtown school had a class the size of 900 and was intimidating to say the least. As I trained and continued school my parents and brother moved from Houston, TX to Rochester, NY. After a year of training, my family decided it would be best if I moved home.

While packing, I forgot my diary. The diary was well hidden between my bed and mattress of the second-floor bedroom. I called the mother I lived with and told her I'd be back in Indianapolis for a competition early in fall. Would she keep my diary safe and please, please, please don't let her daughter see it. Well, her daughter saw it and read it, and read passages of it to the rest of the cool kids about my first boyfriend and anyone I'd ever had a crush on and all the other petty things one puts in their teenage diary.

During the first year with Toys on Ice while on the East Coast USA we played Richmond, VA. I don't remember much from when I lived there since we moved when I was five, but there are snapshot memories of the house I lived in. My parent's favorite house, neighborhood, and next-door neighbor were in Richmond, so I thought I would look the house up. I went up to the house knocked on the door and told them who I was. They stared at me with suspicion and an incredulous look. As it turns out the same people who had bought the house from our family in 1985, were still living there in 2001. She told me they still received mail for my mother. After she showed me around the downstairs, I had her take a picture of me sitting on the stairs. I want to compare with the photo Mom has of me as a naked three-year-old imp sitting on the same staircase.

On tour Richmond offered the Penny Lane pub as our favorite hangout and a river side picnic on the rocks, where we made our own water slide out of the currents and smoothed rock mini waterfalls. I wore my favorite sundress to the rink one day and walking down the loading ramp I was greeted by one of our trailer gypsies and their dog. The puppy dog came bounding up for his usual greeting, jumped up and ripped my dress strap, exposing me from navel to neck. Harry saw it and started laughing; he followed this up by running in to tell the makeup room what he'd seen.

All these memories of various places I've lived during my formative years begs the question: Where is home? When you're out on the road for ten months of the year, your mom lives in FL, your Dad in NY, and your boyfriend in TX, where do you lay your head on break? I always loved returning to my Dad's house, so I guess NY was home. Since I would not be home more than a couple months a year, I decided to box up all my remaining belongings. The attic became a danger zone of piles of Tupperware containers, with taped on labels. Heat negates tape and all my labels eventually melted off. My poor father would be sent on frequent missions throughout the year to find some tiny, miscellaneous article of clothing or costume and then mail it to me. It was always 50/50 as to whether he got it right, but that was due to my attic packing and his interpretation of color. I might ask for something like can you bring the purple t-shirt with black stripes? I would either get the right type of shirt or the right color but not both. If purple and black is what I ordered from the attic, Dad would fill the order with say an orange tee shirt.

I am also a severe clothes whore, it was hard enough packing a suitcase, but I love to buy clothes and for a long time my body was always the same size. I could wear shirts from when I was 15. I suppose that is not something to brag about. Then I got upper body strength and a smidge of boobs and had to go through that packed up attic and give half of it to salvation army, but it was like trying to take a chew toy from a hungry dog. Edward had to sit through the fashion show of me putting it all on, and then physically taking it away from me. I was ridiculous, I couldn't even zip up an outdated skirt and I was arguing with him to keep it.

My sixth year, we had a long break mid-tour. I got tired of digging through all my trunks in the attic while living at home, so I unpacked all my things to start living in my room again. At 26, I had to laugh at some of the things I'd packed up for future use. For example, I had stored away all my markers, pens and pencils. Was I worried that wherever I ended up living, there would be a shortage of writing implements? Not to mention most markers were dried out due to attic storage. I also discovered that while on tour, I would forget some of the clothing I owned. So, there were six, identical black tank tops, one for each year on tour. I also realized I have a shopping problem. After looking at the years of accumulated wardrobe items, I vowed I would never buy clothes again. This was of course before Christmas.

Break is always a nice time to relax and regroup. With our type of on-the-go lifestyle, sitting still can become stale quickly. US Citizens can collect unemployment for temporary leaves of absence. It often pays more than a part time job would, and it's hard to get hired for a few weeks here and there. So, we're home, relaxing, collecting unemployment but soon we miss the road life.

Spending so much time and being in close proximity with the people on tour makes them a second family; for better and worse.

Edward's Dad moved into a small apartment, his brother had a full house of his own, his grandparents lived far outside of Houston, his mother is crazy, and his sister lived in Dallas. Whenever Edward would go home to Houston, there was nowhere for him to stay. He'd end up staying in a cheap hotel for most of the break, spending a lot of money needlessly. Logically, I invited him to live at our house in Rochester. He hesitated at first feeling strange about living at my father's house, but finally accepted. The living arrangement was an even trade, I would do all the household chores and cook, while Edward did repair work around the house. He made a laundry chute out of our old, unused chimney and Dad was sold after that.

Most people can't wait to get out of their parents' house. I've been independent since a young age, but I like moving home for short summer visits. It's only a few months a year and it makes the time at home less lonely. We don't have to pay for some place we only use two months per year and plus, my dad is a cool dude. When my dad comes to visit the show, he's very sociable, he comes out to the bars with us, even though he doesn't partake. For my brother's birthday, he bought everyone from the show a drink. That earned him major brownie points.

Everyone always wants to know when he'll be back. He has become his own legend. When he's visiting or spoken about in the ladies make up room, it's with a long drawn out, lower pitched Adriiiiiaaaaan! And it's become a game to the ladies to see who can get a kiss on the cheek first or the most times. Some upgrade to a kiss on the lips!

Eventually I'll repay his kindness and patience with an invitation to live with me. Then I can take care of him as he has always taken care of me.

Chapter 17
The First Time Is Always the Best Time

Touring on skates is a young person's job. You have the occasional performer who has made it into their thirties, forties and one even in their seventies. But you would never know it to look at them. They are youthful in appearance, acting, and energy levels. The only age indicator might be in their eyes. After my first year on the road, I came home and my father said, you look the same, but your eyes are older. It is true, while our bodies and even faces may stay the same, the toll is taken in our eyes. And from there it slowly begins to spread, the crow's feet, deeper circles, or an imperceptible worldliness in some. Still, this is a job for the young at heart.

Saying as much, each year on tour I found more and more new hires beginning at the age of 18. When I was new, Toys on Ice had 7 new hires, only three of which were under 21. My first year on Underwater Fantasy on Ice we had 21 new hires, most of which were 18. As I was turning 24, and most of the cast were new and very young, I felt strangely old. Each year more and more young'uns are hired, and fewer of the old classics stay around. The feelings of people and groups have changed as tour years progress. Being an actor on the ice and youthful, everything is big and overly dramatic. Add in living in close quarters, passion, and libations and it's easy to get carried away. The rotating door of ripe 18-year-olds keeps the fountain of youth flowing, but the drama gets tiring.

Tour culture is one headed for a self-absorbed, dramatic, and destructive direction. I do not aspire to be like that. It's also not sustainable, which might explain why so many burn out in one to three years. However, our active job and lifestyle keeps us all youthful. Despite best efforts, however, you are affected by your surroundings.

On tour, I was in touch with the current styles and I certainly did not look or act my age. I was ID-ed when I bought a drink from a girl who barely looked 21 herself. She said, "Sorry, but you don't even look 21." Wonder what she thought when she looked at my ID and found out I was 27? When I was sixteen, I got away with occasionally ordering drinks and never getting carded. At that time I looked older. On tour, I looked younger than 21, which is a nice problem to have. It doesn't help that my mother often forgets my exact birthday she called one year a day late and said, "Happy Birthday!"

"Thanks, Mom, it was yesterday."

"Oh, really? What are you now, 21?"

"No, Mom. I'm 27." Still, it's the thought that counts.

When my parents were my age, they were married, Dad had finished law school, my mom had finished nurse anesthetist school and they were both saving up to have children.

After my seven years on the road for me and nine for Edward, we had barely saved enough to start a new life off the road. We had spent a big chunk of savings to start the coffee stand. We paid it back with the success of the coffee stand, but I couldn't even afford to quit the ice show, let alone think about kids. And I was almost thirty.

When I figured out what my next career would be, I would have to go back to school, so when would we be financially stable? As it turns out you're never financially stable, you always have less or more, and you always make do. I never did hear that clock ticking, so children are probably not in the future. However, I'm happy to spoil my niece rotten until she turns 18, then I'll take her on a world tour.

The level of skating skills in new hires seems to decline the longer I was in the company. When Edward joined his first show, they had everyone go through their jumps to find the talent capacity for choreography purposes. Almost everyone could do their doubles, and a smaller handful could do triples. Pair skaters were even less available. The longer I was in the company, the fewer skaters could jump and spin and more and more could barely skate. I should be one to talk about basic skills, but with the demise of figures, I see a lack in edge quality, and balance. Where have all the good skaters gone?

This situation makes the principles and those with talent stand out even more. Many of the shows no longer require much skating ability. There are only two numbers on Underwater Fantasy that require jumping, spinning, and actual skating. And then, a show like Royals comes along and it's full of real pair numbers and plenty of skating. Perhaps opening more and more skating shows means talent is spread too thin.

Turnover rate seems to be getting shorter. The classic skaters are becoming fewer, and the newbie skaters are staying for shorter stints. Taking a guess, I'd say the average turnover rate is two years. I stayed for a decade and had been dubbed a lifer. Auditions changed so that a video was sent in and screened before in-person auditions. It seems like the market is drying up since there was a notice on the board that we needed more skaters. If the company is desperate for skaters, I guess they cannot be picky. This seems especially true for male skaters. If you can stand on two blades, you have a shot at being hired.

My brother joined tour my seventh year as a crew member but was desperately attempting to learn to skate after hours. His incentive, female figure skaters who were helping teach him. He quickly grew tired of the efforts and returned to his partying ways.

My second tour year with Toys on Ice, the summer of 2002, I toured Mexico City for six weeks. The first time I was there, the days were exceptionally long for me. It was hard trying to find myself through tequila, late nights, 12 shows a week, only Mondays off and relationship strain. I did not want to go back to Mexico, but there I was once again in Mexico City, round two, with Underwater Fantasy.

I have come to the decision that the first movie or book in a sequel that you read, whether it is the chronological first in a series or not, is usually your favorite. There are always exceptions, but I saw the third Indiana Jones movie first and it has always been my favorite. I think this is true of Mexico, no matter how bad it was the first time through; it was also the best time.

On this tour, we went back to the Teotihuacan pyramids. The last time Edward and the guys got wasted, taking shots out of their flasks every platform of the climb, and of course having a cooler full of free little Coronaitas, sombreros, and corona shirts didn't help. After that, it was a trip to the tequila factory where they found the mescal and 100% agave tequila. They stumbled through the Basilica during a funeral doing an Elmer Fuud impersonation 'Shhhh', which turned all the serious, black draped heads. He stumbled down the steps and fell asleep in the bathroom as we were trying to leave. A real friend pulls your pants up and puts you on the bus. After that, Edward took the bus mike and tried to tell us all a joke, getting halfway through, and pausing, lost in thought only to repeat it from the beginning and never reaching the punch line. What could top that?

I was not as fond of the drink at the time. I had quite a sober head and was a little embarrassed. Over time the story has grown into a fond one with the retelling and embellishments of time. So how could we possibly top that first time to the pyramids? Our drinking buddies weren't there, and the hired tour guide had a nasal voice and was more interested in telling her personal glories than moving along. We quickly ditched her and went on by ourselves. The tequila factory was closed down, so we tried two others, not nearly as good, but we did find a donkey to feed almond tequila to. Edward whispered sweet nothings in its ear and let it wear the sombrero. One of our buddies watched in wonder and asked, "How do you speak donkey?"

We made a return trip to white water rafting during round two of our Mexico tour. On this adventure, there was much video evidence of a well-endowed donkey. Said video seems to re-emerge about every ten years on Facebook enabling us to remember our enchanted time there. But rounds two and three of white water rafting could not top the first trip. After white water rafting all day a few of us were not ready to turn in so we wandered into the little town nearby. We found the only lit beer sign in the window of a house. We went in only to realize we were in someone's house and had interrupted a birthday party! They did not speak much English or seem to mind us so we danced the night away celebrating a cute old man in a local casa. In Mexico, you couldn't drink the water, but there was plenty of tequila and coronas to slake our thirst. We ended the whole Mexico tour with a pool side smash down of a poor piñata, which is also included in the nostalgic video.

It seems as we got older, and the cast got younger, that in many ways everything became repetitive. Not just the repetition of the east and west coast tours but the conversations at the bar always seemed to be the same. The newness had worn off. This is when you know it might be time to leave. For me, I started to notice it after the Europe tour at about year nine, doing our third new show, and during our third east coast tour. I was getting injured more often and a little more disenchanted. There were plenty of fun times and great people, but I knew my time on the road was coming to a close.

Chapter 18
Winds of Change

Everyone says they want change, but I find that people really don't. They get it, and then wish for what they previously had. I switched shows my fourth tour for Underwater Fantasy, which was the hot new show, and destined to travel to more places than just the United States. I was given everything I could be given on the new show, a fun character, a pairs partner, aerialist training, and lead female fish understudy, but I wasn't happy and couldn't figure out why. I was grateful for what I'd been given, Edward was still with me, so what was the problem?

I think the first problem was attitude. Everyone was just a little disgruntled to begin with, and I think this added to the general unhappiness, and as the year went on people continued to be more negative, myself included. My friends who had come with me to this show were mostly done and ready to get off the road. The attitude was the sooner the better. Things like 'this company is going downhill...' were being said a lot.

Another issue was age, my age. At 24, I'm no old fart, but this is my fourth tour and compared to the 20 new people at age 18, I felt old. The younger group could not go down to the hotel bar. This in turn cuts down on the socializing outside of work. The room parties became more prevalent, which made me feel like a closet alcoholic. And, in addition, there were just too many shows and publicities, and not much down time. There was no one older to offer advice; I was the old one. I certainly didn't feel like a seasoned veteran.

It finally felt like the company was weeding out the old pros, making room for the new young and dumb. If they don't know any better, the company can pay them whatever they want, right? At the end of that tour year, they closed two shows and were only opening one. Thinning the heard makes sense, the longer you are here the more money you make. They do give loyalty raises for every year you have been employed, which always came with stipulations. Does not apply after so many years, does not apply if you are a principle or specialty act, etc. While many classic oldies were leaving, there was going to be a lot of shuffling. Everyone felt they had to mind their manners, or there may not be room for you next year.

Perhaps the leading contributor to my unhappiness was my new performance director. I was used to my first performance director, by the books, treats everyone fairly, tough and knows her job. Paul was new to his position, but he had been in the company for 16 years, leading me to believe seniority or last man standing led to his promotion. I tried to be understanding, he was new to his position, but he's also been around the company long enough to know better.

His time management and organization skills were atrocious. He rehearsed all the potential understudies in the show at the same time and made all the rest sit on the sidelines and watch. The poor principle had to teach their show over and over. I kept thinking to myself, "How does one show initiative if we're spoon fed the whole way."

I worked hard for my first understudy on Toys on Ice. I had however, forgotten that I needed to learn more than just solos and dialogue. At the walk through to place me in the finale in my first understudy spot, I had not learned the principles finale patterns. I was taken aside and admonished. I was wasting everyone's time, and they would have to reschedule my walk through. It was an eye opening lesson I never forgot.

From the beginning of Underwater Fantasy on Ice, they treated us in the order of understudy they thought we were. So then why did it take six months to decide understudies, if they already knew? Perhaps I did not kiss enough ass.

Paul is as slippery a weasel as it gets. Especially when it comes to answering questions. He quickly forgets whatever he's told you to save his own neck. He told one of the characters during the making of the show, to add a moustache to her make-up, when photo shoots started, the make-up artists saw the new addition with horror. Paul claimed it was all that character's idea. New and old skaters were not enthusiastic about this new promotion for Paul. And neither was the crew.

He had his favorites and was not afraid to show it. He was not specific enough in notes and he often sounded as if he did not know what he was talking about. After we opened, he would change the choreography that a whole team had created. His job was not to re-choreograph the show, it was to maintain its originality.

Perhaps when he gave correctional notations, he was worried about offending people. His notes were very generalized and vague. So, his corrections fell on deaf ears. Rather than specifying by name the person out of place, he would say things like the pinwheel line was not straight. So, he gave the same notes over and over with no recommendations for improvement. Remind me what the definition of insanity is? In a position of some leadership, you need to have authority and while there's no need to be offensive, you can't always worry so much about everyone else's feelings. Maybe, I should take some of my own advice here.

In Europe, I was an understudy for both the male fishy lead and the fabulous female fish, as well as the aerialist full time. Between split weeks and heavy show schedules we had many six and nine packs. That's three shows a day multiplied by the number of days in a row that you do three shows. This meant rather than get a break from my aerialist routine I would go into my understudies. And since there were ample shows, I had ample opportunities. Almost every weekend I was in both understudies. One nine pack I was in a combination of them three times.

In an effort to make sure we were all replaceable and increase our understudy numbers, we trained the reluctant Crazy Russian in the male understudy role. He had absolutely no desire to do this role but was pretty much forced into it. He did not study the dialogue patterns and frankly did not give two craps. Good for him. However, this does not make the show look so good. One day they had me in the fabulous female fish when he was in the men's lead role. Now I had two choices. Perform my dialogue patter as I'm supposed to and have been doing for the last five years, while the Crazy Russian goes wherever he wants. Or follow his lead. I chose the latter. If we were having a dialogue across the ice, it would probably not look good to the audience. So, I let him lead and tried to keep the show together as much as I could.

Did I get thanks or even acknowledgement from Paul for this adaptation? No. The Crazy Russian and I had understudy notes together and all of Paul's notes were directed squarely at me. I know my pattern. Clearly Mr. Crazy Russian does not know his, but fine. Message received, next time I'll do my pattern and ignore the misplaced male fish. Lesson learned if you don't give two poops, then you don't get corrective notes, I guess. But Paul never put us in together again. I guess he did not want to tempt fate on that one.

But this brings up stage directions. For someone not raised in the arts of performing on a stage, they are very confusing at first. The best way to describe show directions is if you are standing with you back to the curtain, facing the audience. This is your anatomical position. So, stage left would then be on your left. Upstage is by the curtain and downstage is toward the audience. Add to this that you must count headers for your placement in some numbers. I do sympathize with any performance director. The notes from watching a performance are from a mirror point of view. And identifying one of thirty people in the exact same costume is daunting.

Chapter 19
Tequila Poppers

The second time to Mexico City, we made a different trip out of the city almost every Monday we had off. We would leave Sunday night and come back Monday night. We made it back to the pyramids, white water rafting, Taxco, and Acapulco. White water rafting was great both times, but always better the first. The grass huts and grounds were cleaner and nicer. I think our bus driver was tipped to take us to a different place. No one slept much on the nighttime bus trip after three shows. After a short morning nap, we were all prepped for white water rafting. Since it had been raining recently, the waters were up, making the class four rapids into a class six. For those that are not wise to the water world of rafting, six is as high as it goes, and probably not the best idea for a bunch of foreign, drunk idiots. We jumped in our boats and off we went. Several people were bucked off and one raft toppled over, but all survived.

Instead of napping after our cruise through the rapids, a group of us played volleyball. I was out of dry shorts, so I decked myself out in Edwards long swim trunks and went to town. We rappelled down a tiny cliff side, and zip lined over our little huts. This zip line trip was complete with our friend the well-endowed donkey, that is still around and has ballads sung about him and will be forever remembered by video clip. Before dinner, I took a dip in their pool which looked and felt a lot like a warm baby pool. Follow this by food, drinks, card games where the loser wears beer boxes as a hat, and a crash nap that didn't keep us down long. That's how we white water rafted with only one day off.

Our show's bar in Mexico was the Cantina. Any other hole in the wall Mexico bar was cheaply priced, but the Karisma Cantina, strategically placed across the street from the El President hotel, knows the ice show is coming once a year and they get away with charging higher prices. They also give us celebrity status by locking us in after hours and ignoring any age gaps. We even have our own side of the bar.

The Cantina is home of the tequila poppers. Tequila is an acquired taste, but there's something about Mexico that makes you drink tequila and beer. It goes down better with an Oaxaca steak complete with avocados, mushroom, and cheese. A tequila popper is a double shot glass with more than half tequila and a dash of sprite. It's just not the same drink when you're states side. You cover the top of the shot glass, pound it on the table and slam it back. Tequila can bring out strange emotions in people. I get more aggressive on tequila. Maybe that's why there's so much drama when we head south of the border.

Sometimes the Cantina takes care of us with not charging for a bottle or two of liquor. One night with Toy's on Ice, we were the last, rowdies in the bar. They locked the doors and took all the left-over drinks, poured them in what looked like a glass version of the genie's lamp, held our heads back and made us drink. That's Mexico; it makes you do insane things to keep from going crazy yourself.

There is a smell to downtown Mexico City of dirt and garbage mixed in with street meat, rats, and pollution. It attacks as soon as you walk out of the hotel and it takes about three minutes until your sense of smell has deadened. No matter where you're exiting, there is still an adjustment period. It is cooler than you imagine, due to being on top of a mountain and with the altitude and pollution, you can barely breathe. The men hiss at you like snakes, even if you're wearing a nun's habit. They sense that you are different. Even state side, we are like a colorful flock of exotic birds that do not fit in.

But the real challenge for getting to work is playing Frogger. There are two options. One, go below the street traffic, into the smelly, sketchy tunnel, the long way, or...the short cut on top. When you're sleeping off your tequila poppers, every extra minute counts so it's usually option two, despite company warnings year after year. FYI, Mexican drivers do not stop and have the largest variety of car horn sounds I've ever heard, looney tunes has nothing on their sound effects. The traffic to get to the building is fast and dense, 3 lanes each way. You aren't safe once you're on the middle island either, you must jump two fences without falling off the curb back into traffic. So far, we've had no casualties that I know of.

I was always scared of my purse being stolen. I traveled with a tiny purse strapped across my chest, filled with the bare minimum, and clutched in my hand in case someone tried to cut it off me. Can you say tourist? One of my friends went to see the Pope drive by and had her purse stolen, someone is going to hell for sure.

We were also warned off green taxis. Only take the taxis the hotel calls for you. The green and white VWs have been known to pick you up and take you straight to an ATM, where you get robbed. But I did ride in a green VW once with two guys, we were in a hurry and I figured if I was protected by two big guys, we should be alright. All three of us were squeezed into the back seat because there was no passenger seat, just a big leaver that opened the side door. I wonder what the driver's test is like for those cab drivers. I'm sure you must get extra points for speed, aggression and human casualties.

Montezuma's Revenge is no joke. Street meat, water, it seems almost anything will give your rear the runs. And even when your stomachs on empty, your still excreting acid, usually from both ends. Many people lose weight in Mexico. Problems get a little funnier and more intense when you're in full costume, on the ice, during a show, and it hits. When the urge hits, there's no time, and no holding; all or nothing. Trying to get out of some of those costumes quickly is not easy, but we are true professionals. One of our many rules is no using the toilet in costume, and no wearing the costume to the bathroom. Once Edward was struck with the revenge, he figured you can't catch lightening twice. That meant everything including street meat was on the menu. Cheap and tasty, but who knows what you're eating. I did notice a few less rats.

Mexico City was followed by Monterey. We spent three weeks in Monterey. Most of the children had already gone back to school, but we were still performing daytime shows. No audience, plenty of shows, no break, and not much to do in Monterey. We gained back all our Mexico City weight because the only thing around was Carl's Jr. or race go carts. We did make friends with the circus performers across the street from us. Performers are performers, we all know how to party. We were the first ice show in a long time to play Monterey.

We finally lost the privilege to stay across the street from the Mexico City arena in the El Presidente hotel, and with it our close ties to the Cantina. I'm sure there were many tours and many reasons that the hotel grew tired and annoyed with us, but I do remember one night we had stumbled home from the Cantina and continued our drinking escapades. The crew rivalry was in full swing when suddenly they de-panced Gauge and shoved him in an elevator sent straight to the lobby. Thing is Gauge doesn't wear underwear.

Chapter 20
Do Not Disturb

Edward and I have been on the road long enough to understand the maid service for the most part. The Do Not Disturb sign is the only safety you have, and it is not always a reliable one. Some of those maids are so determined that 8 am rolls around and they are pounding on your door, blatantly disregarding the keep out sign. And while we are nakedly yelling no thanks at the top of our lungs, and the neighbors are calling in a noise complaint, the maid comes barging in anyway. Eight am seems like a luxury, but our job hours are more of the evening to late shift. One of these days, I keep swearing that I'm going to answer the door in my birthday suite, that will send them heading for the hills. Maybe then the privacy sign will mean a little more. Other inspirational ideas include doing naked head stands when they come in or throwing food and acting like monkeys.

I understand they have a job to do, but when the door says leave us alone, hey that is like getting a free pass. The sneaky ones do surveillance and wait until they see us leave, hiding behind rows of towels and toilet paper. Then we come home, and our room is spotless, damn them. Sometimes if the maids obey the door sign, when they see you leave, they follow you with towels begging to give your room service and towels. It is very considerate, but you end up running and hiding in shame like they are the paparazzi. I know what everyone thinks, what is so wrong with having your room cleaned. Well, let me tell you.

I do not know these maids, most of whom are perfectly nice, but those few rotten tomatoes ruin the entire bunch for me. Third year Toys on Ice, Edward was flipping through our DVD collection only to realize that many of them were missing. They were strategically removed so on first glance; you would think maybe you had lent a few out. There was the accidental removed of

Edward's universal remote. I really think this one was an accident, the maids probably thought the room had an extra remote, but the front desk never found it. They often threw away food and other items that might look like garbage to the maid but were treasures to us.

It's not only the trust issues, but we also have all our cook wear, which is a big red fire hazard in hotels, and our VCR and DVD player hooked up to the TV, which sometimes gives us the pay per view channels, yes high tech in our day. Not to mention incense and multiple hair drying and styling items. We did set off the fire alarm in an old Boston hotel while cooking one evening. We quickly threw all the cookware into the bathroom and turned on the shower. When the hotel admin came a knocking, Edward said I was taking a shower and that must have set off the alarm. I doubt they believed our story over the smell of burnt meatballs, but they did not demand entrance to the shower.

Another group of girls made the mistake of putting a hot pot on the floor. They burned that patch of carpet. Had it been anyone else they probably would have pulled the dresser over the carpet. But honest as Lizzy was, she reported it and the hotel took full advantage. They assumed the company would pay and said that the whole room's carpet would have to be replaced. And of course, it was a very expensive carpet. Unfortunately, Lizzy, the Good Samaritan had to pay out of pocket!

All our paraphernalia must be hidden from the maids. Not all maids will turn you in, but how do you know friend from foe? That is the purpose of the do not disturb sign. Just maybe, they won't touch my stuff. After all, this is our home for the week even if we are renting it.

I have only run into maids who ignore the do not disturb sign in the states. Japan and Mexico obey the sign and do not seem to care as much about all our extra paraphernalia. In Japan, if you do not want room service, they would leave a giant plastic bag with all the room essentials, towels, soaps, shampoo, coffee, and robes. I reuse my towel, so my little, tiny Japanese room would be filling up with all the extras hidden in the closet if we were lucky enough to have a closet.

I like the cheaper hotels. Not the dirt bag motels, but the cheap ones. Cheap hotels almost always come with a fridge and microwave. The staff is a lot more relaxed. Room parties are more likely to be ignored, there's more complimentary items, and fewer hassles in general. Downside to cheap motels is that the rooms usually face out to the parking lot and so there is some concern for safety. However, if you take over the entire hotel safety is less of a concern. One girl did have her underwear stolen out of the dryer. And unfortunately, one drunk crew guy peed on an air conditioner that he thought was a toilet! That room had a surprise when they turned on the AC.

The importance of a refrigerator was very clear when Under Water Fantasy on Ice went to Japan and Southeast Asia. One of our skaters was a type one diabetic. He had to have insulin to survive. He negotiated with the company, and they supplied a fridge in every room he had. He also finagled them to transport a three-month supply of snickers bars to keep his blood sugar up. Not only did he have type one diabetes, but he also had celiac disease. Try saying no gluten in Japanese!

The Hyatt in downtown Chicago thinks it's high and mighty. They wanted to charge for everything. They charged me for my incoming mail. I had to pay to get it, isn't that a federal offense? I was charged for valet parking a car for three weeks, when we did not have a car. And we were not allowed to bring in food or drinks. I snuck my groceries in at the beginning of the week, but the hotel wanted us eating and drinking their food, the problem with that is all their restaurants were closed by the time we ended the show, and their food must have had gold flakes for the prices they charged. Security stopped Edward and searched his backpack, they attempted to take away his beer, Edward said no way and went to the garage and downed them all.

I do not advise putting a credit card down if you can avoid it and certainly not a check card. They hold vast amounts of money on a check card and once they have your credit card number it is even harder to argue your way out of any creative billing. But if you pay for anything with cash, make sure you get a receipt. I am extremely glad they changed the way we paid for hotels.

Edward tells me that once upon a time everyone was required to pay their own bill at the end of the week. Often his roommates would have spent all their money and he would be stuck paying their combined bill. Now they just deduct it out of our check. Part of our contract stipulates that if we share a room with one other person, we'll only pay $21 a night. Company works a deal for so many people staying at a hotel, if the rooms work out to be more than $42/night, the company covers the rest. I have attempted quading a few times to save money. Edward refuses to room with four people in the same room anymore, smart man. With the right group and a big enough room, it can be fun, but only on a very limited occasion.

It's hard enough to find one decent roommate that you can stand to share tight quarters with, try four. Even though the room was small in E. Rutherford, NJ, we had a good group. Edward and I shared a bed. I took out a weeks' worth of cloths and then closed and piled my two suitcases on their side wedged between the bed and did not open them again all week. Everyone keeps different schedules on days off. Our little Thai skater would never sleep except during the day, like a beautiful vampire. He was skinny as a rail and always hungry. So, he would hang out in the bathroom cooking until all hours. It was weeks before I could get the smell of fish sauce out of my suitcases.

Normally in small rooms when people quaded everyone avoids their overcrowded room, if possible, and we were only a short train or bus ride from NYC. I stayed in to get well and watched TV. Somethings don't translate across cultures. As I'm watching TV, Atid comes in, takes the remote away, and changes the channel. He watches for three minutes and then wanders off down the hallway. That was the last time I could convince Edward to quad.

I had a far different experience in Spokane, WA. The rooms were much bigger and I quaded with four friends, two gay guys and another girl. I ended up being bed buddies with one of the gay guys. He said I was the best bed mate ever because I did not move or snore. Seemed like one giant slumber party every night, giggles until we passed out, card games, Christmas decorations, and of course excessive drinking. Everyone decided that our room was the hang out spot for the week. So, our little quartet was packed to capacity every night until the wee hours of the morning. When Edward and I room together, I always love to invite everyone to someone else's room to party. That way I never have to clean up or worry about noise complaints.

For a party, I am of the mindset, the more the merrier. There is always the unwanted guest, but I figure once I've had a few, I tend to love everyone, or I play my own game: the more an annoying person talks, the longer I drink and eventually I do love everyone! In Pittsburgh, we had a promoter party. A promoter's job in simplified terms entails a region of the states or country and they help advertise us and get us publicities, to promote the show in their region. Once upon a time, before the company became super cheap, there were frequent promoter parties.

The bouncer in Pittsford for the promoter party was a jerk and would not let one couple in after bending they're Canadian driver's license and being generally rude. They told us they were going home, and I was welcome to come to their room for a party after the bar. They had a corner room that week and it was extra spacious. They never said that I could not invite the entire cast, so I got drunk on my free drink tickets and told everyone. We were so drunk and rowdy that they were locking out the people they didn't like, and things were thrown from the sixth-floor windows. Tracey and Adam joked all night that I might not get an invite next time because of my big mouth.

Edward passed out in the party room, spread eagle over poor Suzy's bed. Attempting to move him is futile and in these conditions, he is not a light sleeper. He kept creepily petting her head and saying, "Now just lay there like a good girl" while laughing. Rather than sleep on a tiny corner of the bed she relocated to the couch. I know how he is when he takes up the whole bed, you get one tiny corner and halfway through the night like a big dog he tries to take the covers.

Edward has perfected the art of the pass out trick. He can party like the best of us but when he was done it was instant lights out. Toward the end of the Toys on Ice frozen forgotten tour, the crew had a party out back of the arena. Highlights included Olivia secretly making out with Chester, but it was not a secret and Noah pushing Peters in a hamper down a hill. Luckily for all of them it rolled over before dumping into the rocky SC river below. I cut out of the party early since I had a morning publicity. Edward never came home and upon arrival to the arena at five am, there he is sleeping soundly in his camping chair. He is always prepared. He got up and was more refreshed than I was.

The art of napping was of great importance to Edward, and he taught me well. Among the many things packed away in his crate was a hammock. He would find empty crates after loading in and set up the hammock. His fellow crew member would give him grief, but it was a lifesaver between shows. He even found one hammock critic enjoying a snooze in his hidden set up.

Edward had also earned the nickname, Batman. He would often just appear out of nowhere at the bar scene. A conversation would be taking place and he'd put his two cents in. Shocked bystanders would exclaim where did you come from? And so the Batman was born. He had also perfected the art of the disappearing trick, one minute he was there, the next he was gone!

One week upon arrival in our next city he sat on the curb outside the hotel with a bottle of tequila. As the afternoon progressed others joined him and slowly his bottle of tequila was drained. He was rooming with one of the other skaters. He went upstairs to take a shower, stripped down, and passed out where he lay on the bed. To his chagrin his roommate and Japanese girlfriend that spoke a little English came home to naked Edward sprawled on the bed. Apparently, her response was.

"So big! I like American men!"

Waking him up in the mornings is a nightmare, especially if he can't sleep it off; if he wakes up to his alarm, which I always set, then he goes back to sleep without hitting the snooze. I can't sleep for fear that he's going to oversleep. I pester him until he isn't pleasant. Usually there's nasty sounding non-sense words and more snoring. It's like poking a sleeping bear that might bite my hand off. Later in the day when I see him, he'll tell me thanks for getting him up. Sometimes I just stare at him like are you serious? But turnabout is fair play. When his drinking ways were over, I picked up the mantel and I know he has had to endure his fair share of my hang overs.

My first week in Japan, I roomed with the guy's line captain. After a long day of rehearsals and being messed up from the time zone change, we turned in early. Our room party crasher was not done yet and wanted to be entertained. He came in and jumped on our tiny beds and proceeded to be loud and obnoxious. I turned off the lights and said, "We're going to play the pretend to sleep game."

"I don't want to play that, that's boring!"

"Shh, there's no talking in the sleep game." Luke and I were quiet, stifling giggles while Franky continued to ask us if we were awake. Finally, after about fifteen minutes, the sleep game won, Franky fell asleep, I didn't really think that trick would work on a hyperactive 22-year-old, but it did.

West Coast with Toys on Ice, Edward and I had only been dating for just under a year. One new to tour girl had her heart set on Edward. The whole year we would bicker about it. She was pair height, and he was teaching her pairs. That already rubbed me the wrong way since I wanted to do a pair in-show with Edward and had been begging. I was convinced she was out to get him.

One party night Edward returned to our room to do his pass out trick. I wasn't done partying so stayed in the room party. From what we can piece together, Mandy stole my room key and ignoring the Do Not Disturb sign, entered our room. She tried to crawl into bed with drunk Edward who had the wherewithal to ask her what she was doing. She made some pithy plea about checking up on him. He snatched the key away from her and kicked her out.

He told me about it the next day. At the end of the year, a mutual friend told me that Mandy had talked her ear off all year about how she was going to 'get' Edward. So, I'm not crazy!

Chapter 21
Culture Shock

Having traveled for a good deal of my life, culture shock hit a little late. My second time to Japan, it reached its mark. Our show group never seems to fit in, no matter where we went. Even in the states, where most of us speak the language and wear the styles, we cause a stir. I think it is because groups of attractive young people suddenly appear walking around empty downtowns. There are plenty of attractive people everywhere you go, but here it seems the company is unparalleled in collecting handsome, athletic people who wear loud clothes.

The loud lifestyle almost got us into trouble in Tangier Morocco. We took a short trip over from Gibraltar. This is a Muslim country, so I tried my best to dress conservatively. We did not take the entire group sightseeing this time, but they followed on the ferry. They wore bright colors and belly shirts and Edward and I feared they might be kidnapped and sold on the sex slave market. We later heard they almost missed the last ferry back to Spain and would have spent a scary night alone at the ferry landing!

We took a trip up the Rock of Gibraltar to see the sights. Highlights included a food pit where the evil, wild monkeys were fed scraps of food to appease them. The locals told us that if they were not humored these primates would come down to the city and wreak havoc on the locals. We watched one such ape steal a woman's newly purchased bag of potato chips and look at her like a mobster, *What are you gonna do about it?*

On one summer break, my mom took my brother and I to Egypt. A glimpse of another culture through guided sightseeing is not the same as living in the culture like you do on tour. In Japan, we lived in the country for four months. In most of the big cities people spoke enough English for us to get around, and we also lived off picture menus. Pointing got us a long way, and I learned what I needed to get by.

"Ea onion, Ea wasabi, Beeru kuda sai." These are of course western phonetic spellings, but their meaning for me was no onions, no wasabi, and beer please. They had an amazing train system, and their bullet train went 60 mph. The train systems were easy to use, unless you found yourself lost in a rural town with only Japanese characters and no written words, and no one speaks English. Even then, we managed to find one person who understood our finger pointing and map enough to set us in the right direction.

A popular mode of transportation around town was the bicycle. The smaller cities were overrun with bikers. And they would usually have an extra person perched on the luggage tray or handlebars. We all thought this was a marvelous means of travel, so we bought fold up bikes. These bikes were well made, small with adjustable seats and tiny wheels. It made me chuckle to see Edward's six-foot frame on those little wheels speeding around town. A bicycle gang of us took a trip to a beach near Niigata and played ultimate Frisbee all day. We saw an elderly gentleman who loved his black lab so much that he carried him piggyback style into the water since the dog was too afraid to go swimming. There were no public bathrooms remotely close, so one poor girl had to relieve her bowels in the deep blue sea. I refused to get back in the water after that.

One late night with little to do in a small town found us disturbing the hotel peace by having our usual hallway party. I guess the company manager was fed up with our noise since we were right outside his room. He came out and unprofessionally yelled at us to stop acting like children. Well, isn't that what we are paid to do on the ice? I later found out that this did not sit well with one renegade who slashed the company manager's bike tires!

Another amazing sight was in Kyoto. Once a year the geisha in training make an appearance on the streets of Kyoto to give gifts to their clients. Any other time of year you must pay to be in their presence or see them at all. It was an honor to see the geisha like exotic rare birds in the streets. After this side trip, a small group of us went to Nara where the deer ate my map and posed for pictures. One deer had such an impressive rack that he blended into the tree roots behind him. In the Todai-ji temple, Rachel and I achieved enlightenment for our next life by crawling through the symbolic nostril. This tight fit was through a hole carved in a large wooden pole. The guys felt they were enlightened enough and happy to just take pictures of us. One rainy tourist travel day saw us at the Ise Jingu temple. This shrine is torn down and rebuilt every twenty years for the past millennium.

My favorite side trip in Japan was the floating tori (gate) and shrine of Miyajima. When the tide comes in, the whole shrine and gate are engulfed by blue sea water that off sets the bright red of the gate that is now floating and looks like the mathematical letter pi. While we were sightseeing in Itsukushima, we took the gondola up to the highest peak to observe the bay and I pet a penguin at the aquarium. Not bad for a day off.

I went with the crew to hike Mount Fuji. You leave in the middle of the night and are dropped off with the goal of seeing the sunrise. As all the westerners were huffing and puffing, little Japanese women who looked ancient raced right by us. Edward and I had walking sticks that were branded at each station you reached. Edward had packed a large backpack. I had packed plenty of layers because I heard that at the top it was cold. I asked him what was in his very heavy bag. At least six of the big boy Asahi beers were in there. His bag got lighter the higher he climbed and the more he drank. Toward the top he rethought his brilliant packing plan. Most of the crew called it quits at the second to last station, which happened to be closed so I did not get my last stamp on my walking stick. While in pain, I refused to quit that close to success.

Roger, Edward and I made it to the top about an hour before sunrise. I promptly sat down and cried. Edward said, "Why are you crying?" My response through sniffles was, "Because now we have to go back down!" It was indeed freezing at the top of Mt. Fuji. There were hot cans of soup for sale floating in metal tubs of hot water. Hot corn chowder never tasted so good. Roger, Edward, and I all huddled together and tried to fall asleep. Finally, the sun rose. Sunrise was beautiful but a bit cloudy so we could not see as much of the horizon as I would have liked.

I reported back to the cast about our adventures and warned that it was a little more stringent than initially anticipated. The male bravado poo pooed me and practically ran up the mountain with beer in hand doing acrobatic tricks at the top just to prove me wrong. To each their own. We had accomplished our mission of conquering Mt. Fuji. On our display wall, there is a Fuji walking stick and a Samurai sword.

The kindness and hospitality of the Japanese people never ceased to amaze me. We would mark the whiteboard in the lobby when heading out for the night just in case anyone wanted to join us later. In one small town, Edward and I left later than the group and found a bar with the same name as the one written on our communal white board. None of our friends were there. We tried with broken communication to ask if there was another bar of the same name. We did not think we were going very far in this line of questioning, but the bartender closed his bar and walked us to his competitor's bar where we found our friends.

Heaven, forbid you try to throw anything in your hotel room away. Edward threw out old sneakers and they mailed them to our next hotel assuming he had left them behind. We had to throw them in a public trashcan when no one was looking so that they would stop following us like a nefarious stalker.

Travel days in Japan were nothing like in the states. You would put your luggage outside your room the morning of travel day and they would magically show up in your room in the next city. When traveling by train as a group, you better keep up. Times between trains are quick and the door will close on you and leave you behind. We only had a bus travel day once and saw a waterfall in Nikko national park, a temple, and Rena vomiting out the window as it splatted the windows behind her painting a putrid shade of pink. Having your luggage taken care of, avoiding airplane lines, and fast trains made travel days far more enjoyable.

Although some things do not translate. When our show was there in 2006, tampons and deodorant were hard to find, I don't know if that is an issue any longer. We had been warned by previous shows and packed accordingly. Apparently, I did not know how to calculate my needs and my supply of deodorant and sanitary needs lasted for the next two years. On arrival to the airport to travel home, security searched my checked bags. He held up the clear bag of tampons asking what they were in Japanese. Since I didn't know how to say tampon in Japanese, I pantomimed how they were used. He turned red, threw them in the suitcase, slammed it shut and hurried me on my way.

Architecture in Japan was winged roof tops curved up in a smile, temples and gods different from our stoney churches. After a while, many of their temples began to look the same, but like an imaginary check list I would hunt each one down and drag Edward from one temple or palace to the next.

Fresh sushi is wonderful, until it becomes your everyday meal. And it is not American sushi. There is no deep fried, cream cheese or spicy mayo. The fishy smell of the streets and markets makes you tired of fish twice as fast. The large fish market of Tokyo was eye opening, I have pictures of tentacles, giant fish eyeballs, and many unidentifiable sea creatures.

I liked the novelty of the sushi restaurants that have conveyor belts. They would send around all sorts of sushi and treats, and you would pay by the stack of plates. They always looked us up and down because of the sizable stack we would rack up. If you eat like a westerner, then Japan can get expensive quick. When we tired of the fish, we would switch to the ramen houses, or Japanese curry from Little Spoon or Coco Curry, which were the local chains. Japanese curry isn't to be confused with Indian or Thai. It is thick and brown, mixes well with meat, veggies, and rice.

When we tired of that we could always depend on Yoshinara. There's even one or two in the states. They had rice bowls with different meats, always a tasty treat and open 24 hours. Last but not least, a taste of American fast food, McDonalds and KFC could almost always be found. Surprise, it's not quite the same. Sure, you have your Big Macs, but you also have your shrimp crocket paddies, which for the record Edward assures me are tasty. KFC did not have biscuits and breakfast was missing bacon. While most travelers are aghast when I tell them, I eat fast food while out experiencing culture, let me remind my readers that we were there for four months.

While all these foods were great, we missed the tastes of home. We would get excited over foreign import grocery stores where everything from home was overpriced. In Kochi, we were so excited by a little import shop with Tex-Mex food. We bought everything we could carry back to the hotel with us and had a Mexican feast. The taco shells had been a long time from Mexico because they were stale and the Coronas, while overpriced never tasted quite like they did in Mexico, yeah skunky fiesta! We didn't care, it was a taste of home.

The Japanese aren't big on the dairy products. Perhaps this explains why they are all so petite. All I could ever find was Camembert, a waxy, mushy substance that pretended to be cheese. When I did find a tiny ten-dollar wedge of Gouda or something they called red cheddar, I bought the store out of it. Red cheddar was like a saltier, drier version of our cheddar. Meat was always sliced into thin strips, which was great if we were having our own Korean bar-be-que, but it was hard to make a big fat steak out of that.

Korean bar-be-ques were a fun eating experience. You had a hot little cook surface in front of you. Sometimes it was mesh wiring or a flat surface over an open flame. You would order different meats, seafood, and vegetables and cook it yourself. Little cubes of grease fat would lube up the grill surface and add some flavor, we became crafty and flavored the meats with beer. Finally, you dip your cooked meat in soy or a variety of sauce and down the hatch they go.

I am an adventurous eater; I will taste almost anything once. That year in Japan there was an over population of jelly fish. The jelly fish were killing a large number of sea life, but the resourceful Japanese utilized the jelly fish. I even saw jelly fish ice cream. That was one I could not bring myself to taste. Everyone has heard of Kobe beef. I made a day trip there to try this illustrious beef. It does not disappoint. I found heaven in a bite of beef. The Kobe beef is worth every, expensive yen. These cattle have been grass fed with beer and given daily massages. Whatever they are doing, the beef is magical and I wish to be reborn as a Kobe cow in my next life.

Rehearsals for Japan were in the tiny northern town of Tomakomai. The show soundtrack is pre-recorded so we lip sync our lines. Most of us were not native Japanese speakers so often I said my aquatic lines by making fish faces and blowing bubbles. We spent three weeks getting ready to open. They didn't speak much English and grocery shopping was like playing Russian roulette. There was not a lot of public transit, so the local equivalent of a drug store was where we shopped for food. There were putrid-looking, hot, hard-boiled eggs that had been at it all day in a brown liquid, or a variety of packaged food with foreign characters. I never got up the nerve to try the all-day eggs. Cell phone cameras were not as common as today so I would buy a prepackaged treat and if I liked it try to remember the coloring or characters. We would often buy these premade rice triangles that had a meat inside. I always considered it a win if it was identifiable like tuna and cooked.

Over four months you find your favorite items like the milky tea and melon cream soda by Fanta. After the creature comforts of home food wear off upon your return, you find yourself missing your Japanese treats. You always want what you can't have.

Chapter 22
Come and Go

Perhaps with everyone getting younger in the company, it seems I pay less attention to first impressions. Gut instinct will usually tell you what's right. There's the old adage, "Don't judge a book by its cover." That's what I hoped for but that's not how it worked. Becoming the 'lifers' on tour has its advantages. You're in a stable relationship so you get to watch the new meat roll in and dress up in sparkles and high heels. Everyone looks so hot and fresh with their best personalities on display. With the whirl wind dating scene on tour you meet, get drunk, sleep together, move in together, realize you're nothing alike, have an ugly break up or just get drunk and sleep with someone else, and deal with the fall out!

The story of the fab four is a similar story. When I first joined tour, I made fast friends with three other girls, Tiny, Catty, and Eva. Catty turned out to want any male that I or anyone else liked, some self-esteem issues there. Eva was going through an emotional roller coaster, riding shotgun to some dark demons. There were rumors of foursomes and an affair that ended in divorce with a side trip to the ER from a forgotten tampon followed by its retrieval mission. She would go through major mood swings, and her friendly pal-around playing was often a bit too violent even for me. We ended the traffic skating number, where there were 16 car drivers in bulky plastic cars of red, yellow, blue, and seafoam green in a traffic jam. The scene called for angry play fight acting. Eva wasn't playing, this was usually her therapeutic anger management time. I would steer clear of her green car and the punches she threw. This is often where she would dole out her not so playful revenge.

Later in tour life, as years and maturity rolled on, Eva and I met up and found a renewed friendship with a fond memory of the past and less violent tendencies. Tiny was my best friend on tour, after the honeymoon phase I realized we weren't really suited for each other. I think it was a forced match out of my desperation to fit in and feel like I had a best gal pal. What we were really missing were the nice little courtesies.

For instance, I had an early morning publicity of the 4:30 am pick up variety. I tried to be polite by leaving the lights off as I attempted to get dressed. This led me to acquaint my shins with the side table and blindly search in drawers for something to wear. After many loud, exaggerated sighs of suggestion in which you could hear her rolling her eyes, she finally sits up in bed and asks me if I could be a little more considerate and be quiet? My retort was something sarcastic about doing it on purpose at which point I turned on all the lights! We would butt heads on everything. Aurora borealis, which is not only the northern lights but also a stone, I took up one side of the argument, she the other and there was no common ground. And of course, we could not both be right.

Tiny was Canadian. I'm all for pride in one's country, but she took it a bit too far. Tiny like her name, is short, barely five foot nothing but her voice more than makes up for her size, it's full volume. There is no inside voice. In the DC holocaust museum, she's saying things at her projected volume about why didn't the US get involved earlier and do more?

At dinner in DC, that my dad treated us to while he was in town, she got on her pedestal about South Park and how sick she was of them making fun of Canada. It's a cartoon! On and on she went. Then there was some debate about whether the writers were in fact Canadian. About this time Tiny did a 180 change of opinion, since the now humorous cartoon might have been Canadian made. By the end of dinner, she was saying how funny they were. Boyfriends solved an unseemly friendship break-up. I started dating Edward and she started dating Blake. I politely left out the fact that Blake had hit on me, and anyone else he could corner, the week before they started dating!

For all our issues we did have fun, especially if we quadded. Bouncing on beds and reenact WWE. You get a false sense of knowing the people surrounding you. Yes, you work, play, and live with these people. However, it takes longer than a week or two to really know someone. Everyone jumps into bed with a false sense of intimacy, wakes up in a serious relationship, and then breaks up. Imagine having to see that person daily for another ten months. So often on tour a one-night stand becomes something it never should have because of our lifestyle.

Edward and I were on the show Underwater Fantasy for five years. We watched with amusement and sometimes horror the dating progression of Mimi who ended up touring with us for seven years. She wrecked one long term relationship soon after she crashed his new SUV, although we don't know, nor do we want to, all the details to that affair. There was a feline fight over her newest fling in Bali. Next up she played English teacher and nurse maid to the Crazy Russian. And finally, she stole her prince while he was on breakwork away from Giggett. Her prince had his own wandering eyes and after moving shows where she might be heard reminding him, by screaming in the hallway for all to hear, that she had given up the role of a lifetime to switch shows for him, she whipped him into shape. Finally, after trading up as my brother would say, she has forced her very own happy ending. Many show people would never have sought each other under normal circumstances. Family Fun on Ice hires attractive people so, 'Love the one you're with', I guess. Dad always says you end up loving the person right next to you.

Chapter 23
Newbies Forever

Everyone is new and certainly clueless at one point in their lives, but there are some that provide us with countless weeks of humor on their transition to independent adulthood and some never achieve it. New Boy for Life came to work in Mexico and had forgotten his dance belt yet again. He was well aware he had to wear a dance belt, so he borrowed one from his brother. He also knew this was not the most hygienically sound practice, but he found his own solution around it.

Sid, the men's line captain came in to get dressed and noticed that New Boy for Life had put his boxer shorts under his spandex show laundry. The boxers were noticeably buckled and bulged, on top of all this he put his brother's dance belt, over the boxers and show laundry. After getting over his laughing fit, he told New Boy for Life, yes, he had to wear a dance belt, but under his show laundry and no boxer shorts.

New Boy for Life was in a number that starts about ten minutes into the show, called school of fish. He had plenty of time to get show-ready since this was his first number. He comes strolling out to the guard rack, already very late for school of fish, and wardrobe is waiting. The performance director (PD) had radioed back, so now wardrobe is looking for New Boy for Life assuming there's a costume malfunction. Nope, no costume problems, but New Boy for Life tries to take off his dirty guards with his costume gloves already on, wardrobe doesn't approve of this, the PD is shouting ultimatums backstage as the number is going on and New Boy for Life says, "I don't really want to do the number." He doubled up on several hefty fines, touching guards in costume, late for a number, insubordination, and more than earned his title of new boy for life.

Edward earned a reputation for training the untrainable. They would send him assistants that were on their last chance. If Edward could not mold them, then they were gone. Most of the time he did not mind. He was a hard worker and a patient teacher. He puts up with me, he must have endless patience. But one year they sent him a problem child he could not fix. This assistant carpenter Dudley started tour life as a concessions vendor and moved into crew. He was not the sharpest pencil in the box, which doesn't bother Edward if they are eager to learn and work hard. Dudley would set up a chair backstage between cues and fall asleep, often missing his cues. Characters would be batting at the curtain begging to get out.

Edward saved the day one time by knee sliding across the ice to pull the curtain open. Then there were the countless load in screw ups that would cost the head carpenter hours to fix. Like putting the curtains on backward. In exasperation, one day Edward made load in and show cues in crayon, thinking that perhaps pictorial learning might solve the dilemma.

Dudley was the solution to himself. He got himself fired at the end of tour for too many drinks and free flying fists. But this was not to be his end with the company. Long after we had left the road, we heard that desperate times called for desperate hires and Dudley got a job on the crew about ten years after being fired.

Then there was Wanda who has won the new girl forever award at closing party every year running. She was the principle's understudy, for a role that depicts a child, but that didn't stop her from lying to impress in Mexico. In Monterey, we were partying with the circus acrobats that were performing across the street, and quite a few of their performers came to watch our shows. Wanda was leading one guy around, proclaiming she was the principle, in front of the real principle. Stolen valor and lying to get a guy?

As irony would have it after several years no one wanted that role any more so by default she became principle.

There was one year that a new girl had never done her own laundry. Rather than ask for assistance she mailed her dirty laundry home to be done by her parents. Another had a soft spot for animals, all animals. Every stray she came across she tried to rescue, especially cats. At one-point, Edward refused to stop the car while she was clawing to get out and rescue a cat. Her boyfriend silently mouthed 'thank you' to Edward in the rearview. She made a few trips home between cities to deliver stray cats she had saved and I'm sure her parents were thrilled. Now she has three, three-legged rescue cats and is the best cat-mom ever.

Devon didn't last long, half of West coast and part of Japan. We were standing in line at a gas station before travel day. The store was full of colorful redneck types, who might not have been particularly ice skater, or gay, friendly. Devon says, rather loudly, "I like sausage." We all turn and look at him and he continues, "I like big, red, sausage." He says it in a matter-of-fact way as he's holding up big red sausage jerky and eating it suggestively. We had already questioned Devon's sexuality.

We had the guys and gals "falling fine" party in Lafayette, LA. The crap hole of a motel, in the middle of nowhere had many New Orleans refugees from hurricane Katrina, not to mention a state trooper convention. Girls had claimed the pool area. The day of our party it poured buckets of rain. The boys leave it to last minute and get a hotel room, no planning, no problem. I get reject phone calls all day from harassing boys commenting on the weather, because of course, I am the party planner. As luck would have it the hotel manager bumped into me and the trailer home behind the hotel wasn't being used, would we like it? At this point anything would do.

We had our infamous ice cube tray races. The girls race each other to finish their alcoholic drink that is in an ice cube tray holder. This concoction must be slurped through a straw, cheating and head butting is encouraged and speed wins. Amanda won final death match for the women's champ. This was celebrated by singing the theme song from Rocky at the top of our lungs as we parade her to the pool. Edward on the other side of the hotel heard us; he came out, shook his head, and went and hid. The men presented their champion and he beat the pants off the girls. That's right he sucks, literally. This caused losing side retorts shouted at full drunken pitch mostly about his sucking abilities.

At that point, we were all hopelessly loud and drunk. Not a whole lot of brain power but a whole bunch of drunk underage ice skaters, making way too much noise with the state trooper convention sharing the hotel. The parties had collided as they usually did. To gain entry into our party the guys had to do condom shots, but the only condoms we had were lubricated, this was apparently not a deterrent. We had a sidewalk puker that I happened to slip in covering my toes in pink puke. Rumor has Devon passed out in the party room in a pile of vomit, but not before gossip had him sleeping with a man and then a woman.

The next day our company manager had to lecture us on hotel etiquette and the best line was, "Air horns are never a good idea!" No one would fess up to the air horn, but it was a new boy Devon.

Chapter 24
Drugs

The first year on the road, refilling my prescriptions was a bit of a challenge for my father and me. I would call Dad about five days before I needed my next month of birth control, he would rush to Wegmans and overnight it to my hotel. There was always the danger of my previous preventative getting lost in the mail, lost in the hotel, or not making it on time. Health insurance was a stickler for buying your prescription one month at a time. I do not want to cheat them; I just wanted to buy one whole years' worth at a time.

I temporarily solved this problem in Mexico City. I took my birth control to the pharmacy, showed them the contents and they gave me their equivalent. Not like I'm playing Russian roulette with my birth control in a foreign language. I bought a year's supply and anytime mine was not on time, no problem, I had plenty of back up. My third year in the states, I tried to be clever. I filled my prescription at Walgreens. I figured there were plenty of Walgreens all over the country and I could waltz in and get a refill. In theory, this was a sound idea, but collecting my prescription in another city, had that city's store calling the NY store. Then that week's Walgreens pulled three of my 12 prescriptions instead of one. By the time I got back to Rochester for the summer, I had multiple prescriptions in different stores around the country. Ultimately it was a big mess, and I could not collect on my full 12-month supply. Modern pharmacies are now much better equipped to dole out drugs to travelers.

The best secret I learned was that if you are going overseas and you know the right number to call, our company will call the insurance company and you can fill a year's prescription at once. Wegmans tried to help me out when my doctor wrote my prescription for three months at a time. The pharmacist called my health insurance company, and she had a startled look on her face when she put the phone down. She told me they were some of the rudest people she'd ever had to deal with. Bottom line, even though my prescription was written for three months at a time, insurance would not fill it for three months at a time. Why is being a sexually responsible adult so difficult? Maybe my health insurance company thinks a baby is cheaper than several months of birth control.

We have a very strict no drug policy in the company. I can understand, it's part of my job. The drug rules are based on illicit drugs in the US. Even if you are overseas, if it's illegal in the US, it's still illegal. If there is something that is over the counter in Canada, you must have a prescription once you are working for the American company. If you are lucky enough to be in Amsterdam with pot on every corner, it is still not legal while employed by our company. This was also years before legalized pot in some of the US states. All these rules and there is still a lot of grey area. Some of the Canadians have flu medicine for nighttime with codeine in it. They still take it, they still give it to their friends in need, but if any of us were randomly drug tested and it was found without a prescription, we could be fired.

We had one tour coordinator when we opened Underwater Fantasy on Ice who had a real stick up her bum. One of my friends was having back trouble and I offered her my left-over meds from my own back problems. The tour coordinator was hiding behind a corner and popped out like a crazed, self-righteous jack in the box and said, "That's illegal and you could be fired if you take her medicine without your own prescription." While this is true, who skulks around corners looking for excuses to yell at people? Someone without a life of their own. Maybe she needs my pain medicine for the removal of said stick.

There's always rule breakers, one guy on Toys on Ice, came around to Edward's room when he was injured asking for his leftover drugs. Edward hadn't even recovered and yet here he comes seeking drugs. Sometimes you can smell the pot drifting under the door. Usually, this occurs more often overseas where drug tests are more expensive and have to be sent back to the states, or so I'm told.

One young, new hire smoked pot all the time. He took one elevator trip that was to be his last. He reeked of pot and was clearly high. He had the bad luck of getting on the elevator with the company manager and performance director. He was drug tested the next hour and sent home the next week.

The rotation of random drug testing seemed suspect to me. There were some who never got tested, some who clearly should have been tested and those like me who you knew would have a clean bill of health, who were always tested. We had one company manager that liked to party like a rock star with a select few. He had one evening of fun the night before our last show day for the year. Whispers of the night's activities got out and to divert attention away from himself he tested his best friend who had partaken in the night's festivities. His friend was of course fired.

Chapter 25
End of Eras

I could have stayed on Toys on Ice after the first three years, but many things pointed to the new show. Edward would be able to keep the skate sharpening crate. Toys on Ice was not doing Southeast Asia or a full European tour, and we needed a change. He did specify that we were a package deal. His crew boss asked him how long we had been dating and when the answer was three years, he said he'd do his best. I wonder what the magic number is, if we had said less than three years would they have split us up. I've known married couples that the company couldn't keep together for various reasons. Tour life is not conducive to relationships.

Edward was eventually offered the stage manager position several times. That is a move in a direction he did not fancy. You are pooped on from all sides, management, crew, and the local city stage unions. You no longer practice carpentry and there is a lot more drama and micromanaging. He said no thanks respectfully and repeatedly, but they kept offering for several years. Then he worked for a guy who should not have been promoted and relished power. I guess that leaves no room to complain.

If we had stayed and gone to an abbreviated European tour with Toys on Ice, we would have opened and closed Toys on Ice. There's a nice, rounded feeling to that, but things worked out the way they were supposed to. First year Toys on Ice was a magic collection of the right people to bring together and the best group I have ever worked with. I've worked with many great people over the years, but my rose-tinted glasses remember the first year as the best year. Toys on Ice cast had slowly been changing, change can be good, better than stagnation and it was hard to leave that group. Had we stayed; I don't think it would have been the same. It was an end to an era.

Endings and beginnings work together to make the circle of our lives. Performing in Australia on Underwater Fantasy on Ice was another ending. That show needed change, but like the ominous rain clouds that grow heavy with rain, the longer you wait, the bigger the storm when it breaks. We waited three years and when cast and crew changes came, it poured. The company opened three shows and only closed one show. A finder's fee was offered for anyone we could suggest that would audition and last through their probation period. Desperation grew, notices on the board and by email for male skaters and finally US men, since visa time was up. Considering how cheap we think this company is, we knew from the finder's fee that they were desperate. My question is what happens when they close three shows and only open one? Time to clean house.

At the end of Australia, we had four people quitting and only a handful returning. Sved, who has been in the company for about nine years, sold us the coffee stand and moved on with his Russian life. We all got together the last night and after too much champagne and vodka I was an emotional mess. I must have cried a bucket of salt water. I might get just a little emotional when I drink. As my headache subsided the next day, I realized it was the end of another era.

What was awaiting us at rehearsals for the fourth year of Underwater Fantasy on Ice? Only a dozen returned to the show and most of the key players gone. Some of the dirty laundry needed to be shipped elsewhere, but you never keep all the good and get rid of all the bad, it's a bit of both. I got a call during break from Chaz, he said our cast list wasn't very full to start tour. Would we get a lot of new girls and boys fresh off the high school boat? Or transfers from other shows? Mature individuals or more baggage focused on drama?

We received far more girls than boys. I mean boys and girls are interchangeable right? They wanted me to try doing pairs with a girl, that didn't go over well. I might have been strong from aerial training but not strong enough to pick another human up over my head safely. They had girls doing heavy lifting in other areas. The sting ray was a very heavy prop held up by three guys originally. The center used to be held up by a strong 6 foot guy. Well, when we were really strapped, I became the center of the sting ray.

We were out of jumpers and spinners. So, my favorite fat puffer fish who was paid extra for character work was taken from me so I could jump and spin in the tiki number. And like rabbits the number of short girls multiplied. It seemed the company sent our show all the short girls.

Underwater Fantasy on Ice fourth year was a big change. We had another swarm of young, underage, short girls. And my brother Adam joined tour. I was very excited about his addition to the crew, Edward had his reservations since he was used as reference to get my 24-year-old, freshly graduated from Carnegie Melon, partying brother hired to the props department.

Adam made a splash when he joined tour, and his wake was more of a Sunami. My brother is a looker, and he didn't have any qualms about flirting with all the ladies. Even if some of those ladies were not available. During rehearsals in St. Charles MO, he made the mistake of passing out in the Crazy Russian's room. With his mouth wide open, he was open to invitations, or so the Russian thought. So, he obliged Adam with another shot in his yawning, sleeping mouth. We thought it was hysterical, Adam as he coughed, sputtered, and spit it back at Crazy Russian, did not like his sense of humor. But that was quickly forgotten by a rap battle on balconies across the hotel. I'm still not sure who won that, certainly not the hotel manager.

Edward was the master of the pass out trick because he did it with class. Adam could pass out, but he did it all in his own style. Still in rehearsals he passed out on the keyboard in the business center. He woke up with letters imprinted on his face. Adam's most infamous black out was in the hotel hallway, with his finger up his nose. There's photographic evidence of this one that found its way to the board for morning notes and public hilarity. He took all this in stride and laughed at himself. Since he was notorious for his narcoleptic ways, he often received the artistic abilities of anyone present with a sharpie.

My brother taught this old show dog a few new tricks. We played slap bag with boxed wine. That is when you take the bag of wine out of boxed wine and drink it as fast as you can while other people apply pressure or "slap" the bag. That will do the trick for a fast drunk and a cheap headache. After a year on the road with us, he switched shows. I'm told he was no longer prime roommate material after he drunkenly kept lifting what he assumed was a toilet lid, only to keep peeing in his roommates' suitcase! Adam could party with the best of them, but he was late on his new show one too many times and partied himself out of his job.

After leaving tour, Adam met up with us when our show played Cleveland. Someone had rented a party bus, complete with stripper pole, which found me upside down on a moving bus and I'm pretty sure a mild head wound on the way down (I never learn). This was Edward's and my third time playing Cleveland and all our favorite bars had been closed down. We managed to find one that had live lobster tanks, that was their selling point. We didn't stay long and found a better bar that had plenty of drinking games. Adam remembered how to party like he was still on tour and toward the end of the night he's calling me on his cell phone in a panic.

"Where are you? Where is everyone? I've been left behind! I don't know where I am."

"Adam, turn around, the bus is behind you!" First, he passed out in the bus and the driver was calling us because he would not clear out of the party bus. Then he collapsed in our room in child's pose on a trundle bed!

Chapter 26
No Sex in the Boom Boom
Room and Virgin Sluts

How do you have sex with a roommate present? A question that isn't usually even considered, except maybe in college, with a scarf tied to the doorknob. But in a moment of chemistry and alcohol, logic and modesty are left at the hotel room door. So again, choose your roommates carefully.

There's the ever-popular bathroom, classy I know, but apparently desperate needs call for desperate measures. The roommate loses all bathroom privileges while it's being preoccupied with sexual endeavors. This can prove a difficult place to express all your bodily desires and sometimes less than sanitary. Listening to these endeavors: you can both sit on the commode or take turns kneeling before it. Then there's usually a nice mirror if you're bent over the sink and the notorious shower.

The Pisces position is a bit more awkward with limited floor space. In your inebriated state, you believe that bumping and grinding into the walls and the toiletries being scattered to the floor couldn't be enough to wake your roommate, even over the grunts and moans. The shower might buffer some sounds, but careful no one slips and falls, that would not be covered by worker's comp. There's always the stairwell. You assume if you climb high enough no one will find you and that your sounds don't reverberate.

Then there's two bodies in one bed, under the covers, while the roommate is trying to sleep single in their bed. The sneaky side swipe of the undies and a quiet quickie is usually more discreet than most. Or there's the blatant thought that maybe they're a really hard sleeper and they won't hear you carrying on in the bed right next to theirs. I have personally encountered a few roommate hookups of every kind. One had the morose afterthought to ask me if I was awake last night.

"Yep."

"Sorry."

"Don't do it again!"

"Can you not tell my pseudo girlfriend about it?" Now I have to carry their dirty little secrets too? Last time we roomed together.

Slutty virgins are my favorite. Talk about two contradictory terms, brings new meaning to oxymoron. There's one every year. A cute little blond, when I say little on the road I'm not kidding, we always need short female skaters and we get them, about 5'. She was instantly popular with the males and became a spotlight whore. She needed attention and if she didn't get it in a good way, she got it anyway she could. Claiming the V-card and changing her personality every week from race car fanatic to bible toting Jesus worship, she was in everyone's bed. But hey, she's a virgin so she must not be a slut, right?

That must be why they would either lie about it or still hold it like a trump card of their virtue. Maybe they think that if they don't have sex, they aren't tramps. People would hear her moaning, groaning, and banging on the headboards (hotel walls are thin), or at a party disappear right in front of us with a Russian in the bathroom for just long enough. There must have been enough friction from dry humping to start a fire, but it kept the men coming back trying to claim that V-card. And a personal favorite, running naked into the bathroom when your roommate comes back to the room early. But hey, you're still holding onto that vestal virgin title so you must not be a floozie.

And let's talk about the male V-card. I didn't think this was really a topic, but we had one that, for unknown reasons, wanted to hang on to that bragging right. He was worse than the slutty virgins. Only one glory hole equated to lost virginity, all others were fair game. And in his own words the tip did not count! I'm not sure where he got his definitions, but I think they need a little revising. This tip comment was uttered originally as a nod toward his dirty virginal status but in later years was heard in utterance as a claim that he was not gay if only the tip was in a male's mouth. Whatever definitions work for you, my friend, live and let live.

I'm sure everyone needs to go through their experimenting stages, but if you're not careful or discreet you become the running tour soap opera. On tour, you get a reputation fast and it's hard to get rid of that initial perception. Don't think you're safe once you get off one show and onto another, everyone knows everyone in the skating world and your rep will follow.

One night an inebriated friend tried to tie tongues with me. I politely pushed back that I was happy with Edward. Like a forlorn hang dog he took his droopy shoulders back to his hotel room and his girlfriend. The next day in the makeup room his girlfriend told us all how he came home and made the sweetest love to her last night. I gagged a little and avoided late night drinking with him the rest of tour life.

We had quite a few with 'wild' reputations the first couple years. They eventually coupled up with one guy for a year or two and the cast changed enough that very few remembered their dirty little secrets. It took one to two years to change reps. But only a few days on tour to acquire a smear title. One free child had the rumor mill circulating over the comment, "Just put it in my butt." Unfortunately for her she had a show line that said the word butt and she never lived that story down until she switched tours. She did not help matters when her roommate woke to the sounds of her electric toothbrush being abused! That toothbrush was never the same and went in the waste basket.

Edward's good at reading people, sometimes it takes me a little longer. We had a lot of wild girls when we opened Underwater Fantasy on Ice, the quiet ones acquired on a turnover year were a welcome change. Most of them were young and willing to pretend to listen. There was a wolf amongst the new sheep. Queen of subtlety, it took a while for some of her slutty, virgin ways to get out. And she liked to play men off each other. She would cry to one guy about another guy who was supposedly leading her on and as she is crying on his shoulder, she's wooing his assistant. Can you see the tangled web she's creating backstage? How about one guy is in her bed, she gets a phone call and tells him it's her boyfriend at home and he needs to get out. He leaves and another guy on tour comes over. My brother calls it trading up. But hey, she's still a virgin! That is a challenge that draws many a suitor, despite rumors.

How do these girls innately know how to act like this at 17 or 18? I'm gonna blame TV, it's an easy target. But remember people aren't playthings.

I've been told I'm slightly paranoid. Actually, it's delayed paranoia. I'll say something and then look around to make sure no one's listening. I probably shouldn't be opening my mouth to begin with, throwing stones, no one's innocent, but gossip is fun. Gossip is also like currency, you share, they share. When I've had a few, I like the blunt verify tactic. "So, I heard…is it true?" Right to the person in question. If it's verified, then it's not gossip, right? We had a pretty boy come on tour with Toy's on Ice and we went dancing, I'd had enough to drink that blunt verification seemed like a good idea, "Are you gay or straight?" He laughed, "I take whatever I can get."

"Oh, you're greedy!" He helped out a friend who wished to lose her V-card to a friend rather than a drunken episode she might regret. He obliged her on the beaches of Puerto Rico. If you get to orchestrate giving up the ghost, then I'd say she did a bang-up job!

The point is that people are always listening or could be. As the tour years got on, it seems people are wrapped up in their own little worlds. They don't see me standing right next to them. I'm still cautious and for good reason, walls are thin, and you never know when someone's at the door or connected to your AC vent. We had a wailer one year, sounded like the character from Porkies. Either she didn't care or didn't know everyone would make fun of her wailing orgasms. People dreaded being her neighbor. When we were playing a small city in France, the hotel was built in a square with a courtyard in the middle. She left her windows open, and the sound echoed up the tower. On purpose perhaps?

I personally would be embarrassed if overheard. We had a short and stout one who got rambunctious one night, pulling down shower curtains and pipes. She came in the next day and was mortified when her line captain asked her, did she have a good night in front of the entire ladies' make-up room. This call out in front of the girls' makeup room is just an example of the nasty little barbs that girls carry on.

Just something else to make me paranoid. So, I practice stealth sex on tour. I check the rooming list when we get in to find out if I know my neighbors. If the bed creaks, bumps, or moans, we turn sideways, a bit ridiculous, I know but, better than make-up room talk with your co-workers the next day.

Not once but twice I've burned myself with gossip. You think I would learn. The first time, I would write these juicy updates about what was happening on tour to my friends off tour. My third year on tour a lot of tour friends had left tour, so I included them in the gossip email. I accidentally included the topic of gossip in the email list! She called me on it and found out who had spilled the gossip to me. She was furious, I had betrayed more than one person's confidence, and I was ashamed. Breach in confidence and friendship, a long 22-hour drive of tears thinking about my wrongdoing, and a fearful call to the most offended party. I apologized; she took me under her wing and eventually things healed. That should have been enough of a lesson.

Years later my dad asked me to make a photo album with the cast and crew's names so that when he visited, he could study up on their names and who was with whom. I use a photo internet site to copy pictures from different albums into a new album. I wrote more than their names, little descriptions, and sometimes history. What I didn't realize is when you copied pictures and change the title and description, it changed on the original album. One of which I had just sent to everyone! So, a couple of people didn't appreciate what I'd written and thought my picture sharing was a vicious gossip circle. It was only meant for my dad, but I had given myself plenty of reasons to be paranoid.

Chapter 27
Go Big and Go Home

If you're going to be out of the show for an injury, you might as well do it right, go big and go home! I would often pride myself for my first four tours that I had never been 'out'. I had never missed shows, been injured or sick enough, that I couldn't make it to work. There were plenty of times I should have been out, but it made me feel tough and of course there were the bragging rights. With the human resources and risk management slowly strangling our newly developing sexual harassment necks tighter, there were many hung over mornings that I should have called in sick. If I had a breathalyzer, I would not have been considered sober. Barfing in the garbage can between numbers, dressed as a lobster, if caught now, plus a blood-alcohol test would get me fired. All the rules and regulations are slowly enclosing on us.

My bragging rights changed a little in Chicago with Underwater Fantasy. My beautiful record of three and a half years was shattered on my return to Chicago. Chi town one of the few cities I couldn't wait to party in, and I got sick. I knew it was coming on Monday and went out anyway. Did the show Tuesday and as a testament of how sick I was, did not even drink as we hung out with the cast of another show that was in town with us. Wednesday I was so sick I couldn't talk, and Edward called in to the performance director for me letting them know I was out. Drugs kicked in and I thought I was fine, did the Wednesday show and was not fine.

Thursday, I didn't argue I knew I was out, I couldn't control the coughing fits, woke up to a beautiful facial of snot and drool. Edward slept on the couch for fear of catching my dreaded cold. It was such a bad cold that I couldn't leave my bed for two days, on the same weekend when many others were also out, and we had a six pack of shows. The men's line captain was heard exclaiming, "It's a cold how sick could she be?" Then someone used my new brag line, "This is the first time she's EVER been out." That shut him up. I came back on miracle Sunday, but I'm not sure I should have been back then. I lay on the floor praying for sleep or death and wheezing in-between shows. Then I got to say things like, "I've only been out once in four years, five years, six years…" On the bright side the weight master might be happy, I'm sure this cold knocked out about 5lbs. Where there is no will there is no hunger.

Then cursed Chicago rolled around again. I really do like the damn city, but my track history there doesn't tally up to well.

Opening night on Wednesday, we finally had one of our ladies back, she had gone home for three weeks for her mother's funeral. We were terribly short of skaters and had cut major group numbers down to accommodate a lack of bodies. Each and every body we got we were happy to have. During the aborigines in the fish tank number, the guy beside me fell, got up, and accidentally knocked my left leg out from under me. I fell back with my weight over my right leg, on a bent knee at a 90-degree angle toward my butt.

All rational thought went out the window. The only way I knew to get out of that position was lay forward on my stomach. I just laid there screaming as the other aborigines skated away. Accidents happen, and pre-programmed 'the show must go on' sets in; everyone was doing what they are trained to do. In my pain induced hysteria, I couldn't figure out how to get up, so I lay there screaming, "Please help me, somebody please help me," within ear shot of first row audience. Any thoughts of professionalism were gone. Time doesn't make sense in great pain, after a very short amount of time, which felt an eternity, a big yellow fish came over and tried to help, but it was a two fish job. They both took me under my arms and helped me off skating on my left foot as I sobbed loudly.

School fish and friends tried to distract the audience by dancing in front of them. They pointedly ignored this like a car crash you must watch and were witness to the aborigine carried off the ice. The worst thing I've ever seen while watching one of our ice shows was an acrobat number that had been performed hundreds of times. The show I watched; two guys jump from a platform onto a teeter board. They launch the other guy, skates and all into a back flip and he lands in a tiny chair, on a pole, strapped to another guy's chest who is on skates. This particular show the chair-pole guy must have been just an inch off. The back flipper landed in the chair but just the front lip of it and slipped off. He landed face first from about a ten-foot drop. The whole show stopped to a screaming audience, and they scrapped blood off the ice. He survived multiple facial surgeries, but I have a hard time watching anything with backflips anymore.

After my accident and once backstage, I yelled for paramedics, which were already on their way and a chair. Then I cried hard, no longer for the pain, but because I knew I was going to be 'out'. And not just for a day or two, for a long time. My brother tried to lighten the mood by asking if we were still going out dancing. Then he decided dancing could still happen if they pushed me back and forth across the dance floor in a wheelchair. I refused to let the paramedic cut my show laundry off my leg, a small amount of control is better than no control, right? But the doctor cut my show laundry off anyway. Funny what you're stingy about in situations like that.

I was rolled out on a stretcher with ice bags, show laundry, stained make-up face and wig cap on my head. The company manager offered to come with me and as tempting as it was, I still knew the show must go on and it would need him, so I said I was okay. I had my first ambulance ride and that was anticlimactic. No flashing lights. I cried again at the hospital in fear of what was wrong with my knee. Knees are funny things and I depend heavily on mine.

I laid around for a while and finally a young doctor came by. He looked at my leg and asked what I would like to take for the pain. I could tell he didn't want to lead me on with available drugs, so he said, "Motrin…" And before he said anything stronger, I said, "Let's start with Motrin and see how it goes." Suddenly I was exhausted and passed out cold. Guess that level of hysteria is exhausting.

X-rays were a freezing and uncomfortable experience. Then I slept for an hour or so and the doctor came by again, he said nothing looked broken but there was a shadow on my right tibia. I said I'd broken my right ankle twice. The shadow corresponded with where I had previously broken my right ankle. He said there was a possible sprained ankle and internal knee damage, but I'd need to see a specialist as soon as possible.

Then they brought crutches over and asked if I knew how to use them. I've had two broken right ankles and countless skating injuries; crutches are old friends. A few years before this I'd cleaned out my attic closet and thrown away the lam's skin crutch covers that pad the arm pits. I had hoped I'd never need them again. They wrapped my right leg in a soft air cast. It looked like a giant yoga matt that was Velcroed around my leg and then I was forgotten about. Another hour goes by and finally someone asks if I've been given release papers. Like I'm a wild animal that needs permission to leave.

Edward came and picked me up. Everyone called and texted me and it felt nice to know they cared. My brother after the usual questions said, "We're all over at the Irish bar if you feel up to it." I laughed and told him, "Maybe you don't know, but if you're out and people are pulling your weight at work, it's not cool to be seen partying at the bar." He stopped by later at 4 am with some of my other friends who had brought me my requested breakfast of choice, V8. Edward wasn't impressed.

Shocked exclamation was the reaction when I told everyone I was only on Advil.

"You didn't even get good drugs?" I tried to argue that this meant it wasn't as bad, if I was only on Advil, plus I don't like to lie in a muscle relaxed stupor all day. Usually, I could shut them up by saying, "I can drink on Advil!" Some of the guys on concessions argued that you could drink on any drug, but after a trial period with muscle relaxants for back pain, I knew I couldn't handle that, it ended in puking.

Out of respect for my co-workers I would stare at the multiple birthday bottles of booze in my room, strategically placed right in my sightline above my injured leg. I would wait until fifteen minutes after the last show to have my first evening drink. I claimed that this was ten percent respect and mostly so I could claim I wasn't a closet alcoholic, because I have self-control.

As my UK friends liked to tell me if you drink alone, or go to meetings, you might be an alcoholic. I was the friendly, loyal dog waiting patiently until everyone was home. After the first two days which were swamped with visitors, flowers, and chocolate, no one came over. So as soon as I heard the doors slam on our floor, I would take a crutch walk up and down the hall until someone came out and talked to me.

There are so many unspoken rules of conduct. I knew it was okay to go out Sunday night before I went home. How do you explain that to someone new? If you've been around long enough, you know what is tolerable in the etiquette department. I had stayed in all week, I wasn't faking an injury, and I was going home on Monday; that makes it okay to go out my last night. We always end up at an Irish bar, proximity plays a big role in bar choice when most people don't have a vehicle on tour and pre-uber days. I played one-footed darts, had a drink with the company manager, and did a lot of hopping from one table to another to talk. When I had beer spilled on me, visions of being the beer smelling, homeless woman in a wheelchair at the airport filled my head. My friends had better visions of me living, drunk, in the TV room at my Dad's house, he would just close the door when guests came over and say there was nothing to see in there.

My brother's first airport travel day, I made him nervous. He couldn't leave his terminal and wheel me and my bags to the next. American argued that I could get Jet Blue to pick me up in my wheelchair at the next terminal. Adam argued that I needed the wheelchair to get there. Little bro got it all settled and waited with me despite his growing anxiety that tour people were moving on without him.

First flight was smooth, had two seats to myself and was able to put my foot up. I was wheeled to my next gate by an unaware attendant who left my leg in the line of fire at a crowded airport. My leg was hit twice, so I put on my backpack and crutched over to a less congested area. My second flight was painful. I'm sure their intentions were good, however in the first row, the arm rests do not go up, and there's a barrier wall in front of me. I couldn't elevate or fully straighten my leg. A little achy and agitated, I made it home.

Even though I had packed my bags after seeing the orthopedic doctor, I couldn't just buy my plane ticket and fly home, I had to go through the proper channels. Risk management looked at the cities coming up and where my home was. I logically thought seeing only one doctor and physical therapist, plus the company would not have to pay for hotel rooms was the simplest solution. It boiled down to a lesser of two evils. It was harder to get workers comp and physical therapy in Quebec, than in NY. Still, they tried to warn me that NY was a pain in the foot. If I did not actively keep my claim open, I would lose it. I had to have weekly updates and doctor's reports. This seemed a better option than following tour around sitting listlessly in a room by myself.

I ended up being out for two months.

Chapter 28
Recovery: Time Home

I was upset about not being able to start physical therapy right away. I wanted to stick to the time frame the Chicago doc had given me, 3–4 weeks. I tried to make a physical therapy appointment; they said fine come in over the phone. We get there and they tell me that NY state law requires a prescription or referral from a NY doctor, they won't take an out of state referral. That's ridiculous, so even though I've already seen an orthopedic doctor, now I must see another one just to have physical therapy. Now I begin to see the issues the company warned me about.

Dad got me in the see the orthopedic assistant the next morning, which was wonderful luck. She took more X-rays and said it didn't look like a chipped ankle bone; however, it did look like there were old fragments in there from a previous injury. That sounded wonderful. She was worried about the knee, so the next step was to get a MRI. Upon check out at the doctors, I was not getting anywhere with the receptionist, she wanted me to be seen in a months' time because workers comp would take a while to get an MRI.

Now my mission was to prove her wrong, I got a MRI for the next day after contacting my workers comp representative. Workers' comp can be a nice set up, paying about 80% of your check while you are at home recovering. I don't do well just sitting at home, I wanted to get back on the road as soon as possible. I got back in to see the orthopedic assistant again a few days later. She thought that there might be a meniscus tear and wanted me seen in a few weeks when the swelling went down, to decide on surgery. The tears were threatening to come out again, surgery and then recovery. Now we are talking for a few more months at least.

I decided that if I needed surgery, I wanted it done ASAP so I could recover sooner. I kept trying to move my orthopedic doctor's appointment up instead of waiting two weeks. First my workers comp rep was on vacation for a week. When she was back, I could no longer get in to see the doctor any sooner. I finally saw the doctor; I had liked the personable PA but wasn't sure how I felt about the doc. He didn't really say much about the meniscus, except that I didn't need surgery, finally some good news. He said there was a tear in the medial knee ligament and a sprained ankle. He also said I could start physical therapy and it would take about two more months to fully recover. Two more months? My workers comp and job position security ran out in that time. That's a long time in a tour year. I was scheduled to see him in another month and my response was, "We'll negotiate that time frame when I see you again." It's not that I wanted to go back before I was ready, but I am a hard worker, and I don't want to sit around for another two months. I went home and immediately scheduled physical therapy.

My existence up until this point had been a quiet, lonely affair where I had scheduled my daily activities into a semblance of routine. I would get up after nine or ten hours of sleep. I would write or attempt to write on this book for at least an hour. Then it was lunch, with extraordinarily little physical activity I kept calories down to an all-time low. Next, it was onto craft projects. I took to scanning all the old scrap book photos that had no digital backups and made CDs for Christmas presents. Followed by reading time. And finally, dinner. No drinking or TV until after 5 for fear of becoming the dreaded coach potato. But I lived for the weekends when my friends were free.

One highlight was the story of Adam's encounter in Montreal. He was out at the bar and as a gentleman he went in to retrieve a lady friend's coat. He came out with the coat and a large, ripped man followed him out shouting at him in French. Adam said, "What" and promptly received a slap in the face by the man who continued screaming in French. Adam was shocked and said, "I don't understand, I don't speak French." This received him another slap across the face. More screaming and a third slap before the man grabbed the lady's jacket that Adam was holding and said in perfect English, "Asshole!" I guess Adam had taken the wrong lady's jacket.

That was the same year Edward and I had purchased the coffee stand and decided to drive tour. Now Edward was having to run our new enterprise alone. Not only did he have to load in, load out, run his shows, but he would also have to get up early to cook breakfasts and lunches as well as spend his days off at Costco or Sam's club mass purchasing for the hungry horde. Word of his cooking prowess spread and there would be a line for three show day breakfast and lunch. If you did not line up fast enough, Edward's hot lunches were gone.

We would put up a menu for the week and there was a lock box that you could pay cash in or a book with your name that you were supposed to pay off every week. It was based on an honors system since during the show we could not always guard it. We had one electrician that promised and pleaded to pay his bill the next week and then the following week. Finally, he skated off and skirted his bill seeing as it was the end of tour, he got away Scot free and belly full. He also did not get a return tour.

Edward would have to police Rori's intake of cheese when he had the baked potato bar, otherwise she would build a mountain of cheese and the hangry customers behind her would have no dairy for their poor spuds. In Detroit, someone broke into the coffee stand after hours and stole several pounds of cooked bacon! Who steals bacon? I hope they have a tummy ache. They did not even steal the lock box full of cash.

One morning, Adam came over to 'help' Edward at the coffee stand, which really meant eating free breakfast and began reading labels aloud to stave off his hangover. He became increasingly agitated over the marketing slogan of the soda company that proclaimed a 36 pack is 50% more than a 24 pack.

"That's not a deal! That's just good math!" They both watched a hot-headed concessions vendor who wanted to try Edward's ghost pepper hot sauce. The recommended serving was one drop. He dumped about a tablespoon on his breakfast sandwich, despite warnings from on lookers and his assurance that he was a spicy sauce connoisseur. Not only did that cure his hangover, he ended up in the ER because he also got the sauce in his eye!

As Edward packed up the coffee stand for one load out, he had several sandwiches he was throwing into the garbage and Adam literally dove in after them. Adam was known to often wander over to our hotel room, usually at four am as we tried to sleep, to have drunken, philosophical musings. As he made his grand proclamations, he would eat all the food he could find in our room. We kept my brother well fed!

When I got injured, Adam told Edward that he would help him drive tour. Adam's version of helping drive tour was often to stay up late while Edward drove, good naturedly talking his ear off, and then he was too tired to drive the second leg of the trip. The crew only had about two days to change cities. The city-to-city drive was usually reasonable but occasionally there were long ones like Orlando to Providence. The rest of the cast and crew would fly, but if you're driving tour that is a tight turn around. Adam was notorious for his sleeping farts. Edward would be trapped in the SUV with a farting, sleeping Adam!

One frozen forgotten travel day between cities, we would be passing by colonial Williamsburg, VA. Edward did not think colonial Williamsburg looked intriguing and he wanted to get to our next city and relax before he had to load in. As our driving arrangement often happened, he would be amped up after loadout and drive for about three or four hours. Now it's one am, I've had a nap, and he's exhausted. So, I take the wheel. He's sleeping soundly and wakes up to sunrise and bird chirping.

"Are we there?"

"Yes, we are at colonial Williamsburg, I bought you a ticket!" So, I got to go to colonial Williamsburg. After that Edward was understandably hesitant to hand over the wheel.

The physical therapist said I should schedule two appointments a week and I could come in whenever I wanted and do my stretching, exercises, and use the gym. I told my PT I wanted, without hurting myself, to get back to work ASAP, and was to see the doc in a month. By the end of the second day, I was slowly getting my legs around on the exercise bike. At the end of the first week, I was allowed to skate with no jumps. The second week I started adding a different double jump every day and doing leg weights in the gym.

With the start of physical therapy, my daily routine was forever altered, I would drop Dad off at work, only allowing myself eight hours of sleep. I was a model of safety driving one legged in the upstate NY winters. Then I would work out for an hour and a half, skate for an hour and then go home to write and scan pictures. I made friends with all the rink staff, and the old men who were regulars for the noon session. They were like a friendly, gossiping bunch of hens. Whenever anyone new would show up they would share my ice show history and recovery story with them.

The physical therapy exercises were interesting and effective. I would hop one legged on a half a medicine ball, do quarter revolutions on the same medicine ball, side skips with a therapy band on, and my least favorite a cardio machine that was like cross country skiing, causing a butt soreness I'd never experienced before. The physical therapists gave me a hard time about everything from the IQ of a skating fish to the next family ice show being Saw III on ice.

One weekend when the tour was in Scranton, PA, Dad and I drove down to visit and watch a show. It was great to see Edward and my brother, but I felt like an outsider looking in. I wasn't back and as such wasn't a part of the shenanigans. I felt I had missed so much in tour years. Unless you're in the daily show grind, in the trenches so to speak, you're an outsider.

Finally, graduation day came so I gave the PTs a show picture for their wall of shame and went to see the doctor. After establishing a comradery with the PA and the PTs, I received a chilly reception from the doctor, he didn't read the physical therapy report, asked if I was skating, and did a quick scan. I asked if I could go back to work after one more week for a little more time to skate and stretch my knee. I asked him to put it in writing and for a sports knee brace. He just nodded along and out the door I went. I was going back to work in half the time he had recommended. The extra week also meant I could spend thanksgiving with my family.

100% is a funny thing, as far as what I need to do for my job, I'd say I was close enough, maybe 95% recovered. I was not good as new. Some things are due to injury and age. 100 percent is not needed for the ice show. One of my concerns was fully bending my knee to hook it on the silk for my aerialist routine. I was stretching every day, but there were still little twinges when I was squatting. However, I could sit all the way back on my haunches. But I wanted to go back to work, and I could at least skate, so I gave it a twirl.

Chapter 29
Fakers

Miracle Sundays, that's the term used when someone's out for most of the work week and then miraculously gets better for Sunday. That way they can party and enjoy their days off. If you are out on a Sunday, even if you feel better on your days off, Monday and Tuesday, the unspoken rules still apply. Until you have gone back to work on Wednesday, you stay out of sight and out of mind.

Amusing and infuriating were the fakers. The ones who were sick or injured a little too often. Not to be confused with the skaters with a streak of bad luck or repetitive motion injuries that are hard to fix. Side bar, the legal portion of our company was based in Virginia. In VA, repetitive motion injuries are not covered by our company. That means even if you wear a giant dog head for two hours and develop back injuries, workers comp does not cover the injury. Does that make any sense? This individual attempted to sue the company to get his injuries paid for. That left a bad taste in the performance director's mouth. Then he had the gall to ask for his skating job back. He did not get his show gig back but did come back to work as crew.

One injured female went home and had to have multiple knee surgeries ending her skating career. The company got tired of paying and hired a private investigator to follow her around trying to catch her in the act, of what I'm not sure, just so they could stop paying her medical bills!

Faking a call out on the weekend is an even bigger insult. Weekends are multi show days which means even more work for the rest of us. When someone is out of the show, we don't have an extra person sitting around waiting in the wings to fill a role. Everyone else must jostle their show track around to pick up extra numbers. Sometimes this means quick changes or whole track changes. We have understudies for when a principle is injured, they have learned and practiced that role and are ready to jump in. This is made more difficult if an injured party is a pair skater. Some pair skaters have worked with back up partners. But most come as a package deal. Then that whole team must be swapped out even if only one partner is injured.

When the flu hits, the board is a mess of crazy different multicolored dry erase markers. I can remember triple quick changes, wearing two pair of costume leggings for rapid changes because the show wasn't designed for that. Flying out of one number into a quick-change tent set up backstage, sweating through the next number and bumbling into the third. Tangled in uncomfortable fishnets that get zipped into costume legs and knowing you'll have to hand repair them because that doesn't fall under wardrobe jurisdiction. Not to mention you only get one pair of precious fishnets. And there is no extra mullah for sparing extra numbers unless it's a principle's understudy.

I remember the first time I was flustered from a quick change into a large chorus number. In this chorus number, you have mesh over your eyes and it's in black light. You have about twenty people wearing the same costume and you can hardly see or skate since the crotch of the costume only rises to your knees. Trying to identify the person next to you is impossible yet you are supposed to follow one person then the next. A Russian thought it would be amusing to give me directions, so I followed them across the ice and ended up on the wrong side and was lost for the remainder of the production number. I wonder if the audience could tell. I know the performance director sure could. I didn't get a fine, I wonder if the humorous Russian did?

As far as miracle Sundays I'm talking about someone claiming to have an injured ankle; the company manager comes back to the hotel on a three-show day and catches Mr. Z running across the street with a six pack of beer on his 'injured ankle'. Other people are pulling extra slack for you, it does not make us happy to see you dancing and drunk at the bar when we've got to get up and do your job the next day.

Mr. Z was also psychic, he could predict the future, but only his own. He would waltz into the show office Friday nights and say he was 'probably' going to be out the next day. What made it ridiculous was that it happened on a regular basis, he was a principal, and he would miss Saturday, the three-show day and be back on miracle Sunday, rather routinely.

When we first met Mr. Z, there was genuine concern for his wellbeing. When his health always seemed to be in question and there was always something new and more terrible than before, we began to roll our eyes. Part of the eye rolling might have been because he was a principle, being paid more than everyone else. This meant that everyone else picked up more slack to cover his show; the same show he was always bemoaning about was 'so difficult.' Since I was one of his understudies, it almost guaranteed me going in every weekend, which was all right by me. As long as I didn't have to wear his horridly dirty costume. One of the times wardrobes washed his principle costume the water ran gray.

We had hypochondriacs abound, like a contagious disease. Luckily, they were not usually out of the show, but it was one complaint after another. It was hard to escape when it was the center of make-up room discussion. You have twenty some girls in the same room, half naked, discussing all their health issues, many having the contagious out-do-each other syndrome. Who has it the worst? Then we must physically compare, you think men are bad. Dancers are not the only ones with ugly feet, skaters have not only nasty, smelly feet, but also some ugly cankles or stout ankles. Our petite line captain would joke about her cankles, so when I was out with an ankle injury, I texted her and said, "You think you've got cankles? Check this bad boy out!" I obviously caught the one up syndrome.

Foot issues become a real problem overseas in warm, humid countries like Japan and S.E. Asia. We performed so many shows that our skates never fully dried out, add a bit of smell, and combine all skates in one storage hamper for travel day and you get a wonderful breeding ground for foot fungus.

Foot fungus is a mild term for this mutant crap that grows into and on your skate, not just your skin. Even if you kill it on your foot, it loves to feast and fester in your smelly, dark, damp, boot. Many people end up chucking their skates after that tour. If the foot fungus doesn't do your skate in, the humidity warps the wood looking leather at the bottom of the boot, strips the screws, eats the tongue and generally breaks down very expensive skating boots. This is not an item the company pays for even though we aren't worth much without our skates.

That's where Edward, handy man-carpenter extraordinaire comes in. When he joined the road, he thought he was just an ice skating, skate sharpener. Ice skating is the second most expensive sport. At this point in time, good boots and blades cost a thousand dollars and in the competitive world, needed to be replaced once a year. Boots and blades are expensive and getting more expensive. They're also falling apart faster these days.

If someone has an easy show track, breaking into new boots is hard and no one wants to do it. New boots are needed if you have a jumping or spinning show track. No one likes new boots, they're a pain in the feet. This makes us reluctant to throw out old boots and buy new ones. Eventually everyone must, but there are some, nameless Russian males, who just refuse. One such male went to land a double Lutz only to land flat footed with no more blade attached.

So, Edward became much more than just a sharpener. He carries plenty of bolts for stripped screws, extra leather to attempt to re-build the inside of boots, he's even hand stitched a tongue back together. He's a skate doctor. His Mr. fix it attitude has made Edward the guy to go to when anything breaks. Broken luggage wheel? No problem, Edward shaves down an extra roller blade wheel and voila, suitcase rolls like new. How about custom, lightweight shelves in your suitcase? He's done it.

That leads back to our fakers. Everyone screws up, especially when balancing on thin blades and twirling in the air. Excuses are like fire ants, once one shows up, the swarm isn't far behind. They've always got an excuse for everything. It was my boot's fault, or the ice's fault, but never their fault.

Chapter 30
Make-Up Room Antics

Many women, half undressed, in one room can get up to no good. F-you February is a term to describe that time of year when everyone hates everyone, you're tired of each other and tour. Sometimes to keep our spirits up during the F-you Februarys, we would all perform little side shows for each other. February blues are usually cured once we go south to warm weather, open pools, and open bars. I am sure it helps that the end of the tour is in sight by then. I contribute the 'peep show,' it is not as dirty as it sounds. Someone will end up buying me a package of marshmallow peeps. I make them sing and dance, then I stuff as many in my mouth all at one time, while making a monstrous roaring, screaming sound.

This strange ritual started on Toys on Ice when Suzy and I were bored in-between shows. Eventually, I went to Underwater Fantasy on ice with Suzy, she informed my secret Santa of my extra talents. Secret Santa though this was a great idea and made me perform at company meal in front of everyone to win my gift of the week. After that it became tradition, there was always someone who had been around for last year's peep show, and I would perform once or twice a year. Funny thing is, I don't even like peeps. They make my teeth ache and give me a short sugar rush followed by a big sugar crash, which usually coincides with show intermission.

I realized how strange this ritual was during my fourth year of touring with Underwater Fantasy. We had about four new girls and I did a peep show for the make-up room early into the tour year. It takes time for some newbies to come out of their shells and realize we're all weirdos and its okay to be your own crazy self. Everyone else was laughing or applauding and the new girls just sat there batting their doe eyes without any understanding.

I think it takes a special type of personality to join an ice show, especially the ones that become lifers, like me. The Company hires unusual beauties on the women's side that are also a bit kookie. Ice skaters are a strange flock to begin with, then you get them all together in one room, for ten months at a time, it's a different type of crazy. I guess that's what kept it interesting for ten years.

Make-up room discussions cover quite a range of topics, and just because it is the women's make-up room does not mean the conversation is lady like. We had at least one who loved to talk about her bowel movements. It became contagious, the entire room was one big potty mouth. Sex and period talk are never out of place in a women's make up room. Current issues are pop-culture related, favorite sports picks, and food is always a popular topic. What we ate, what we plan to eat, where we are going to eat. Pain and injuries are another common theme, but during February, we all get a little quiet, put on our I-Pods, and leave the room a little faster.

The lady's make-up room was not the only room for shenanigans. I once came across Chaz feeling the brail on all the hallway signs. He was pretending to be visually impaired and making up what the signs said. He apparently also had quite the toilet talk time. Chaz would ask the toilet questions in the men's make-up room, early in the mornings.

"Good morning, Mr. Toilet, do you want me to pee in your mouth?" Then he would raise the lid of the toilet and make the inanimate object respond in a high-pitched squeaky voice, "Why, yes, Chaz, yes I do!"

Of interest, often women who spend so much time together, find their periods beginning to regulate to one another. Many of us are on birth control, but that does not seem to control much of anything, except for babies. But not for all, one bright eyed and bushy tailed eighteen-year-old skater who had been handpicked by the choreographer, got pregnant six months into tour. She left and lived her happily ever after with her boyfriend-now husband and a handful of children. I ended up stopping my pills and re-starting again to sync cycles. This means twenty plus women all being on the same emotional roller coaster. Once a month everyone better steer clear of the lady's make-up room.

New girl pranks were another excellent way to pass the time. Even these semi-innocent pastimes have become virtually non-existent with more HR restrictions put into effect. On my first show, we would tape costume hangers to the rack or pack out new girl's costumes, which consisted of zipping and hooking everything together. Packing the costume in its garment bag and tying that closed. These antics fall under that rule, check your costume at half hour, which not even the old pros adhered to. This doesn't sound like much of a prank until you run into the costume room last minute because you've gotten your show routine down to the last second with no time to spare. Then you glide in to realize your costumes are packed out or you can't get them off the rack.

Another favorite was for the rock bot girls. Each show they would sit in their rocks, in costume for the about 15–20 minutes with your robot buddy, so that we could pop out and attack the male superhero space toy. Most of us passed the time by sleeping, talking, or once one rock called another rock. As a prank we would soak the crotches of their costumes, forcing them to sit on a wet crotch for about ten minutes. When we entered our rocks backstage, it was always dark and sometimes we'd put little paper cup of water where the robot was going to sit down.

We lost wet crotch privileges when we wet a new girl's costume and a spare wore her costume. When the spare took off the costume, she had someone else's soiled crotch stains on her show laundry. Some new girl had a feminine accident in their costume and had not reported it or cleaned it up. I'm going to stop and dry heave at the memory now. Anyway, no more wet crotches as a prank.

Make-up spots were always fair game. Re-gluing the whole personally organized make-up spot either under the table or on the ceiling in the exact way we found it was great fun. In retaliation for this one time, I found my make-up spot covered in baby powder with a loving message written in it. Most girls took the pranks in stride but occasionally some didn't take the antics well.

In Mexico, round two for me, the guys had a falling fine party and invited a few girls over only to splash them with water balloons. To retaliate the ladies line captain and myself baby powdered the men's make-up spots at work. The men's line captain, the crybaby that he was, could dish it but couldn't take it and we ended up in the performance director's office. His argument was to leave it outside the building. The only thing I felt bad about was I had accidentally powdered a friend's insulin pump.

The new girl Ali couldn't take it and made her situation worse. She joined us in Puerto Rico, where the weather was unbearably hot and humid and there were plenty of shows with nine pack weekends. She found out Edward had a little bit of martial arts in his background and wanted to spar with him. Edward's 6ft, she's a scrawny 5'6", so he put her off for most of Puerto Rico. Toward the end we were all drinking by the pool and finally he gave in. Everyone was watching and she meant to show off. He easily blocked and dodged most of her shots, which infuriated her. Her face became one big, angry cherry and she wasn't playing or sparring any more. When she had her claws all the way out, she full on punched him in the face. That was it for Edward, he kicked her legs out from under her and made her eat dirt in front of everyone. She was angry and mortified but that was the end of the sparring match.

From the start, she was digging herself a hole. She wore her gators, fancy term for costume boot covers, into the make-up room, a big No-No in wardrobe rules. No costumes in the make-up room this is due to the potential for food and make up to meet costumes. The line captain wasn't in the room so we all told her politely that she was breaking rules and could get fined, she shrugged her shoulders and said she didn't care. The line captain had to drag her from the room and make her remove her gators.

When it came time to play pranks on Ali, it was all too easy. We hid her make-up in a locker right next to her make-up spot, she came up at intermission, couldn't find it, didn't look around, stomped downstairs tattled to the performance director and told her she wasn't going to do the next show number because she no longer had enough time. The performance director looked her in the eye and said she expected to see her on the ice and wasn't going to hold the show. She marched up the stairs and said, "Fuck all, you bitches!" Well, any allies she might have had, were gone now. Then the pranks escalated, ending with tooth paste in her skates. Needless to say, she didn't get hired back after Puerto Rico for the West Coast tour. She did call us and ask for tickets to the show later that year, but no one returned her phone calls. Most of our pranks are relatively harmless and other than angry Ali, everyone laughed them off or got even.

One of the best prank wars I've ever seen was between two veterans. Edward lowered a fake spider into the quick-change room on a fishing lure and scared "little girl screams" out of two grown men. Edward followed this by removing Todd's skate blade, interlocking it with his other blade and re-bolting it. Now his skates were locked together. Todd got them undone barely in time for the show. When Edward came back to his crate after the show, he went to pick up his note pad and Todd had bolted it to his crate. As he looked around, he noticed everything had been bolted down, including his piece of pizza. To finish the escalating war Edward took Todd's new cowboy boots and covered them with tons of saran wrap and used a heat gun to melt and harden it around his boots until it looked like a big, clear, ball. Then he hid them in the make-up room.

To add insult to injury it was a pack out show and everyone wants to get out of the building as fast as possible. If you're driving, you want to get going and beat the bus for hotel check in. If you're on the bus, you want to get a good seat with your friends on the best bus, and if you don't fly out until the next day you want a shower and beer ASAP. Todd had to sit there and figure out how to free his boots.

On my first show, I would get packed out quickly and I was almost always in the make-up room with one other girl. I would quickly undress and be in nothing but a thong and fish nets, so I'd walk across the room and drop off my show laundry in this scandalous outfit. She hated it and every time we'd get a new girl, she'd warn them that I liked to walk around naked. I do not like to walk around in this condition, but since it bothered Olivia, I proceeded to do it as often as she was around.

I was also notorious for sitting in my show laundry in an un-lady like position. My first ladies line captain was a very proper English woman, and she would often be heard saying, "Maddie! Is that any way for a lady to behave?" We are still good friends but I'm sure I caused her an eye twitch or two my first few years. I was smarting off as she was giving notes one time. She was talking about crossing a line. I asked her where the line was, she drew one on the floor, so I got up and put my toe over it. I of course thought I was hysterical, she was exasperated.

In hot and humid Taiwan, I harassed a friend for wearing a top that showed off way too much cleavage. During rehearsals I would yell as many different names for boobs as I could think of at the top of my lungs, others picked up the game and she laughed but I never saw the shirt again. All these games seemed perfectly reasonable on tour.

Baby powder wars, this game wasn't just for new girls. My second year on tour the old show pros had had enough of my lip so they ganged up and baby powdered me. I had a faint aura of white exhaust cloud around me until I was finally able to get to a shower.

On a frozen forgotten tour of the US, we bypassed boredom by having a mascot. We had a Ken doll, no one knows where it came from. Wardrobe made him miniature fish costumes to match all the different characters in the show. He would sit at the board as the super spare of the week, and we would paint his tiny face to match all the elaborate fishy face makeup.

Another pastime was to make our show laundry as gross as possible. Sometimes this was showing off sweat marks. I bet you didn't know you can get nipple sweat rings. Or sewing fake fur in anatomical places on your show laundry. One time I came back, and someone had taken our line captain's clothes and stuffed them with a variety of items, the face had been made from hair and plastic bags and sunglasses. I sat down next to it, and it scared a scream out of me.

The love, hate, family relationship of tour means you're hardly ever bored and rarely ever alone, but sometimes you can still be lonely.

Chapter 31
Aerial Arts

I was one of the lucky few to be chosen for aerialist training before Underwater Fantasy opened. A month before rehearsals started in Lakeland, FL four of us headed to Gainesville, FL. I luckily roomed with Suzy, both of us had come from Toys on Ice to the new show. I arrogantly thought only four hours of training each afternoon, that doesn't seem like much. And then, we had our first training session.

I have never had much use for upper body strength. I might have done a small amount of cross training with light weights, but I'd never relied on my arms to hold my own weight. Four hours a day was all my body could stand. I was bruised and aching, my hands were raw, and I could not wait to get back in bed. We were informed that the new show would have a jellyfish number and at the heart would be two pieces of silk attached to a motor. With our skates on, we would devise a routine to do death defying drops on the silk. This would be the aerialist number.

Franny was the principal and Suzy and I were the understudies. None of us had any experience in the acrobatic world. Franny's roommate, Sydney, came from a show that had a ropes act. She had climbing experience and would be our guide and mentor. She was the bridge between the skating world and our two silk instructors.

Rehearsals were at odd hours, often 6:30–10:30 pm. I have thought about this in retrospect and believe that perhaps the gymnastics gym utilized their other hours or maybe our instructors had their own lives. We would do as little as possible during the day to save up our strength for training in the evenings. One of our instructors was from FL but had experience with the circus and other aerial arts but not specifically silks. Our second instructor was Brazilian. She was very strong and very talented. She spoke English well enough but often could not tell us the names of the tricks she was teaching. That was fine by us. We would name our new tricks by the body parts where the impact was felt. There was the De-Virginizer and the Brazilian wax twist, just to name a few.

Our second day of training saw us tied up and falling face first to grab the silk between our legs. If you did not catch the silk, it was a swan dive to face plant. Our instructors held onto the silk, so face plant was an unlikely scenario, but the fear was very real. There is a video of me floating around somewhere and in it, my instructors have ahold of the silk and are encouraging me to fall. I'm reaching out one hand like a toddler trying to grab the fabric before the fall, while the pain in my crotch is getting excruciating. Realizing this is futile and that the pain would only stop if I dropped, I finally held my breath and dropped. Then there was a new pain and I survived.

I do not care for roller coasters. If they go round and round, great, I'm all in, but if they drop, like most of them do, I am not interested. My stomach falls out from below and I silently scream, unable to breathe. This drop was similar, initially. Many people ask me if I'm afraid of heights and if it is scary. It is, initially. With training and strengthening, the fear falls away as you trust your body. Then it is exhilarating. All the work of climbing and tying yourself into twisted knots of silk is rewarded by the release of the fall.

The hardest thing for me to master was getting my own ass over my head. I could climb thirty feet of silk and do death defying drops, but I could not move down under up top. I was so excited when I had built enough core strength that I could hang from the silk and finally flip upside down. Then they had us put on our skates. With the extra weight, it was back to square one.

We trained six days a week for at least four hours. During daylight hours we would do yoga to try and ease muscles and aches. We were disappointed that the hotel had no pool and would sneak into the Marriot's pool. Once we almost missed practice because we were locked into the pool! At the end of the first week, we were all in tears of pain and frustration. Sydney took us for ice cream. From then on, we had a weekly tradition. Ice cream made everything better. We celebrated Fourth of July with sparklers in the parking lot and made photo documentation of our bruises. My father told me they looked like old lady legs! Dad came to visit for a weekend, and I spent a weekend with Mom.

Putting together an imaginary number, not knowing the big picture was no easy task. Add trying to find tricks that can be done with sharp blades on our feet and without slicing the silks or ourselves made the job even harder. We settle on what we called the butterfly. This was no graceful, winged thing, this move would sinch tighter and tighter. Then you swing your legs back and forth until you have enough momentum to do a back flip. Don't stop upside down or the tangled web that's been woven will come undone and you will land squarely on your head. We learned this the hard way, demonstrated by Sydney, who luckily has a hard head. Landing with the silks catching you underneath your armpits and ribs is a painful adjustment. If you do it long enough, it stops hurting (new scar tissue). We quickly learned that when doing death defying drops on the silks its best if you cover all body parts. Moving quickly on silk causes burns. The masseuse asked me if I had fallen down or was being abused when he saw the burns and bruises covering my body.

The second and most impressive trick was the Brazilian Wax Twist. In its final transformation, this trick has you fall face first and then do a full rotation on your side as if you are log rolling down a hill. When I got good at it, my goal was to have as much impact as possible at the end so that I would bounce up and down like a teeter board for a more dramatic finish. Finally at the end of three of the hardest weeks of my life we performed for the Director of Talent, and we went out to a celebratory dinner. They were impressed with how much we had learned and the strength we had gained in such a short amount of time. We said tearful goodbyes to our instructors and to Sydney who returned to her own show. Then it was off to the start of rehearsals.

Rehearsals changed things. We had built a comradery during the pain and struggle of aerial training. In Lakeland, all that was undone. We did not realize that Franny had a deep fear of being replaced. Having been a principle on another show, she wanted more money. But her performing track record was not on par with what she wanted to charge. The powers that be were not impressed and said no. She threatened that if she was not paid more, she would not perform.

Sydney was back to help the new show open, and she was becoming more aggravated with Franny. She told Suzy and I to always be ready because you never know what changes might be coming. Franny started trying to add new tricks to the number but refused to teach us, her understudies. She wanted to try these new tricks without a crash matt while over the ice. Franny grew angry and accused Sydney of treating her like a child because Sydney would not let her try new tricks unsafely.

I think Franny realized she was talking herself out of her specialty act and took the original deal. The rift that was created during rehearsals never healed. She would learn new tricks but became secretive about sharing information or training. She trained her own hand selected understudies but luckily, she could not take away Suzy's or my understudy. And when she decided to leave Underwater Fantasy on Ice for a different show I was promoted to aerialist, but only after they brought in a talented new Russian skater and acrobat that I trained and made me wait over a month during rehearsals where I trained all the aerialist understudies and taught climbing classes between shows to finally tell me yes, you are now the aerialist!

While training with Suzy backstage during show run-throughs, the owner of Family Fun on Ice came over to watch. He saw us practicing flip overs and finally asked if he could try that. We said sure. He was surprisingly agile and strong. When he was upside down, all the change fell out of his pockets like a piggy bank, irony?

Many shows play Minneapolis on their first east coast tour. Our schedule was changed because that year a circus had an accident in MN. One of their aerial acts had a performer fall to their death. After that, MN wanted all specialty acts to have nets under them. This was more easily accomplished in big top type shows but on the ice with twelve moving skaters, you can't feasibly stretch a net across the ice. So, we did not play Minneapolis for several years until that regulation was changed.

Chapter 32
Physically Fit Challenge

It is difficult to get in a good work out on the road. Seems crazy right, our jobs should keep us in shape. That's a logical assumption, but there's plenty of reasons to fall out of shape. Your body adjusts to the same routine. If I'm doing the same show track for five years, my body finds minute ways to use less muscles, less cardio, less brain power, which equals auto pilot.

On Underwater Fantasy on Ice, my first three years I had a pretty comfy spot once the costume was broken in, and I liked my porcupine fish, it was like a big shaggy dog. To get my back adjusted to this new costume was an arduous task which took muscle relaxants, severe back bruising, new stomach muscles, and six months to counter the back strain. After which, the costume felt great, and I was on auto pilot for most of the show. Between shows I climbed the silks and would get a good muscular work out, but not much cardio; that all changed my fourth year. Act I became a whirlwind of jumping, spinning, and costume changes and I lost ten dollars of character pay for my efforts. Some of the heavy or difficult characters receive compensation for wearing their cumbersome costumes for two hours.

My thigh muscles were screaming from all the pumping and jumping they were suddenly expected to do. My hammys and groin weren't keeping up well and would constantly whine to me. I began running while home on break. This should have helped my wheezing lungs, but I couldn't tell a difference. I had mixed feelings about the change, a good sweat every show, and the chance to skate for the first time in a long time.

After two weeks of rehearsals and a week of shows, my body was used to the abusive show track. I was still sweating, but not as much, the changes while fast were no longer stressful, I had found places to breath. This meant my body, had settled into a routine. By the third week, the only thing I noticed were the shaky hands when I changed my make-up at intermission.

Still, I wanted to lose a few pounds, so I thought I'd add running to my show skating, silk climbing and finally lose those elusive five to ten. Regular exercise is not conducive to our lifestyles. Even when you're home telling yourself, I'll run Mon, Tues, Thurs, and Fri, you get to tour, and the whirl wind hits. Monday you could be traveling or recovering from a travel day. Tuesday I was often recovering from going out Monday night, plus it was sightseeing, grocery shopping, and errand Tuesday. No excuse on Thursdays. And Friday I blamed early morning publicities, rehearsals, and kiddy shows.

If that wasn't excuse enough, have you seen the ancient equipment, locked away in the dungeon of hotels? It's not fit for an abandoned mongrel to run on. It groans under me like I'm the elephant, doesn't work half the time, and tells me the wrong time and distance. I can't work in situations like that. How about a run outside? That's fine until it's scalding hot, humid, raining, or winter, or when we stay in the ghetto or near busy streets. Where's a girl to run?

I thought I'd solve this problem with my birthday. I bought a fancy I-shuffle with no wire headphones, so now I am wireless, no whipping wires or annoying arm bands to deter me. Then Edward bought me a GPS watch that tells me how far I've run. This was probably the original Garmin watch that looked like a car GPS on my wrist. Now nothing was holding me back, except my injured right leg. I had such good intentions and so many better excuses.

I reached maximum upper body beef cake status on the Japan tour. I was quite proud; the scale and my performance director were not. I was finally the aerialist and not an understudy, we had what felt like a million shows a week in the heat and we'd climb at least once a day, since it was always a multiple show day. Add to this walking all over Japan in the sweaty heat for sightseeing and I slimmed down and beefed up. We had quite the silk group, about ten people would always be around the silk, and we'd have music playing and climb for an hour or more. I finished off the tour with a three-minute silk performance, just me on the silk using my arm muscles to hold on for dear life. I was pretty proud of myself. Before learning the aerial silks, I'd had no upper body strength. Three weeks of silk training brought me up an entire t-shirt size. This caused muscle weight gain, so the scale started to become an enemy again.

Four months off after Japan, the closest circus school for aerial practice was a three-hour drive from Rochester and a border crossing to Toronto. I would go with my dad once a week to learn new tricks and try and keep in shape. My first week at Toronto's circus school I was discouraged to feel so weak. I learned there are two kinds of silk. The kind we use and learned on is easier to climb. Our silk is less bouncy, but hurts more on drops, and is easier to get bruises and silk burn, which I had plenty to prove. The second type of material is stretchier; it's like trying to climb up a bungee cord. It's harder to climb but gentler on drops. After being at top beef cake status, I came to a new place to show off and realized in the circus world I was a beginner all over again.

To add to all of this, the silk was slippery, and I felt I couldn't get a good grip, I tired more easily, and they didn't heat the place in winter. Trying to show off I got tangled in the silk and stuck in midair with the silk acting as a python squeezing tighter. They had to get a ladder to get me down. That's when my dad started waiting in the car during my lessons. And that, was when I decided to invest in my own set of silk. I finally found someone online who would sell it to me, but only when she had enough orders. My solution was to purchase two just to get one. It turns out it's the super stretchy stuff. I figure I'll go back stronger.

Having the silk wasn't enough. Now I had to find somewhere that was thirty feet high with a ten-foot clear radius and a crash matt. After extensive searching, we finally found a gymnastics gym that was about 26ft, Edward rigged it up, but having to put it up and take it down every time was not efficient and time consuming. The gym was worried about being sued for injuries, and when we did rig it, rosin dusted everything, and to add insult to injury, it wasn't a high enough ceiling. I even investigated a place online that would build something to hang it from outside. I laugh to think about the neighbor's expression if they were to see me over their backyard fences.

The aerial rig was too expensive, it would have been a constant eye sore taking up the entire backyard and it's NY so nine months of the year I wouldn't be able to use it. I never solved the problem of hanging my silk in NY but by the time I left the road an aerial school had finally set up shop in Rochester NY. I sold them one of my silks and continued climbing after tour life. Eventually when we settled in NC, Edward made a rig between the trees for my very own place to hang the silk. This required shooting a bow and arrow over two trees to tie ropes. Building his own rope ladder all to hang C-spans complete with a pulley system for putting up and taking down the silk.

When Underwater Fantasy was a new show, I was given a pair partner that arrived late because of visa issues. We did well together, he was 6'3" and Edward says that's actually tall enough to skate with me. At 5'6", I'm a giant in the pair world. My new partner opted for a five-foot skater and would do scout clinics and practice with her. Scout clinics take place after the evening show where boy and girl scouts stay for a presentation and demonstration about the show. My pair partner wasn't exactly stable on his feet, and we would giggle through the entire pair number. Add into this that he dropped me at least twice, which was luckily on a low spin where I was already close to the ground, and I wasn't too sad to see him go to another show. Also, Edward may have threatened him if he dropped me again. And why lift 5'6" when you can lift 5'?

Next year they did not replace my partner, while I was okay at pairs there were not a lot of very tall guys, and the shows have plenty of trained, short pair skaters. So, I became pair wench. I was the pair back up when any of the pair girls were out. I would skate with three of the guys from the different pair teams. Any time one of the pair girls had to spare, understudy, or was out sick, I got to go in. This was trickier with the guy who did spins and lifts in the other direction.

Being pair wench kept me from a permanent turtle spot which was a different burden. That tricky 5'6" height was just short enough to make me baby turtle size. In actuality, I looked like a Giganta turtle with all the other shorties. So now I must know all eleven turtle spots to spare-with costumes that floss my privates painfully since they were made for someone short, four pair spots, countless jellyfish spots, and aerialist. A girl's work is never done.

Chapter 33
Loon Mt.

Snowboarding had been an essential way of life for Edward and I before we came to Underwater Fantasy on Ice. Our trip to Loon Mt. was the tour trip to talk about. Morning round-up took many phone calls and banging on the door to get the crazy Russian and his roommate awake after a night of binge drinking that had ended with a toilet broken by a Russian head, a flooded room, a room change and eventually a divorce. Crazy Russian was making out with someone else's wife in front of a bar window in full view of her husband!

Eventually they all crawled into the van. There were eight of us leaving Boston at an excessively early hour on a day off. We proceeded to New Hampshire; it was going to be a two-hour drive and most of us passed out. I stayed awake to help Edward stay alert. We heard some interesting sounds coming from the back of the truck. Edward looks at me and says, "Who brought the alien?" It was the crazy Russian, not even making words, just unintelligent, Russian gibberish. Everyone woke up when we pulled into McDonald's for breakfast. The Russian alien grabs his flask, orders breakfast and a short orange juice which he pours vodka in. It's a day off, gotta keep the party going.

I later informed the group that I needed the facilities, since I have a 90-year-old bladder in a young person's body, this is not new information. We pull off NH-93 where there's nothing but trees around. I run into the bathroom and off we go, except there's no north entrance, so we stop and ask direction from this eerie creature with very few teeth, who looks like something out of *The Hills Have Eyes.* We hardly understand her, we think it's a her, but realize that we need to double back to find an entrance.

We're driving through thick woods with nothing around in the grey fog and Slap Stick says, "This is like one of those horror flicks where we ask

149

directions, and some creepy woman leads us to her place where we're going to get kidnapped and killed." We all laughed uneasily until we were back on the freeway. After we were safely on the interstate again everyone harassed me for getting us lost and needing the bathroom. In my defense, I never said we had to get off immediately.

Already the trip was off to a great start. We pull up to Loon Mt. and everyone gets out with more crap for a one-day trip than I've ever seen. While the pros head off to start renting or changing, the crazy Russian is rummaging through his stuff and muttering. He becomes more and more agitated until he burst out that he had forgotten his shot glasses. He gives up and puts his flask in his pocket.

The crazy Russian, Slap Stick and Suzy had never skied before, Sid took Suzy for the first few runs to the bunny hills. We took the insistent crazy Russian and his skis up to the top of the mountain with us. He looked down and said, "I don't want to drink no more!" After Suzy's warmup runs, everyone kept up pretty well. The crazy Russian took a few side trips over the snowbanks. We have pictures of him and all you see are his feet sticking out of the snowbank like the Juggernaut.

Slap Stick was our endless source of amusement for the day. He's like a cartoon character, singing the mission impossible song to himself as he sets off at breakneck speeds. We come to moguls, and he goes right over them eventually gaining air and yard sale: everything goes everywhere. With the amount of pain he should have been in at the end of the day, most people would have quit. After every wipe out, he'd get up with a wave saying, "I'm alright!"

His crowning moment was when he followed Edward and Roger into the woods, still singing the Bond theme song, Roger goes over a ten-foot drop and waits for Edward at the bottom, Edward goes over and they both watch Slap Stick who later told us his thought process went like this;

Bond theme song, oh look there's Roger, hi Roger. There goes Edward, oh wait that where I'm Go...ing...!

That wasn't the end of Slap Stick's woodland excursion. He got up, assured us he was okay, and followed Edward and Roger. Roger went left, Edward went right, Slap Stick could not make up his mind and hugged a tree, hard. I am sure his little boy bits were not okay.

Lunch is always spent in the bar, and we get there right as it opens at noon. Bring our food up, which is less important than liquid lunch and buy several rounds of drinks and shots, toasting our misadventures. My favorite snowboard drink is hot chocolate with baileys and either butter schnaps or gold schlager. After this intake of liquid courage, it was back to the mountain, with another tradition accomplished. After imbibing, we'd find the snowboard launch site and do jumps and half pipes since we felt invincible, and our joints were a little looser. Today we just explored the other side of the mountain with the new skiers in tow.

At the very end of the day, we all tackled the half pipe. It started raining, that slushy, melting, heavy rain. We were all soaked and watching each other go down the half pipe, Suzy just went straight through, a safe choice. Slap Stick decided if Edward could do it, he could do it. He stabbed himself in the chest with his ski pole that got stuck in the side of the half pipe and yard-saled all over, effectively blocking the entire half pipe so no one could go down it. In the process, he had also pissed off two kids waiting their turn to tackle the terrain park. We're all standing there laughing in the rain waiting for him to pick himself up and get on with it.

Dry clothes for the drive home; I'd forgotten a change of clothes and end up wearing borrowed sweatpants. The crazy Russian finds his shot glasses at last. Last one in the car gets locked out, Sid takes pictures out the window and is cursed for his photography. And finally, we head home, everyone is exhausted and passes out except Edward and me.

We get back, shower, change and all go out to Chili's for family dinner, creating another snowboarding custom. Edward had load in the next day so after dinner he went home and finally got to collapse in an accommodating bed. This was not the fate for the die-hards, we go out to the Foggy Goggle, where they serve fishbowl drinks of grain alcohol. I realize now why first year on Underwater Fantasy I did not have to worry about weight, I was highly active, always drunk, sometime forgot to eat, and didn't sleep much.

Chapter 34
Letters from the Far East

S.E. Asia Tour
2/4/07–3/6/07
Taiwan

After a three-month break at home in western NY where it refused to snow, which meant no snowboarding, I had my longest travel day. I left at 2:30 pm on Sunday, flew to DC, LA, and finally Taipei, Taiwan. I arrive in Taiwan at 6 am on Tuesday, a great deal, dirtier, smellier, and grumpier. Our travel day did not end there. We took a little van to the domestic airport in Taiwan, it is separate from the international airport, something to do with China. There we were to wait until 4 pm to fly to Kaohsiung, Taiwan. A ten hour wait did not seem like fun to me, so I called the company manager, and played tour coordinator for the little group that had flown with me, and we left at 9 am, I counted this a small victory as I made it a step closer to a bed and a shower. Finally, I had made it out of the US and to Taiwan.

Kaohsiung, Taiwan is very industrial, dirty, polluted, and bustling. It is located at the south, western tip of Taiwan. In Japan, it was the bicycles that would run you over, here it's the scooters. Everyone drives a motorized scooter, and you can forget about lanes, lines, and lights. They are just guidelines that nobody follows.

One of our days off I went to a little island off the coast of Kaohsiung with another couple. We drove scooters along the beach and at one point I knocked over my scooter and the battery fell out of the floor. When we rented our scooters, Jeff walked up with a beer in his hand, we paid, didn't leave them with anything for contact info and road away on scooters. Nothing to stop us from taking the scooters to our hotels or knocking the battery out of them.

The natives on the beach all had on long pants and sweaters. I guess it was winter, but we were blinding white people in our bikinis, and this made us somewhat of an attraction because they all wanted pictures with us. I don't think they see many westerners on the beach of Taiwan. Another day we went to the Lotus Pond and saw the brightly colored statues, along with the tiger and dragon pagodas. The statues and pagodas had a Chinese feel to them and looked fairly new with brightly colored paint.

Taipei was a five-hour bus trip across most of Taiwan. Their buses did not have bathrooms, a fact that only made my need greater. Toilets in Taiwan are predominately squatty potties. Squatties were not new to us, we were assimilated to them occasionally in Japan, but in Taiwan, they are the majority. These little gems have no toilet paper and are mosquitoes infested. Imagine having to take care of business at intermission of a show, balancing on skates, over a squatty with mosquitoes biting your bum. Isn't tour life grand?

A group of us went to the Taipei Tower, which was the tallest building in the world for a brief period. Not long after another country erected a bigger one, it always comes down to size, doesn't it? As a consolation prize it does have the world's fastest elevator. I also went to the electronics district, which has everything you could ever want for very cheap.

This was followed up with snake alley and a night market, where we watched our friends drink snake blood. This aphrodisiac is supposed to have mythical qualities like sexual virility, or some such powers. It is also very unhygienic. They don't just hand it to you in a little glass, they kill this little snake, by whacking its head on the table, hanging it on a hook and draining it into your glass by squeezing it like an old toothpaste tube. Very appetizing! I settled for taking a picture with a boa constrictor. For the Chinese New Year, we had a show bar-be-que behind the arena. They had fireworks, parades, and we got ten days off. At night, every few hours we would wake up to what sounded like gunshots as more fireworks went off.

Our final stop in Taiwan was Taichung. It was a grueling two days of loading in for the crew, only to perform for two days, followed by a challenging load out. I went to see the Fat Buddha statue, he was cute, obese, and golden. It is interesting to see all the different faces of Buddha since each country depicts him differently. The crew finally had their first day off in about a month and Edward got to sleep for most of it. Then we flew to Singapore.

The Bay of Thailand

We had a 10-day break before Singapore. One of the best perks of a S.E. Asia tour is that occasionally you get these long breaks, and everything is cheap over here, except in Singapore. Instead of trucks for transporting the set, grid, props, and costumes overseas we have shipping containers. After loadout, these containers are shipped to the next location, and this can take longer than a truck driving to the next city. This led to some long breaks between cities.

A few of us wanted to go to Hong Kong and China, but that didn't work out because of the Chinese New Year, everyone was flying, and it cost too much. Normally, the way things work on this side of the world is last minute often works better for booking flights. There's Tiger Air and their round-trip fares are so cheap it is unbelievable. When China fell through, we went to Phuket Thailand. Our round-trip tickets at last minute were about 100 US dollars. We found a cheap room for $42 a night. Our room already had its own visitor, a lounge lizard. Then it was off to the bar.

Phuket is the gateway to Southern Thailand, home of some of the most beautiful beach islands around the world with full moon parties that movies are made from. Each island and beach have a unique feel all their own.

A group of four couples took the ferry to Koh Phi Phi Island. Pronounce pee pee, que giggling. White sands, aquamarine water, and hot enough to roast you. Within half an hour, my shoulders were burned as we walked around and looked at bungalows. How much and do you have AC, were the only important questions. We got a room for $38 a night with plenty of AC. It came complete with a small electrical current in the shower. I complained to Edward that I had lost feeling in my right arm when I moved the shower head and my feet would burn, he wrote me off until he also became a human conductor, grounding the electrical current to the floor. Luckily arm numbness was the extent of any damage and we left the shower head where it was.

We went on a water taxi, snorkeling around Koh Phi Phi Lai, where parts of the movie The Beach were filmed and then over to monkey island. These cute little monkeys came up to us and we fed them. Mistake one. They would take food right out of your hand, but once the food was gone, one swung on my hair and the other bit my leg. I did not live down the rabies jokes for the rest of tour. Second mistake do not look them in the eye it just enrages them. Then they all ganged up and chased me around the beach. My only escape was waist deep water, they don't like the water. They would hiss and then gang up and run at you, barely knee high, but they were not to be trifled with. We filled empty beer bottles with fresh water and took pictures of them drinking what looked like beer. With the bigger beer bottles, they had to use their feet to gain drinking leverage.

The cost of living in Thailand is very affordable, divide everything by about $40. We climbed to the highest peak to watch the sun set, played on the beach, and watched fire shows at night. People would light both ends of their sticks or chains on fire and perform. They sold booze in kiddy sand buckets. After one of these buckets and watching staged kick boxing, Giggett and I decided we could do it, in full pads of course. We put on a much better fight than all the staged ones, or so I am told. They called it a draw, but I'm fairly sure I won.

While putting on our padding we both agreed no face shots, as soon as we got in the ring, she punched me right in the nose so that was the end of civility, her head looked like a tether ball. She pinned me to end the match, but it was kickboxing not wrestling. The next day her neck and other various body parts were sore, but I felt great. I was told by the rest of my girlfriends that they would never get in a ring with me.

After a few days on Koh Phi Phi, four of us split off and took the ferry to Krabi. Krabi is a beach peninsula. To get to many of the different beaches you must take a water taxi, so they feel like islands. It was amusing to see Edward with our luggage balanced on his head, wading out waste deep, with his towel wrapped around his head like a turban, just to get to the boat. He had his pooka-pouch on one side with his camera and tripod on the other and a holstered bottle of Malibu. He is certainly, always prepared. I definitely over packed for a beach vacation. We stayed on the cheap beach right next to Hat Rai Lei West. We thought our room with AC was a steal for $25/night until we asked them to turn on the power. Power is only on between 6 pm-7:30 am. No AC during the hottest time of day, what is a westerner to do?

Krabi had a chill full moon party, it was all the young hippies smoking weed. We just had our drinks and danced on the beach under the full moon while sending off floating lanterns. The next day we went into Krabi and climbed a waterfall that does not see too much tourist action, the locals were staring, again. After that, we rode elephants. Our elephant pulled up two baby trees, roots, and all, for a snack. On our last day, we hung out at the beach until it was time to take to ferry back to Phuket. I don't think Thailand has the same standards for emissions that the states do; every boat and car I got in I felt sick from the smell of exhaust. I don't think there are the same codes for bathroom hygiene either. I used one of the bar bathrooms and was not surprised by the lack of toilet paper. I was surprised that there was a sponge on a stick in a bucket of water. A communal douse? I'm feeling ill just thinking about it.

For our final evening in the bay of Thailand, Edward & I had dinner on the water, we chose a ten-pound lobster, he was shimmering rainbow colors and was beautiful. The lobsters over here do not have front claws instead he had long whiskers, when they told us the cost, we chose two little lobsters instead. Everything this far had been ridiculously cheap until our rainbow lobsters which held a price tag of $100 each! Keep in mind that we don't get paid on our breaks between tour cities.

The next day a few of us met in the lobby to go to work and discovered that we had one more day off. Understandably some of us were pissed because we could have stayed on the beaches a little longer. That's all for now, see you in Singapore.

Love, Maddie

SE Asia Tour
3/7/07–4/20/07

Singapore

Singapore, home of the Singapore Sling, an overpriced frou-frou drink. We partook in the touristy tradition at the Raffles hotel, made famous for inventing the drink. Singapore is exceptionally clean and very safe. I found it a little boring, but there was lots of shopping, which was outside of my budget. I did make it to the zoo but missed the infamous night safari. Little India was a bit dodgy and might have given me food poisoning, or it was a left-over souvenir from the bay of Thailand. There is a cool club scene called the Canary, with many different bars and restaurants, which was also out of our price range. In one bar, there were more skinny, six-foot-tall women, than I have ever seen anywhere else. It looked like a ballet dancer's convention full of gazelles.

We had one day off in the middle of our show week and went to Sentosa Island. It is commercialized, but we quickly found Casa Del Mar. Swim up bar and beds on the beach, does it get better than that? Actually, it does, we met the navy who was in port and partied with them until the evening. They all jumped into the pool to find Edward under the water with six straws connected, to make a slurpy bridge to his bucket of jack and coke. The guys took one look and said we'll have what he's having. Instant, expensive friends. Ten hours of day drinking cost us $800! We found an Irish bar for St. Patty's Day and I had my first taste of Brazilian food. Any kind of meat you like on a skewer. Each meat comes around to your table, and they feed you as much as you want. Don't forget to put the red flag up or the meat just keeps coming!

Bangkok, Thailand

There is a game the guys played for years on tour. You ask unsuspecting or drunk guys what the capital of Thailand is. If they say Bangkok, then you punch them in the nuts (Bang Cock!)

Dad and his girlfriend came to visit in Bangkok, Thailand. Everything was cheap, but you had to deal with the hecklers and haggling. Dad likes this type of bartering, but I do not. I dislike it so much that when my mom took my brother and I to Egypt, I left the bazaar in tears. We went to dinner and had real Thai food. It was interesting, Edward and I like Indian and Japanese curry, but not the green coconut Thai curry. They use a sweet coconut and something with a black liquorice taste.

We checked out the night market and bought a couple of souvenirs. There was one beggar missing legs, pulling himself through the streets asking for money as we are being assaulted by sellers on either side.

The next morning, we were all up early and off to the tailors, this was the number one thing on Dad's list. The airlines had lost his luggage and Dad refused to buy more cloths until the airlines agreed to reimburse him. So true to tour life he washed his undies every night in the bathroom. They had lots of suits and shirts made that were kindly paid for by the airlines. A few of the guys from tour also had suits made for cheap while in Thailand. I'm all for a good suit but what occasion calls for a maroon and gold suit? The 70s porn stars called and want it back!

After the tailors, it was off to the Grand Palace. Everything was gilded in gold and shiny cut glass. Thailand has a different take on Buddha and architecture. But beware of the scammers. We asked for directions to Wat Poh from a soda vendor who pointed the way but said it's closed until the afternoon. Immediately another guy comes up trying to help us with our map and says it's not open, but he could take us elsewhere. We were so close and had been warned by the tailor, so we went for a look. Sure enough, we found the temple was open. Wat Poh had a giant, gold, reclining Buddha. After that we were all sweaty, hot, and tired, and we finished the day with a Thai massage. The women use their entire body to massage you. She would sit on my leg and use her feet to massage my thigh or hang from bars in the ceiling to walk on my back. One of the girls on tour was used as promotion. They gave her a massage and propped her up, exposing her boobs in the front window. Free advertising.

The next day we were up early and off on a grand tour. We had our own air-conditioned coach and went to a coconut plantation. I climbed up a tree to truly experience coconut gathering and we discovered many different uses for coconuts. We took a little water taxi boat to the floating markets, vendors selling on boats, and boated along the intricate canal system. A stop at the war memorial, lunch on the water, the JEATH war museum and finally the bridge over the river Quai, built by the Japanese war prisoners. We were all surprised by the train that unexpectedly came down the tracks and almost ran Dad over. After that, we took it easy in the five-star Dusit Thani hotel, that the tour put us up in.

By the end of our stay, we were highly annoyed with the concierge. One way to make a little extra cash on the side is by sending the tourists to your friends' shop. Shopping in Thailand they are a little too helpful, personal space is debatable, and they think on a slower time frequency. I made sure Dad got the full Thailand experience when we went to the Super Pussy, Ping Pong show. Talented girls, with amazing muscle control, new uses for darts, and birthday candles, but they were not very excited about their jobs. Edward would do impressions to make me giggle of their zombie like dance while they waited their turn to show case their talents.

They were clearly excited about our money. Edward pulled some money out to pay for his drinks and they tried to grab the whole wad out of his hands. Their aim was impressive, hitting balloons with darts and Dad's experience was complete when some of that talent hit him in the head. A banana was shot like an arrow, and my dad was told it was lucky to be hit by a banana. To purchase this luck he would need to eat the lucky banana and that too would cost extra. He politely refused. They even cut paper dolls with razor blades hidden within! I would not want to be the boyfriend that pissed them off.

We made it to real Thai Kick boxing, which was exciting with the crowd yelling and screaming, and the match was complete with one bloody nose. We had lunch at the Oriental Hotel and Dad and his girlfriend came to see the ice show. I was sad to see them leave but I'll see them in another six weeks. It also meant back to work, lots, and lots of shows.

We had two days off in the middle and Edward and I went to see the Marble Temple, the Democracy Memorial, climbed the Golden Mount, and the Temple of the Dawn. There is a great roof top bar on top of the Dome Tower and one of the sky bars leaves you feeling like you are floating over the rest of Bangkok. There was more on my never-ending sightseeing list but unfortunately, I did not make it to the old capitol or the north of Thailand. Edward was secretly grateful for the reprieve and at some point, we had to sleep.

Malaysia

Kuala Lumpur, Malaysia. I buy country flags for all the places I go and will eventually put them on my letterman jacket. When I tried to buy Kuala Lumpur, in Orlando, the store owner and I were confused when we could not find it. I finally bought a Southeast Asia map because I was tired of not knowing where I was and realized that KL (Kuala Lumpur) is a city in Malaysia. That was today's geography lesson. We pulled up to the Palace of the Golden Horses Hotel and Resort. Sounds wonderful, opulent gold horse statues, its own shopping mall, which is difficult to get to, several restaurants, what more could one want? How about a capable front desk staff, who charged us for many imaginary things, extra restaurant or bar bills, phone calls, extra internet?

Or we could do without the moldy rooms, and AC vents that have never been cleaned. In the states, if a hotel has black mold, it is immediately condemned. Not so in Southeast Asia, they think nothing of it and leave it. You can die from inhaling black mold. I thought I was imagining things, but I continued to get increasingly sick in my room and many others were expressing similar health concerns. Sure, enough we found some black mold. We were far from the city, but close to the arena, so we were stuck eating the expensive hotel food, and after two weeks anything gets redundant.

KL is a nice clean and modern city. We saw all the sights in one day and did not have time or resources to explore the rest of Malaysia with shows starting. I went with friends to the National monument, some different mosques, the KL tower, and the Petronus Towers (featured in Entrapment) which had a connecting bridge in-between. We also explored the Batu Caves. Huge caves with a giant golden statue at the front and 272 steps to get in. Unfortunately, we missed the colorful Indian festival.

It was that time of year once again for girls falling fines party. We had it at the pool, I made my trash punch and pizza. Trash punch is so named because it can be made in a trash can and you put everything in it (like a trash can), and possibly because it gets you trashed in the end.

We had a three item, theme party. You draw three random, cheap items that you can either find or buy and make an outfit out of it. Mine was money, socks, and wash cloths. I made a top out of coins, a skirt out of socks and money, and a washcloth hair veil. I did not spend as much time as some of the other ladies, because I was busy party planning. Some of these girls looked like magazine models, a channel looking dress made entirely out of straws. Or an elaborate head dress made from trash bags and CD cases. We had three prize categories, best outfit, most creative, and funniest. I always won funniest without even trying! As per norm, we crashed the boy's party at the bar after we had ice cube tray races. We lost to the boys again; they still suck. Then we had eight days off.

Cambodia

Once I saw pictures of Cambodia, I had to go; it was my number one goal while in Southeast Asia. We flew into Siem Reap, with our best travel buddies, for about four days. Our first day there we took a tuck-tuck to the killing field's memorial. The memorials are ornate boxes with glass windows, filled with gruesome bones. We followed this with a trip to the land mine museum, which was the backyard of someone's house. The kids begged for my water bottle and tried to pry it out of my hands. From there, we went to the famous Angkor Wat and climbed all over this incredible temple. There are little warning signs about the uneven, steep steps, but unlike most ancient ruins we are still allowed to climb all over. These huge temples and city ruins are very impressive and different than any other sights I have seen.

Even tired in the heat and travel day we climbed up another ruin to watch the sunset. Edward had extraordinarily little sleep with a long load out before our travel day and unfortunately left his camera in the tuck-tuck. The driver disappeared quickly and our camera even faster. When he was back to pick us up, he claimed he didn't know anything about it but stared at where it used to be and said in perfectly good English that he could not speak English. The police were no help.

Cost of living in Cambodia is cheap, they take the US dollar because the conversion is about 4000 to 1. The people are very friendly, they will steal your wallet but are genuinely nice about it. We found a great tuk-tuk driver the next day and he took us to Angkor Thom. This complex has many ruins on it, but the most impressive is the Bayon. A Bayon is a stone with three faces looking out of the rock at you. It is eerie but beautiful.

Promh was our next stop, I think some of Tomb Raider was filmed here. This was Edward's favorite temple; they have let the trees take over. Massive trees with roots that look like seeping puddles are climbing and rooted all over this temple. The people here still like tourists, since tourism is new, but man are they persistent. Seems to be the way they sell things in Asia. They learn at an early age, little kids following us heckling all the way. Personally, it drives me away. I did manage to buy a few souvenirs and some extra clothes since for once I packed so little.

On our last day in Siem Reap, our tuk-tuk driver took us to the floating villages where there are floating homes out in the middle of the lake. We saw one little boy, naked, and paddling around in a bowl. Out of the city, people live in little shacks propped up on shaky looking stilts for the monsoon season. They do not even have electricity, but we did see one child with a game boy.

We found a couple fun bars; The Red Piano claims it was home to the Tomb Raider cast and crew and our personal favorite was Angkor What? A play on the famous temple Angkor Wat. We were there for the Cambodian New Year celebration, but luckily did not partake in their tradition of getting doused with water and talcum powdered.

Bali

Bali, Indonesia, was a relaxing change after climbing around Cambodian ruins in the hot sun. We crossed over the equator, my first time on the other side and if possible, it got even hotter. Our hotel was amazing, a canopy around the bed, which I got into a fight with, and lost, an outdoor shower, big tub, and a full kitchen that opened to a patio.

I road on the back of a motorcycle for the first time, Edward was driving and considering anything goes with the driving here, it was scary. Edward is a great driver, but my arm muscles were tired of holding on for dear life. We couldn't locate a map, or street signs and never got to the sights we wanted to see. We did see a lot of rural, rice paddies and then got rained on. We were just in time for the tail end of monsoon season in Indonesia, and the hottest season in Cambodia. We always have great timing. After five hours on a crotch rocket, my butt was sore.

We spent the next day surfing and getting sunburned with 50spf on. Edward was in the barrel of ten-foot waves. I was proud to say I finally stood up on the board and got rash burn. Of course, I stayed in the baby waves. Life is also affordable here; the conversion is 100,000 to 1. We collided with some of our tour family and partied together for one night.

Our last free day we chilled at the pool and swim up bar. We finished the day with some tiring, heckle filled, shopping. In the evening, we went to Tanahn Lot a temple on the water and saw the sun set. Their pagodas here look like they are made from thatch and horsehair. We did not get to see as much of Bali as we would like but it is a place we would come back to, after we see the rest of the world of course. Dinner on the beach and finally back to KL and the horrible hotel.

Brunei

Up next was Brunei, a dry country, wonderful place to finish tour with a bunch of party animals and nothing else to do. My large tourist book has about five pages on the little country of Brunei; in comparison, Thailand has 200. On our first day, we took a taxi, took pictures of two mosques, and bought groceries.

The sultan of Brunei had an amusement park made for his people and it is free admission. But he did not spend the money to maintain it and it is not fully operational. The amusement park is eerie and run down. I commented that all we needed were some psycho clowns and the picture would be complete. Right after that a car full of clowns drove by. That was our exit cue.

When an arena cannot support our rig, it means a lot of extra work for the crew. This is called ground support. Not only do they have to build the set and grid like usual, but now they must build legs to support our show ceiling full of lights and special effects. They decided to practice in Brunei.

Ground support is not a new concept to our company but the added twist was the aerial act. The bigger the drop, the more torque, and the more strain on the grid. The company did not know if ground support could withstand my thirty-foot drop. How to solve this problem. Rig ground support, then put a crash mat on the ice and perform the drop that has less torque, do it closer to the ground and see how the ceiling holds up. That passed, so now let's do the drop that causes more torque, okay, good to go. It's a very scientific process. Just please don't do any of the extra drops and rocks that you like to do, the bowing of the grid does not look reassuring.

Brunei is divided into two parts, a group of us went to the rain forests side and climbed up to see the canopy. We did not dress appropriately so I was swimming in the waterfall in my sneakers, capris, and sports bra. We all snuck in extra booze bottles to help celebrate Rachel's 21st b-day. The hotel bar would sneak in as much beer and wine as they could each day. Alcohol is illegal so you would knock, and they would look at you through the peep hole before allowing you in, just like a speak easy. We performed plenty of shows and said our goodbyes until Australia.

Chapter 35
Birthdays in Providence

Providence, RI the first time through with Toys on Ice, I turned 21 and got kicked out of Dave and Busters. I had a lot to live up to the second time around and I was coming to terms with spending a lot of time without Edward with his hectic work schedule and my new drinking buddies. We arrived in Rhode Island and immediately went out to the men's line captain's home. His mom threw us a party with cake and all. We drank, ate very little, except cake, and made up a new game with a soccer ball and 30 people. It was a variation of monkey in the middle with several monkeys and if you served the ball and it was captured you become the monkey. We added to these rules with tackling and precariously perched drinks, who says we aren't creative in our down time? All the fun, running, violence, and alcohol went to my head. Since Underwater Fantasy was a new show, the crew was doing a two-day load in and unfortunately, Edward was busy.

I have vague recollections of being dragged down the hallway and tickled to death, drinking card games where we screamed profanities at the top of our lungs, inebriated talks with the smokers in the stair well, and pre-gaming our dual birthdays 24 hours in advance. Crazy Russian and I had the same birthday, and we were both the same age, this means double the parties, right? By the next year we had added a third birthday to our ranks, triple birthday threat! Sharing a birthday with Crazy Russian never disappointed. The year we had birthdays in Toyama Japan after sloshball playground take over, they found the only Russian family in the city and we had an authentic Russian dinner with imported Russian vodka in their new friends house!

In Providence, Crazy Russian and I started drinking at midnight of Tuesday, the guys had a cracker spitting contest that gave great pictures, I think we sobered up for our opening night show, and then we went out for the real birthday celebration. There wasn't a lot around that was open on Wednesday, plus we had a bunch of 18-year-olds, so I finally found a bar that would let us in. The bar turned out to be a hole-in-the-wall gay bar, which is a tour special. I was already limbered up, so I had a good time dancing on the speakers. The crazy Russian was not impressed with the bar choice, or the crew, Edward would not come in and waved from the door. Once upon a time Edward used to go to the gay bars, but he wouldn't come in even for the birthday girl.

This brings to light crew versus skater. Most shows the divide was small. And often the mostly male crew was chasing the female skaters. On Underwater Fantasy on Ice, the divide was much wider. If you were a long-time girlfriend of a crew member, like I was, you were grandfathered in. They would often complain about the cast believing that they were snobby and whiney. Edward would often have to clear his throat to remind them that I was there. This was not much of a deterrent. But on a rare occasion I would hear a comment about why can't they be cool like Maddie?

Thank you, my friends, but I have not always been so 'cool'. This reminds me of the mayonnaise story. Edward and I were newly rooming together in our relationship and I had let many little things build, festering beneath the surface. Poor Edward had no idea of my volcano waiting to erupt. He had grocery duties and I had written out a list. He brought home miracle whip instead of mayonnaise. Proof to my mind that he was not listening. The argument ended with miracle whip smashed against the wall and Edward saying something like "So, no miracle whip then?" which brought laughter out of the situation and from that point on only mayonnaise.

My, middle school friends came for a visit from Boston and a break worker left us to go back to his show at the end of the week. All good reasons to get drunk so it was a blurry birthday week in Providence. Mission accomplished I out did my first birthday bash, trip to Providence, RI.

Chapter 36
The Secret Room

We performed in LA during the 2005–2006 tour season. The company took away our week off near Christmas to drag us back to LA to play a different building. LA twice, a week separating the two different arenas but bridging a year between them, happy new year. LA is a great party city, but we stayed so far away from the bar scene that a taxi would cost us all our drinking money.

When you get home from a show and want to go out, there are several dangers. First, don't sit down. Keep moving, immediately jump in the shower, with drink in hand, which takes acquired skill not to waterlog your drinky-poo. Don't sit down in the shower, which is hard for me because that's my deep think time. Make it a quick wake up shower, when I had long hair, I used the shower cap on going out nights, slap on clothes and make-up. I later discovered the wonders of dry shampoo. I was usually slowed by the clothing selection process, not able to decide or trying several outfits on. I strongly believed that in my over 50lbs of clothing, I had nothing that was new or looked good enough. This destroyed any semblance of organization in the room and became a giant dumping ground of clothing.

Make-up is easy for me. I liked my bright lipsticks. It was the one thing I always wanted to wear as a kid. I'd be in front of my mom's light up make-up mirror, like a puppy dog who has gotten into Mom's lipstick, smearing it across my face and my mouth and in a pout at being found out.

I am usually still first to the lobby for our arranged outings. I end up waiting for the herd and begin breaking my cardinal rules. I sit down. I have a few more drinks on an empty, dehydrated stomach. If we were done at 9 pm with the show and not back until 9:45 pm, I would end up waiting until 11 or 12 for everyone. Finally, we go out and it took so long to get where we're going, we stay until the bar closes. If that's 2 am, then we come back and drink until the wee hours. I usually end up in my PJs after all that effort.

The second danger is when the phone calls start coming in as you are rearing to go. They all cancel on you or want to change the plan so many times that it falls flat. It never fails. It is not one person that calls and says they're tired and not coming, it is all or none.

LA was a hard schedule. Even with my brother visiting and excited about going out, sometimes I just couldn't muster the energy. That did not stop him. He was full of energy after sleeping all day with no shows to perform.

When we first pulled into LA, I get a call telling me to come up to the top floor. The elevator won't go to the top floor, so I have to take the elevator to the second to last floor and take the stairs, from there. Then the directions get complicated. I head up alone and after the flight of stairs things get a little eerie. Going through dusty, pipes, renovations, back rooms, tight quarters, alone in the dusk was a bit scary.

The secret room was worth it; a circular room with windows looking out on LA, small dance floor in the middle, couches, and an empty bar. We had small parties all week. When we are not at a bar and we have enough space, we all tend to get really silly. We had table rolling races around the circular room. Threw papers in the air that the Crazy Russian tried to catch with his mouth, staying up and drinking much too much. The way down was much easier, the elevator would come to call if the button was pushed from the secret room.

You know you're with a group that can let loose when one of our first room parties on Underwater Fantasy ended with Sid and the Crazy Russian with pots and pans on their heads. Singing at the top of their lungs and beating their headwear as band instruments. Another never ending bus ride we rewrote the lyrics to Bohemian Rhapsody to the tune of our show life.

Like anything else, we wore out our welcome. First week we'd gotten away with it, when we came back, we invited more people to the secret room. They used the glasses at the bar and the elevator traffic increased so much that we were noticed. A security guard came up and politely kicked us out. So much for our secret room. But it's there if they ever let us stay at that hotel in LA again. That's pretty much our MO, we get great hotels, and no amount of money can convince some hotels to let us back in.

This became a real issue during the hurricanes of 2006. Many refugees from Louisiana were staying in surrounding hotels in Bossier City. We had an infamous golf party that ended with one guy pissing off the second story balcony onto hotel cars and pissing off the hotel. There was lots of shouting, and vomit everywhere. The company manager had to beg forgiveness for us because every hotel for hours around us was booked full of refugees. He was understandably, fuming mad at our misbehavior.

We were good at finding hidden areas, roof top access, and secret rooms. In Cleveland, with Toys on Ice, there was an entire floor under renovation. At night, that's where we all partied. The bathtub in one abandoned room became someone's vomit trough. Frenchie dragged a small, strangulated tree he'd found while out on the town, through the lobby. The front desk asked him what he was doing with a tree in the hotel. His drunken response was that he was taking it to his girlfriend to prove that he loved her. This became one of the hotels that we were not invited back to.

A different Cleveland hotel saw me inebriated and unable to form the words to ask Edward who was comforting me, to get off the toilet. So, I clogged the bathtub with bright pink, chunky vomit. No amount of apology to the maids would earn their forgiveness.

What is a golf party? I'm glad you asked. You have 9 to 18 rooms participate. Each room has a different alcoholic beverage and rules on how to drink that beverage. Each sip was counted like a stroke. The lower the stroke-sip count the better your rank. Toys on ice had an outstanding golf party in Fresno, CA. One room had those plastic straws that do loopty loops. The meanest drink was the LJ Shaker; red wine and tequila. If you were still standing after the eighteenth hole at the arena across the street and had the lowest score you won. We had a tie so there was a putt off. The boyfriend and girlfriend who were tied had a fist fight over the putt off. People were passed out or making out in the bushes, but the hotel did not care since we had our sloppy finish in the arena parking lot. The next day Edward was told that golf parties are not allowed in the company. He received this memo from the performance director who had participated in the illegal party.

So, in Bossier, LA we did not have a 'golf' party. We had an Epcot party. Each room had a different country theme, same golf scoring, and we drank around the world and almost out of Louisiana.

Chapter 37
Frozen and Forgotten

A Frozen Forgotten tour is a states' tour that plays mostly small cities because it has either done everything else or isn't selling well. The show isn't ready to close or be revamped into a new show, so we entertain the smaller cities of America. There are many different levels of frozen and forgotten, just as there are many levels of margaritas. There are classic shows that have done everything, so they play rural tiny towns with Thursday openings and one show Sundays. There's also the fourth-year frozen forgotten tour after a show comes back from overseas and plays half small cities and half big cities that may not have been covered by the original tour.

My third year with Toys on Ice, instead of going overseas we played a frozen forgotten tour, some of the city highlights were Tupelo, MS.; Albany, GA; and Biloxi, MS, amongst many other little towns. I personally thought the show was dying but as I jumped shows the next year, they went to the UK and did half Europe and another dying states tour before finally, closing. One highlight was the front-page news upon arriving to Bangor, ME. The headline was about a man having an inappropriate relationship with his horse, I guess there was a ladder involved. In Bangor, the show converted a high school gymnasium into an arena. That was a pretty impressive feat.

I've found that frozen and forgotten tours are some of the most fun tours. More time off means more time to get in trouble and less money. You don't get to see everyone at work, so you actually want to see people outside of work. There's nothing to do in these cities and no moolah, so you become very creative.

Sloshball was a popular solution to our boredom. In Tupelo, MS, there was a field with a soccer net right next to the hotel. It was like a shining beacon, calling to us. We filled a trash can up with ice and everyone brought there drinks over. Running low on booze, not a problem, there was more than enough, and we were happy to share. How to play sloshball? Rules are simple. Kickball with a full drink in your hand. You must finish that drink by home base, without puking, for the point to count. Beer cans and red solo cups keep score for the teams. It is a sweaty, messy, exhilarating game.

Then we moved on to hanging out by the empty, winterized pool in the cold. Only one set of boxing gloves, no problem. Two guys, one glove each, and go. Edward did pairs with a skinny six-foot guy. There's photographic evidence of Edward holding Peters upside down over his head. There was also a miniature pool table and a tournament. Finally, there were the many drinking card games.

There was your classic butthole, but we would get drunk and argue about rules. Later there was F the dealer, a much simpler game that even when inebriated is easy to understand and achieves its goal of getting you very drunk, very quickly. Sociables became a favorite, but often there were too many rules so some lost patience and the game of choice my first two years on tour was three men with dice. Don't ask me the rules, they are lost in a history of haze.

In one city we heard of a foam party. That was a new one for us. So, we piled in taxis and off to the gay bar we went. While I frolicked in the suds, Edward was hit on by a dud, who then wanted to know why such a straight guy was in a back woods foam bash. By way of answer, he just pointed at me dancing on a platform covered in soap. At exactly the witching hour, the bar closed. No warning, just get out! All of us are standing outside, shivering, and waiting for a taxi that was called for us. We waited an hour, and we were too far from the hotel to walk, not to mention my hair was frozen by that point. We did eventually make it home and many of us had rashes from the foam that had dried on our skin. That was our last foam festivity.

Edward eventually stopped going to the gay bars with me. I think he was tired of fending off amorous advances, and I was of little help. Sometimes he got his revenge while watching me squirm waiting to buy a beer and getting hit on. I kept looking at him to save me and he sat there chuckling because I was stuck in line.

When Edward first joined tour, his costume rack was right next to Paul. Edward was bent over changing and as he stood up he was eye level with male junk wrapped in a candy cane thong for the holiday season. He was greeted with, "It's a hard candy Christmas! Do you like my new underwear?"

Bad strip clubs were a classic on a tour like this. Sved had a birthday in Albuquerque, NM and so we all went to the only strip club open on a Monday. While the boobies were slouching and the pot bellies were present, there was fun to be had. They dragged Rena up on stage and she got a face full of cleavage. Next it was the birthday boy's turn. They sat him on a chair and all the women took turns hanging from a bar in the ceiling and humping his face. We were concerned he might suffocate or have a broken nose, but he just had a goofy grin on his face!

This brings me to male strip clubs. I have only been to one, and it was not a good one. I have heard there are fantastic ones, but after my one and done, I cannot bring myself to go. This little gem was in Toronto and these guys were very impressed with their dick slapping abilities. They did not need to be in any sort of physical shape, the only requirement seemed to be if they could get as close to you as possible and make noise by slapping their members back and forth on their thighs. The entire thing was a painful process.

Assassins was another favorite on a circuit like this. We played with water guns. The only rules were you could not kill in the arena, and you could not have a witness. I made it to the final five but did not win. I thought I was so clever because I would use a knit sweater with a front pocket. Through the mesh I would assassinate. Everyone thought they were safe as long as there were witnesses but no one noticed me shooting out the front pocket of my sweater and I could kill in public. The winner would stage elaborate set ups. He would disguise himself as a homeless man on a route that we walked to work and strike the unsuspecting by standard as they strolled past.

One of our favorite hotels was Jumer's Castle. It has changed names over the years but resides in Peoria, IL. This old-fashioned hotel was rumored to be haunted and was creepy with old carriages, fireplaces, and hidden nooks and crannies. The portraits in the hallways seemed to follow your movements and the armor appeared to shift positions. We were usually there near Christmas and they did a great job of decorating. Large tree in the atrium and the balcony overlooking the tree had Santa's workshop. Apparently one couple found this too irresistible and christened the workshop. The lodge would display giant inflatables in the yard and apparently the pull of these large fluffy objects was too alluring for one individual who was caught humping them! Idle hands on easy tours.

There was plenty of time to dream and scheme pranks or just good old-fashioned revenge. One crew guy Sceavy, had pissed off the ice guys so badly, that retaliation was required. The ice guys took his crate and filled it top to bottom with popcorn. And not just the light fluffy air popped kind. No, the buttery, salty, slimy kernels. When Sceavy opened his crate, the mountain of corn buried him waist deep. There was no appreciation of the hard work put into retribution just angry sounds. Unfortunately for Sceavy, he had beef with so many people that he could not pinpoint who the counter blow came from.

We drove that year and found any hill or mountain within a three-hour radius and went snowboarding, took road trips, found craft projects, and there was always time for in-shows. The only downside to a frozen forgotten tour is with more time off, there's also more time to spend dwindling money.

In-shows are usually performed twice a year. This is when we either audition for an understudy or we often show case our own creativity by creating novel routines or group numbers. My favorite was the cell block tango from the musical Chicago that I choreographed as a group number. Edward created a backdrop with fabric over curtain rods on rollers. We back lit these and started the number with the six women as silhouettes.

Organizing everyone for a group outing is difficult enough, now convince them to spend their free time learning new numbers after hours. It did not always go over well. My father on one visit in CO stayed after the show and watched me leading the group and teaching my choreography. He said that's the first time he realized I was a leader in my own right.

Another favorite was the last group in-show I created. It was to '99 red balloons', and 'I got a feelin'. We had our talented skaters that could also sing and play instruments perform the songs live on the second story stage while we skated below. We even strapped skates on the crew as they show cased their hockey skating abilities, sticks and all. It took all my powers of persuasion or begging to convince the company manager to put his skates back on with us. He joined the day we performed the finished product. Those that couldn't skate, no problem, they danced on the platforms downstage. When I finally decided to do this swan song group number, I only had a few weeks left on tour and no one would trade sunshine for extra rink time. So, I took five minutes out of our warmup before each show, and every day that we had shows, we would warm up with the flash mob choreography. The flash mob may have found its way into my wedding reception. This number was completed with professional level lights and effects.

We had a week off before we played Puerto Rico after the frozen forgotten tour with Toys on Ice. Many went home but a few of us stayed in the Sunrise, FL hotel. Sunrise was a good time. We put all the plastic chairs and tables in the pool and played cards in the rain. I had purchased some clear, plastic playing cards so if you dropped one in the pool it was a lost cause, but the cards could withstand beer stains and a little rain.

Before I joined my first tour, the only money I'd had was from a part time, minimum wage job. I thought I'd hit the jackpot, even on first year probation pay. Money seemed so easy back on tour days. No bills to pay so you kept everything. Most of my money in the early days was spent on food, booze, and clothes. My brother came on tour as part of the crew after college graduation and even though he partied like the best of us, he managed to pay off his half of an Ivy League four-year college education in two years. That is impressive.

In later tour years, we finally began to save some money, especially when the end was near and collegiate dreams were ahead. I often wonder if I had saved from the beginning how padded that account would have been. But Edward reminds me that we enjoyed tour life and would not trade those memories for anything.

Chapter 38
Yosemite

We would take road trips whenever possible. Fresno doesn't hold much in the way of entertainment, an old hotel, hole in the wall bar down the street, small dingy rooms leading to an outdoor pool, looks like time for a road trip. Lucky for us there always seems to be a party planner. I am usually the default planner, but if someone else is willing to put in the work, then I am happy to go along for the ride. Edward thinks he'll never be able to throw me a surprise party because I will have already planned it myself.

One of the commando party planners had arranged three cars and two connecting cabins in Yosemite, we ended up with 15 people. I was one of the lucky few who got to drive. Never having rented or wanted to rent a car until I came on the road, I discovered that some dealers will not rent to anyone under 25. So, I can vote and drink but am not responsible enough to rent a car until 25? The first few years on tour I would run into trouble because I had a credit card but was under 25, Edward was over 25, but didn't have a credit card. They don't like check cards and hold ridiculous amounts of money. By the time we did this Yosemite get away, I was one of the few in the over 25-year-old club, so by default one of the drivers. On tour, time moves on, some of us age but the continuous influx of young adults keeps us looking young and sometimes feeling old.

We headed out of town Monday morning after travel day. Right before entering the state park, we stopped for supplies and essentials. We had arrived at Fresno on a Sunday night, left Monday morning, and were coming back Wednesday morning. That makes two full days of eating, drinking, and merry making. You take 15 people into a grocery store, add a grill, two days of food and more importantly alcohol and see how long and how much it costs you to get out of the store. I think I must have spent $200 on my food alone, for a two-day trip. Must have steaks, cheese, skewers, and mixers for the next stop at the liquor store.

Side notes on buying liquor in 50 different states, it is difficult when everyone changes the rules. It is the United States, can't we all just agree on the same guidelines, except for the dry counties and no liquor on Sunday, we can just skip those rules. In NY, you can buy beer and hard cider at the grocery store. At the liquor store, you can buy wine and hard alcohol, but not beer. So, when I am home, I have to make two stops. I like the states or counties that not only sell all kinds of liquor together, which makes sense because they're all related, but also sells all of these selections at the grocery store and at any time of day or night. One stop shopping makes me happy. Don't get me started on Utah's diluted beer rules!

Early into tour life I had a friend who believed himself a wine connoisseur. I was barely 21 and knew nothing about wine. He would sneak it out of his backpack at parties, hidden away because he didn't want to share, I would slosh it around which would aggravate him. Mr. Wine Connoisseur would order wine each week and have it waiting at his hotel when he got in.

After the winding roads up and into the mountains, we all scrambled out of the cars and ran around our respective houses laying claim to beds and couches. We reveled in the simple pleasures, a fireplace, kitchen, grill, hot tub, and a pool table. We stocked one fridge with food and the other one top to bottom with booze. We opened the freezer and fridge door and took a picture of our proud booze fridge. It became the cover picture for our closing night party DVD. After getting up way too early on a day off, many people took naps, but not the diehards, about four of us, cracked open the fridge. Every time the fridge would open it would make angelic sounds in my head. No food, a pool table, and almost unlimited amounts of alcohol, by the time everyone else woke up at dusk, the four of us were well on our way.

Attraction and alcohol, chemicals at their best. My friend liked one of the guys on the trip that was still involved with someone else. He was also into her. These two were trying to have what I call social alone time. That is when you're in the room with other people, so the rumors can't start, but you're not really interested in anyone or anything else happening in the room. My amusement at watching these antics rose when the remaining single male felt he must compete for this female's attention when she was clearly not interested in him. Sometimes I have perfected being invisible, add to this all the photos I take and watching this unravel is better than reality TV. On the road, everyone wants what they can't have.

The houses woke up and we began seriously drinking and started up the grill. It was cold outside, so we started a fire and wore our hats in the hot tub, because that's what normal people do? It was decided we needed an aerial shot of the hot tub party, so I crawled out a window and scaled the roof for a great shot of what looks like a cover photo for an 80s rock band, complete with flying champagne. Then everyone turned around and mooned this photographer. As if asses were not enough, we have a picture of two guys naked with hat on and junk in hand who took my spot on the roof.

I was introduced for the first time to the game of sociables. For this particular round, you had to do anything from rhyme time and categories, or any embarrassing thing one can think up and of course changing seats whenever possible. Each king card and foul up of the card scaffold meant dumping a generous portion of your drink in a big silver cooking bowl at the center. The person who drew the last king had to drink a full cup of that crap. It was filled with beer, wine, and every hard alcohol mixed drink we could think of to imbibe upon. We had several brave souls, but we would all help whoever had to drink the slop.

Gay men get away with everything. Women feel safe because normal rules don't apply to gay men and straight women. I have seen plenty of make out sessions and some of my bigger breasted women friends with their chests practically violated by gay men and think nothing of it. Other shenanigans that night were leg wrestling matches where a six-foot guy lost to a five-foot girl. And finally, we roasted marshmallows in the fireplace, it was a good night.

After an early morning, the day before, no nap, a late night, I was up early the next morning to go out and see nature, with dark sunglasses, Advil, and a pounding headache. Our time here was limited so we thought we should go out and see Yosemite. I tried to start the morning with breakfast and got a bacon grease burn that left a scar, bacon is dangerous on a hangover. We caravaned and took pictures of waterfalls and climbed a little in the cold. I made my anti-nature friend roll around in the grass while yelling at her.

"You love nature, you love nature, say you love nature." The only thing we did not get to that I still want to see were the giant red woods. In the winter, they close those roads and it's a mile walk. It was getting dark and cold so that was our cue to get back, start the grill and warm up with a drink or four.

A few drinks later and shivering after the hot tub, I proceeded to cover my hands in splinters marinating and stabbing my kabobs, but they sure did taste good when I was done. We drank, washed, and repeated the night before. There were piggyback rides, and my piggy backer would fart every time I moved, so I used him as a weapon, point, aim, move. The professionals were of course the last ones standing at some unreasonable hour.

We woke up, hung over and cleaned the house, packed up and left. The god like booze fridge was completely empty. We had impossibly, eaten and drank everything in the houses. We took a group picture out front, putting the 10sec timer on across the yard and racing across the ice and up the stairs to capture this weekend in a frozen moment. The winding roads did not feel so good on the mid-morning drive back. We all got in, took a nap, and skated a show; like the professionals we are.

Chapter 39
Wild Goose Chases

I think there are two types of tourists. Those who read their books and must go see the landmarks and museums, and those that feel experiencing and living with the culture is the way to experience a place. Our lifestyle forces us to exist within society, but at heart I am a reader, planner, doer. I can improvise and have been known to go with the flow, but that has come with experience and not naturally. I do not feel like I have completely seen a place until I've gone and seen the sights in my tourist book or in my mental check list. Edward rolls his eyes and says so you want to go see what some guy in a book told you was important in a city. Well yes, I do.

There is a hit of dopamine when you check a box off a to do list. Like the mouse rewarded with cheese it can become an addiction. Check lists and I go way back. I now have a journal with the 1000 things to do before you die and it has a check list in the back. The first thing I did was not to write in the journal, but to go through and check off everything I've done. I got the journal at 26 and I was disappointed in how little I had done.

Edward also wants to know why I must do these things, "Why do you want to do these things, to brag that you have done them?" Maybe, but this is how I feel I have experienced a placed. Checked it off so thoroughly that if I never get to come back, I'm okay with that. Plus, I need photographic proof because my memory is short, and I have a sick obsession with check lists. I got tired of Edward's exasperated face in my photos and pestering every passing person for a couple's picture; mind you this was pre selfie era and so it's either him or I in those sightseeing, proof pictures.

I knew I had a check list problem, but it became really apparent when I went to a beer sampling. They gave you a cute little plastic card to wear around your neck and you got a sticker at each of the 48 samples. And by sample, I mean about a half pint. You do the math. Lunch with my Aunt and cousin saw some projectile vomiting and Edward carrying my to-old butt to the car with a reminder from family that I was not 21 anymore. It wasn't my fault; they gave me a sticker check list. I was quite good at my journals for a while. Since the age of 8, my journals have had journals. Except for the occasional year I didn't write, I have a trunk load of journals.

My first two years on tour were the worst for my sightseeing lust. There really are some cities where there is nothing to see. If there was nothing listed to do in my book, I would go scope out the postcards to see what they recommended. I also sent out 8 postcards a week. Father, Mother, Brother, ice rink, and then the last four were rotated between my friends so that they got one once every three weeks, simple.

Lubbock, TX; if you have seen a tumble weed go by and been to the college bars, you really have seen it all. I did not believe that was it, so I found a postcard that said prairie dog park. Edward refused to go with me so I dragged my girlfriend with me, we got dropped off by the bus and walked for two miles but couldn't find a way into the outer border of the park where we thought the prairie dogs were. Finally, hot, sweaty, and dusty we had to give up and face a long hike home with no prairie dog sighting or photos. When I started tour, there was no Google Maps on my bulky cell phone that Dad paid for, and I was only allowed to use in emergencies. I also had to buy and develop film, an expensive habit.

In Chicago, I dragged a group of four of us to the navy pier, in February. We even rode the giant Ferris wheel in the bitter wind and freezing cold, but now I can die happy having nearly frozen to death to see Chicago. I should have held out for the navy pier in warm weather when stores and vendors were open as I discovered the next time I was back.

In Puerto Rico, Edward and I had barely any days off. I did skater crew on top of the shows, helping load in and out. I was always working and always sick. Added to this our hotel lost power when we arrived. Imagine dragging two, fifty-pound bags up ten stories of stairwells in the dark. Fun times.

With our bunch, people either loved or hated Puerto Rico. Those that loved it wanted to move there or date Puerto Ricans. Edward and I did not enjoy all of our time in Puerto Rico. However, that was not going to stop me from sightseeing. I purposely bought the smallest tour book with colorful pictures so that I would decrease the chances of our wild goose chases, but it didn't help.

In Ponce, I had a picture of some quaint outdoor market that I had to see so I dragged Edward through the heat on one of his only days off and finally found the picture that was taken of some poor open air farmers market, that was not worth it. A picture guidebook does not solve the problem. Then we climbed all the way up a hill to some cool building that was shaped like a cross and a famous house with a great view to find out they were closed. I thought Edward might want to bury me up there at that cross.

I planned a trip to the rainforest and invited a few people. Soon the word spread and if someone else is willing to do the groundwork, everyone else might as well jump on board. I took the entire show to the rain forest. I rented three cars, one of which was a van and I refused to drive. We got stuck in traffic and were about an hour late picking everyone up. We ended up on back roads ghetto vanning through Puerto Rico and finally made it to the rain forest, which was a disappointment, it had become too pedestrian, lots of sidewalks and concrete everywhere. The highlight was the waterfall we hiked up to and swam in. My outfit looked like some butch version of wonder woman in my bikini bottoms, t-shirt, bandanna, and hiking boots. Everyone seemed to have a good time including Edward who scaled the waterfall. I know because I have picture proof.

Then the plan was to go to the red beach, cleverly named because of the sand color. We lost the other two cars which eventually found the correct beach, we ended up taking a pizza detour and finding a different but pretty beach and then we all returned our cars. The other downfall to organizing big trips, is not everyone pays. Then I end up being the bitchy collector. Somehow, I always end up in this role. No one else wants to collect for donations.

There are always little signs from fate that sometimes things are not meant to be, but usually I don't listen. I am learning in my older, hopefully wiser age, but I am a slow learner. At the end of our S.E. Asia tour, I got approval that Edward and I could change our flights home, which would cost $100 dollars, so I would be up until 4 am trying to call and change flights at the right time in the US from Kuala Lumpur on Skype. Skype was a wonder in our Stone Age days. I could find cheap flights into China but flying once inside China was expensive and potentially dangerous in 2006. The country is so big that train rides can take days. I worked hard on this for four late nights, it should have been the first sign. Finally, Edward says, "I don't want to go to China."

"Yeah, but we're already over here in Southeast Asia, we might as well."

"I don't hear good things about China, everyone who has gone there says they don't ever want to go back, and they tell me not to go."

"Well, if you don't want to go now, when we've already flown the 17 hours here, you're not going to want to go when we're off the road for one of our vacations."

"I promise I will go to China one day."

"But I've already paid $100 to change our flights!"

"I am tired of S.E. Asia and just want to go home. China is not my idea of a vacation. If we're starting a new business of the coffee stand next tour, we can't afford to be spending the extra money."

Always my voice of reason, he won; I changed our flights back and wasted another $100. One of our adventure buddies tried to go anyway. He landed in China and didn't have the right visas; he was detained for a while but finally made it back in the nick of time for his tour. After $200 and so many flights changed, Edward suffered the brunt of my meddling. It took him 24 hours of flying and nine lay overs to get home after a very long tour.

When Edward became crew, he no longer had the time to go on wild goose chases with me. In Japan, my travel buddies Sid and Rachel were always ready to go, and we'd have a great time. I have gone round and round the US tour and my idea of sightseeing has become finding the next bar and immersing myself in the local cultural flavor. Overseas it is all new and I must go, see, and do everything.

In Japan and Southeast Asia, one travel buddy made a mock video, her interpretation of my sightseeing. Running full sprint and videoing like a Blair Witch movie, while narrating, because I must see all. It's pretty accurate.

We were in Paris for three weeks during our European tour. I had gone with my family in 2001 but was back with tour. With Edward's busy schedule, I tried to save the must see for his limited time off. We had off one rainy Monday and so I dragged half the crew to the palace of Versailles. We were cold and shivering and excited to go in. It was closed on Mondays. Tour guide Barbie did not do her homework. But fun was still to be had as we raced golf carts around the almost deserted gardens and found alcoholic hot chocolate at the café.

I know there is debate about French snootiness toward Americans, but I have firsthand accounts. The first time in Paris they refused to seat us at a pizza place because we were American. They tried to seat a couple behind us after we had waited an interminable amount of time and the couple politely said these people were here before us. Not only would they not seat us they made us take our box of pizza and eat it outside like barn animals, no utensils, plates, or napkins. Not to worry our family friendly lawyer and Dad's girlfriend wrote an informative letter about the inhospitality to tourists and the pizza place got in trouble with the tourist bureau!

On our return to France, I took another friend to a small nearby city and got lost. My French is broken at best, but I was trying. They do not give As for effort here. I asked where the bus was in French, not perfect enunciation but understandable. She made me repeat it three times like she did not understand me. Corrected my pronunciation and accentuation and then rattled off fast French directions with some finger gestures. We found the metro on our own.

From London, I took a group to Stonehenge but had read about the monoliths in Avesbury that were even older and less well known. They did not seem too far apart so an extra stop seemed reasonable to everyone. Tour guide Barbie strikes again, going off halfcocked with only fifty percent of her tourist research done. Avesbury was a one pub town where we looked at big rocks scattered around a field and the highlight was when I got in trouble for chasing sheep around. As the afternoon moved on we were ready for the main site of Stonehenge. But there's no bus, or train, or taxi that will get us there before Stonehenge closes. I have a lot of angry sightseers that only wanted to see the main attraction. We came from London and did not have many days off to sightsee. A sketchy BW van rolls up complete with bead curtains and a hippy looking guy gets out. He sees our distress, all eight of us and offers to give us a ride.

Now normally I do not get in a stranger's car. Stranger danger and Mr. Yuck stickers have been burned into my childhood memory. But there's eight of us and only one of him and damn it I'm going to Stonehenge. So, we all pile in, and politely ignore the smell of wet dog in the back of the van that looks like his home, minus a dog, and we make it into Stonehenge right before they closed, so it was fairly empty and there was only one fluffy dollop of a cloud in the sky for a spectacular photographic backdrop.

I have learned that even on wild goose chases, half the fun is in getting there even if there is nothing to see. If I look around as we are trying to get somewhere, I've probably seen more in that city or country than if I had not left my hotel room. Edward has followed me on many wild goose chases and misadventures now for almost twenty years. We alternate between going to do crazy challenging things I want to do and relaxing things he wants to do like lounging on the beach. It is a comfortable compromise for me. But he's still going on wild goose chases with me after all these years.

Chapter 40
Flakes

While home on injury leave, my brother called. Usually with him it's out of sight, out of mind. He has a built-in radar that reminds him you're alive as soon as you are in driving radius of him. When we're on tour, he comes over and vents about this girl or that girl or we get drunk at a bar and go in the corner and gossip. I figure it was obvious to everyone that he was my brother because I had talked up his arrival and because we look so alike. Those that were not clued in must have started the gossip mill. It did not help matters that we had a few drinks and got on stage and danced the night away. Our Japanese skater sees us in the corner whispering away and knows I have a boyfriend, she came up to me right before I went home and said, "I just found out Adam is your brother!"

When I was home with an injury, I did not hear from Adam very often. As soon as I was within a half hour of his location he began texting and calling. When he called, he said that it was strange that he felt like he didn't have any best friends on tour. There was a girl that he felt close to with a similar personality. He made it hard to be friends with her because he was also chasing her for a date. Attempting to add to the conversation or saying I understood resulted in him snapping at me. Sometimes you just have to let him ride it out. So, I shut up and remained happy that we didn't have sibling drama to add to tour.

There is truth to what he is saying. Some of the people we met our first few years were quality friends. Even if I have not spoken to them in a few years, I could call them up in an emergency with no hesitation. While they are great friends, none of them were best friends.

Most of my life I have been fortunate enough to have a best friend. Those friendships that stand the test of time. When you get together, it's the same silly jokes and you giggle tell sunup. On tour, or maybe as an adult it seems harder to find that connection. A couple of times on tour I came close. Most of the friends I considered best friends did not feel the same. I was not their best friend. When I complain of this to Edward, he always says, "You're my best friend."

Now there are fun people, a few great people, but the drama seems to run rampant, and most are flakey people. They're not there when you really need them. When times get rough and it is no longer the good times, they're out of there fast. We have all lost friends to boyfriends and life. Even if you find good friends, can they survive FU Februarys? This expression accurately describes what happens around February. It is dark and cold and before we head south to warmer weather everyone is tired of everyone else. People have short tempers that are on shorter leashes. Then we go into spring and sunshine, everyone is happy again, but you notice as the end of tour draws near that different friendships and alliances form, usually people you never would have put together are best friends.

It got harder and harder to organize group outings. I organized a round of slosh ball for fun in Rosemont. We were going to play in the arena parking lot, which wasn't being used. Of course, there were questions of will we get in trouble? Trespassing? Open drink laws? Should we ask first? Ask? My policy is do first, ask later, I'd rather be told no after the fact then told I can't do it at all. I went head-to-head with a friend who had a publicity and would be late. I got upset and called another good friend and said, "Just tell everyone slosh ball is off. I don't need to plan it, everyone else put me in charge. If they don't like it, they can plan it themselves!" He calmed me down and said not to call it off, he would be out there drinking with me at two, even if no one else was. Everyone wants someone else to organize so they can knit pick.

Two o'clock rolls around and we had drinks, grill, and sidewalk chalk. We were having a good old time. Most people came an hour or two later. My friend that talked me off the ledge did not show up until almost five, good thing I wasn't relying on him. Why are people so flakey? Another lesson that took me a long time to learn and I keep relearning is that you can't please everyone or anyone for that matter.

My brother told me a story about going for Philly cheesesteaks after sightseeing. One or two people said they weren't sure they wanted one, and then the whole group began hemming and hawing like clucking hens, if they're not going, then I don't want to go. Adam and about two others went on for cheese steak and said screw you to the rest. The group collective is hard to deal with.

As I got older, I had a harder time relating to the rotating door of 18 year-olds. We had one little wide-eyed girl come on tour in Europe. Her first tour at eighteen and she makes it to Europe! We were sitting at company meal, and she asked me a question. I began to answer her question in a thoughtful manner. When I was done, she responded, "Whaaaattt?" and my retort was, "Did you just ask me a question and not listen to the answer!" Who is the old fart now?

Chapter 41
The Art of Falling

Figure skaters are supposed to be graceful works of art. With a finished package, you never see the countless falls, the sweat, the tears, the injuries, or even the athleticism. But doing a dozen shows a week, if you look closely, you can see all that and more. Toys on Ice had the klutziest bunch of girls, which included myself.

I love the expression of innocent bystanders when I say falling fines, "You get fined for falling?" Disbelief plastered on their faces. Paying for our own hotel rooms also gets a good reaction. No, the company doesn't fine us for falling. We keep track amongst the girls and guys and at the end of a tour, collect money for each of our falls and have a party. It's a good remedy for show flukes. There is even a rating system.

There is your typical fall, that's $1. A $2 fall was backstage or in the costume room. Those happened all the time, trying to get these tight costumes over your skate, putting the leotard on before the pants, or don't get me started on the zipper burns that would leave a rainbow of hard to explain bruises on your inner thighs. No sitting down in costumes so you had to stand to acrobatically change costumes in skates. There were quick changes to consider, when you had little time to go from one number to the next and had to under-dress several costumes and change hastily.

A $3 fall was achieved when you earned audience reaction. An example was going backward in a four spoked wheel, attached to three other girls, falling straight on the tail bone, and trying to scrabble out of the way of the oncoming spokes as the audience, in unison said, "Oooooh." You also got the $3 fall if you were in character costume and there were not enough ensemble on the ice to pick you up and the sound board had to play the toy down music.

"Toy down, we have a toy down, will our toy technicians please assist the toy?" Then the crew would run out in their shoes trying not to slip and pick up the poor toy. One of our Trolls went down by the headers during a scene change and none of the ensemble skaters saw it. The next number had six large costumes with no hands. The Performance Director couldn't see the troll from her seat and the radio crackled back and forth.

"There's a troll down stage left."

"Where? I don't see anything?"

"By the headers." By the time the Troll was spotted, it had inched its way toward the upstage curtains on its back like a little inchworm.

We also had $5 Fridays, so if you fell on a Friday, it was compounded interest. A fall backstage on Fridays became a costly mistake, adding up to $10. And then there is $10 Tuesdays because we rarely had Tuesday shows. If you fell on Tuesday, you were out of luck and money. The winner of third year's most falls was Catty at 42 falls.

Opening night of our first year on tour, my line captain, in the beach doll box next to me attempted to get out of her toy box for our big toy reveal and slightly tripped. She was staggering around as if she'd been at the bar. In the confusion, I got locked in my box and just watched poor Georgina stumbling about. I loved to hear her high pitched and loud laugh, followed by her lady like snort when she retells the story.

Usually, we have a minimum and maximum so that one or two clumsy people aren't paying for the entire party. The boys have all sorts of convoluted falling fine rules that I could not follow. Escalating prices on multiple show days and discounts for falls on jumps and tricks. The crew has their own version. They call 'six pack' anytime anyone falls and the one calling the shots is owed a six pack of beer.

I heard after leaving the road, as the HR noose tightened, that the company did away with falling fines because one crybaby did not want to participate. We always had an understood clause that if you don't want to pay then don't go to the party. One tattle tale always ruins it for everyone else.

Moments of embarrassment were also found when losing parts of your costume. I was the brush in yard sale and loved to move as much as the restrictive costume allowed. On my highlighted entrance, I swung the handle of the brush around only to have it fly off. There I am, exposed, showing off a wig cap with half makeup, no hands, and no professional facial expression. I run over to my handle and must put my hands up over the top of my brush backpack and carry it off like a little squirrel. The message to backstage must have been delayed because I was jumping up and down yelling at the curtain, "Open the curtain, open the curtain!" I didn't know whether to laugh or cry, but the *trumpet* found it amusing.

Our Brazilian dinosaur ran down stage for his big roaring entrance and lost his head, literally. The head of the beloved dinosaur went flying downstage left. One of the soldiers retrieved it as a frantic dinosaur ran upstage for the safety of the curtain.

The dinosaur wasn't the only one to lose his head. One of the times Edward went in to perform his understudy of the principal cowboy, the head flew off during a jump. He was disoriented and accidentally kicked the head. His real head looked so small in comparison to his toy body. He battled and batted the curtains to escape. Backstage they quickly found his head in the curtains. And his show must go on.

Most state tours luckily end in southern Florida. So of course, when at the beach, you sunbathe. I decided to borrow my friend's suntan lotion, 8spf. I don't think it was very waterproof, and then I attempted to learn "skin boarding". I fell off the board onto the hard sand and skinned my bare right hip. Without good SPF and a skinned hip, I burned real crispy, several layers deep on my sand burn. I was not a happy camper on three show Saturday, when I had six costume changes, times three shows, over one lobster body. Edward had raccoon eyes from his sunglasses and had to wear base makeup to cover it up.

Costumes were also prone to popping, breaking and busting. I was self-labeled, Zipper Bitch, because I was always breaking zippers. They would put a new stopper on it, but each time the zipper stopper got lower, it was harder to put my foot through and easier to break the zipper. Second act, one show day, my zipper busted getting into my robot costume and there was not enough time for the panicked robot or the poor wardrobe to get me done up or sent off. So that shows the evil robot lord only had seven robots. I am positive the audience was devastated. One beach girl illusion spin found me hard on my butt with my shorts ripped open at the crotch. Then I had to explain it to wardrobe who just laughed at me.

I was also well known for missing yard sale. If people are understudying other roles, or out of the show, we have a certain number of spares for each show number that can fill in. I was a spare for yard sale. And at least once a week when an understudy was in the principle show track, I filled in as Peppermill. Peppermill and I were not friends. I was almost always up on the board to spare yard sale, and I almost always seemed to miss it. The first time in D.C. the performance director gave me a warning and shortly thereafter I missed it and got my first fine. The amount of the fine varies depending on the severity of the offence. At the end of the year, the fine money is donated to a charity decided on by popular cast vote.

One show, it was Dezi's turn to spare Peppermill but at the last minute I realized she wasn't in the costume room and would have missed the number, so I jumped in for her. Olivia watched me hurry into costume and asked why I did it? She said she wouldn't have. I begged our ladies line captain not to tell the performance director so that Dezi did not get a fine. In return, Dezi did the baggage number I was sparing.

The next show, not two hours later, I was supposed to spare the Peppermill and guess what I forgot to do? The Peppermill. I could not exactly say anything for my good deed the show before. No good deed goes unpunished. I earned a fine for my troubles.

Opening night in East Rutherford, I forgot my skates back at the hotel and was waiting for an extremely late taxi to take me back to the hotel. He did not know where he was going and I didn't either, we finally found our way and then hit traffic in the giant parking lot. My name and numbers were up on the board to be spared in case I didn't make it back. I made it into costume on time and into all my numbers. However, I forgot to read the board. I did not get a fine for being late for half hour call, but I did get a fine for missing, the Peppermill.

This lovable yard sale item became named the Pooper Mill when Lizzy put it on and there was poop inside. It had been stored on the floor and we speculated a little animal crawled inside and pooped in the Peppermill. Poor Lizzy had it smeared on her shirt, shorts, and hand. She got clean laundry for the rest of the show.

Sometimes I must have had an invisibility cloak on because I would think for sure everyone had to witness my goof ups. One beach doll number found me backing up and when I turned around, I tripped over the pig and fell on top of him, sprawled out wide getting a free piggyback ride that was very un-lady like. No one saw it, not the performance director watching the show, none of the 15 other beach dolls, toys, and the pig did not even feel it. Go figure.

Chapter 42
Napa Valley Done Right

It seems no matter where we are going or what we're doing, we do it with alcohol. We are a loud, flashy, fun, or possibly just an obnoxious group. If I'm drunk, we're fun and free spirited, if I'm sober, I'm usually embarrassed. Because we often draw unwanted attention to ourselves, the general pub goer asks what we are doing in town. We can't very well tell them and smear the company's good name, so we had many false answers.

The favorite answer for so many people traveling together was that we were in town for the coat hanger convention. This classy answer serves a variety of purposes. There's not a lot of interesting conversation to be had about such a job and if the inquiring mind has been drinking, they just accept this answer. Why would anyone lie about such a thing? There is always one skeptic but once they ask around and receive the same response, they give up the inquiry.

The Pro party planner, handpicked, a fun group to go wine tasting in a limo from San Francisco. Our limo driver was cool, the car was already stocked, and we were allowed to bring our own purchases in and drink those as well.

Travis had already been drinking late the night before with the Russians and had to be woken up and half dragged to the limo. I was fighting off a bad cold and figured the best medicine was to drown myself and my cold in large quantities of alcohol. Edward always says tequila cures the common cold. I assume the same applies for wine. We proceeded to start with whatever was in the limo at 10am. First stop was Vianasa where we had the free sampler and then a secondary taste tester. Lacking breakfast, Travis went around tasting all the jellies, jams and spreads and that was our only meal for the day. We took our purchases and climbed into the limo.

Most of us were not wine connoisseurs, we were just looking for fun and a limo ride with friends. Travis downright disliked wine, and declared it all tasted the same, but down the hatch it would go anyway.

Our second stop was Silverado, they mercifully only had a small sampler of wine, no food, and they were expensive. Up next was one of my personal favorites, Mumm's, known for their champagne. Yes, to tiny bubbles. We had our samplers and were well on our way to being ridiculously drunk. Now we were even drinking our wine purchases in between wineries and still no breakfast or lunch in sight. Our last tour of Beringer led us through their barrels and we have pictures getting friendly with their statues, one leg thrown up and over our inanimate new friends. We ran around the barrels having a great time acting like giant six-year-olds with volume control issues.

After our last tasting, we noticed there was a big bowl in the center of the countertop. Travis dipped his cup in it and poured some in my glass. I distantly heard the attendants saying not to drink that and trying to get Travis's glass away from him. We both get a sip in and then as they're taking his away, I think I'm sneaky by hiding my glass under the countertop. Through a haze of delayed reaction, I hear some lady saying get that away from her. As Travis got his final sip in, he says, "That's the best vintage of the day." The best vintage of the day was the spittoon where everyone had spat their wine in or poured out their leftovers. This place had a wonderful variety of cheese and seeing as we had not eaten, half of us bought hunks of cheese and in a quiet, drunk stupor of hunger, chowed down. I made the bad choice of a dry, crumbly cheese with blueberries in it, way too sweet to eat a whole block. I stupidly put the remains in my coat pocket for a fun discovery the next day.

The ride home was quiet, most of us passed out, laying draped and drooling over the person next to you. The limo was littered with bottles and bodies, and few people returned with any souvenir wine. I personally went to bed and did not drink any wine for months. The guys took a nap and went out for guys' night at a strip club. Talk about endurance!

Chapter 43
Snowboarding Chronicles

Alpine Valley

We had the itch to snowboard or ski, so when it started snowing in Auburn Hills, a suburb of Detroit, we found the closest 'mountain'. Alpine Valley was really a landfill that had been made into a ski hill. We added an extra hour to the trip by getting lost from bad directions and I was shotgun for the crazy Brit who was driving on his wrong side of the road. Our group was getting bigger every trip. Edward always seemed to have an endless supply of extra snow pants, jackets, gloves and goggles to outfit everyone. On one snowboarding trip, I took lots of picture of Peters wearing Edward's snowboarding clothes. I printed these great pictures and sent them to Edward on break, his response was, "That's not me, but thanks, I didn't even go on that snowboarding trip." Whoops. When Edward's extra supply of clothes had reached the bottom, plenty of first-time skiers were not able to dress appropriately. Some of the Russians were in jeans and after a few falls, they're butts were nicely iced over. Slapstick assumed he had mastered skiing and switched to snowboarding, he also made the mistake of wearing fleece. Snow sticks to fleece, so he began looking like an overstuffed, frosted, blue berry. He ended the day looking like a snowball rolling down the hill.

Since this dump really was a hill, we quickly exhausted all the runs, many people felt this was a great time to try snowboarding. Even the supposed expert skier Travis traded in his skis for a board. We found a gap in the guard rail and went down what looked like a ten-foot, icy waterfall. When one person got to the bottom, we would turn around and watch the next person. I turned around to watch Slapstick and he manages to make it down the hill, then he's wobbling on one foot, lost the ski on the air borne foot and goes on teetering for another twenty feet before finally collapsing in a powdery heap. He really could star as a cartoon character.

Misha was a massively, muscular guy, built like a train. This was his first time, and he didn't bother learning to ski, all you would hear is, "Get out of the way," and cursing in Russian as he steamrolled down the hill until something stopped him. Halfway through the day the Russians could be found warming and drinking by the fire in soaking jeans.

For many people exiting the ski lift is the most intimidating part of skiing. For Slapstick, getting on the ski lift was a challenge. He misjudged the lift timing, amount of people in front of him and spacing. He fell, got up using the father of the family in front of him, and then tried to sit five people on a four-person ski lift. He attempted to sit in the middle of the family of four on the arm rest. It was not comfortable, stopping the ski lift, he found himself face down in the snow again. For the rest of us, he provided endless entertainment.

That was not the end of Slapstick's episodes. We found a few decent size jumps and were laying belly down on the top of the take off ramps with some ten-year-olds. We were all waiting our turn to go down the terrain park, Slapstick cuts everyone off as he enters on snowboard, I turn to the kids and say, "Watch this!" He goes full speed ahead, takes off, feet are over his head and a normal human being would have been hospitalized as he lands on his back. A couple seconds go by, and he sits up waving and yelling, "I'm okay!" We're laughing and the ten-year old's have a look of pure astonishment on their faces.

Hidden Valley

Sounds like a Ranch commercial. The way I would find some of these places before googling, was go to weather.com and click on the ski report and it would list the hills or mountains closest to farthest away from the city I entered. It's not as simple as what's closest, you must look at the vertical rise, (not just elevation), snow conditions, how many runs are open and especially the trail map.

The tale of Hidden Valley actually starts the night before, we flew into Pittsburgh and went down the street to Hemmingway's with my brother who was attending Carnegie Mellon. I made him do seven shots with me and was later told, that was the most drunk anyone had ever seen me, which says a lot on tour. I freaked my little brother out when I would cry one minute and laugh the next, like a severe manic depressive. Then I tried to play darts. This was already a hard enough process when I added alcohol, but they had placed the dart board on a wall right next to the door, a recipe for danger. As if we were not already the local circus, Crazy Russian stood next to the dart board and caught every dart I threw. Drunk minds think alike. Adam and Travis carried me home and tossed me on the bed, Edward laughed at me but as I went to sleep, he said, "You have a lot of people relying on you tomorrow." I laughed and said, "I have 7 hours to sober up." That's when the puking began. Red and bleary eyed, I searched for my brother's car the next day and it wasn't where he said it was. I was cold and irritable, finally I found it and took two guys to the rental car company. Late as usual we started our trip to Hidden Valley, with our biggest group yet of 16.

Hidden Valley was also a hill, but not a dump this time. The weather was sunny, and the snow was good enough. The best part was the free shot glasses we got, they were plastic and had glow gel that moved around in them, lighting the whole shot glass. After a round of courage shots, we headed out to the one icy jump. We took turns watching each other go over the jump.

Tina got up the nerve and took her turn, she got slower and slower and almost made it over. We saw her head and then she disappeared back the way she'd come, not quite enough liquid courage. Slapstick took his board off to climb up and try it again. He sits down to put his board on and next thing we know he's chasing his board down the hill and over the jump. Giggett's family came to visit and went snowboarding with us. She could smoke and snowboard at the same time, impressive. Our favorite was the silver bullet. A little kid with a silver helmet and no fear who wanted to play with the big kids. He'd go straight down the mountain, full speed, and over the jumps.

Mount Hood

First snowboarding trip on the West Coast tour of Underwater Fantasy on Ice was from Seattle. Only the die-hards went. Mount Hood was a nice change from the hills at the end of East Coast. It was cold and so misty that you couldn't see ten feet in front of you. Travis left his snowboarding confidence at home and was having binding troubles. He spent his first long trip down the mountain sledding on his board. He would sit in the middle of the rental with his feet up on the binding and paddle-push with his mittened hands. He had a couple of drift crashes and was less amusing to the locals trying to ski by.

After a warming, liquid lunch we went up to the big boys and girls back terrain. If you went off the wrong side, like I did, it was a steep drop off to a river down below. I was skirting this steep edge trying to get back out on the main side. Meanwhile the guys were above and looking for me. They would shout my name and thought my replies were coming from the river. I ended up waiting at the bottom calling *out of reception* cell phones.

Whistler/Blackcomb

From Vancouver, we drove to Whistler, it took two different high speed ski lifts and half an hour to get up the mountain peak. It was one of the tallest mountains I've ever been on. We were no longer playing around; now we were in the big leagues. At the bottom, it wasn't cold or snowy but by the time we got to the top the snow conditions were perfect. Whistler and Blackcomb are two mountains, but only Blackcomb was open that day. Slapstick took his girlfriend, and it took them an hour and a half to get down their first run. When we saw them next, they were done and taking the lift down as we were coming back up.

I went down a run that was not really open, but the snow looked so fresh and untouched that I snuck under the marked off ropes. At one point, I fell and as I rolled over to get up, I looked at the marked obstacle next to me. It was a board covering a body size hole. That knocked some sense into me. I thought if I had fallen just a little more to the left, no one would ever have found me!

I took another fall and as I was rolling down the hill my board got stuck and cracked! I had trouble staying on my feet that day, I fell, got up, and in the process of getting up, fell flat on my face again. Last run of the day Edward was taking a nice easy, narrow green to finish off his day. Suddenly, he hears a runaway skier who not only hits and knocks Edward over but falls on top of his board pinning him down. The beginner skier sat up and said in a nasty tone, "I was clicking my poles."

Edward in pain says, "What?"

"I was clicking my poles together; didn't you hear me?" Edward almost threw the skies and poles off the side of the mountain. How are you supposed to hear pole clicking when snowboarding downhill? Why wouldn't the guy shout, or better yet, why not control himself! Downhill has right of way and they call all boarders rude! Edward's ribs weren't right for a year and a half. I couldn't convince him to go to a doctor, but we think he cracked a rib.

Crystal Mountain

During our stay in Vancouver, we found a nice little hill literally right outside the door from the hotel, so on a one show day Edward and I took a romantic snowboarding get away. It was the perfect setting, a grey, misty day, lots of trees, empty and secluded, with a light dusting of snow coming down. It was so cold outside that the snow was freezing to my goggles. There is a rewarding silence when a ski hill is empty, and the snow is falling. It suspends the world, and you are left with a deafening sense of solitude.

49 Degrees North

Not even the freezing rain could keep us away. It gets a bit tricky and sticky when the temperature is just above freezing, and it begins to rain. Your board will glide along the snow until it hits a warmer rain drop where it will stick. The feeling is like being on an airport conveyor belt that speeds up and jerkily slows down causing you to engage those little balancing muscles in an effort to fight off going head over heels or heels overhead. I personally do not find it enjoyable. We finally made it to the mountain with Andy. She had been talking for months about boarding. She had worked in skater shops, was from the Northwest, and talked up the terrain parks. We were all excited to be blown away by her mad skills. Her skills remained mostly in the game of talk, but that did not deter us from another day on the mountain. As we rode the ski lift up for our last run I received a phone call from my little brother. He asked me how it felt that he would be graduating college before me? I let the good natured ribbing slide by and said congratulations to him. Then he asked what I was doing? We're snowboarding! There was a pause and he jokingly said, I hate you guys as he laughed. The rain washed us off the mountain and into the bar for warm Irish coffees.

Copper Mt.

We played Denver, CO in December for two weeks. We flew in on Monday and rented a cheap, POS car for two weeks. Tuesday, we went to Copper Mt. a personal favorite of mine because this is where I learned to ski when I was eight and on a family vacation. When I learned to ski, I would take an eight-hour, all-day group lesson for five days. My brother was in a different class since he refused to turn and went straight down the slope until he came to a stop, usually into an inanimate object. Dad was out on the slopes enjoying himself and my mom loved it because we were all out of her hair and she would have the day to herself.

There were at least four cars in our caravan to Copper Mountain. We had the two Russians and a native to Colorado. Everyone wanted to stop and rent their equipment before we got to the mountain to find the best deals. I still do not know how we fit all that equipment in a small car with five people. The Crazy Russian in between hangover and inebriation, kept making horse whinnying sounds.

We hit the mountain hard. I am always anxious to get there, and we are always delayed. I'll plan until my butt is blue, but it never works out the way I imagine, and my impatience knows no bounds. I'm held up by the rental car, traffic, MapQuest is a liar, or waiting on people. If you're driving a long distance, then the directions will be perfect until you get to the fine inner-city details. And time estimates are unrealistic. I don't know how we survived pre cell phone GPS days. So, after the rental delays I put my snowboard gear on and almost ran out the rental car door.

I could barely wait for Edward, but finally, after a small eternity we were all ready and on the mountain. I can be a good teacher, if I want to, but when we get the chance to snowboard, do not ask for my help. If you can keep up and keep us amused fine, but when Franky told me he had never skied before I said, "Meet up at the lodge for lunch at noon." And I was gone. Two others stayed with him on the bunny hill until he was ready to move on, so he was in good hands. At first, he was pissed, but after his first trip down the hill, he immediately called his mother to profess his newfound love of skiing.

The group split again, and the advanced found the back country and black runs and proficiently traversed the mountain. All the groups were evenly matched. Slapstick was pissed because he wanted to keep up with the advanced group and could not. We passed over him at one point and noticed he was uninjured and stuck in a literal hole. There were ski poles and big orange flags marking a large hole in the middle of a run and there's Slapstick stuck in a hole with his head and shoulders sticking out. He was not his usual cheery self that day.

As if being an ice skater is not enough for a profession, we have multitalented people in our ice shows. One of our skaters is also a skilled skier. The first time we went skiing with him, he was laid back over his skis, looking at us with his head upside down, dragging his poles behind him so that he powdered us with snow. That's when I made him rent a snowboard so we would be on even playing ground. We had a guy who was a roller-skater and a well know box car racer. Edward started ice skating when he was eighteen and as a child, he had been a national level roller-skater, we are a group of jacks of all trades.

I took a detour on our last run before lunch and lost the group. I did however find a huge powdery snow drift. While that sounds like a skier's dream, it can also be a nightmare on a snowboard. I was up to my chest, and I could not see my feet to get my board off and dig out. Even when I had found my bindings, I couldn't find the release with froze fingers. When I couldn't get my boots off, I began to fight panic. I was in a bit of a frozen foul temper when I got to lunch a half hour late.

Edward and I had to take off early so he could get to rigging. Rigging is done the day before the crew loads in a show. This is when the initial set up of the grid lights and any equipment that will be hung from the ceiling is done. But with the caravan situation we had to have one more volunteer to leave early. It was like pulling my own teeth to get anyone to leave and it had started to snow to add fresh powder to injury.

Breckenridge

After a six pack (6 shows in two days) and the end of our first week in Denver, a small group of die-hards headed into the CO mountains for our Breckenridge trip. We had rented a dirt-cheap room for the night, $60 per night with three double beds. There were four of us, so it worked out well. I was exhausted after six shows and passed out. The guys went and closed the local bar and then got in the hot tub to thin their blood, they were special when they came home. I woke up to one of them peeing in the corner, next to the bed. When I woke up, he stopped, waited tell I was quiet and started again, so I kept rustling the covers trying to make him stop. Finally, I said, "Go to the bathroom!" He had some unintelligible response about he could not make it and it was occupied. At least that's what I made from the garbled noises emanating from his mouth amongst the shhhs. I gave up and went back to sleep, we were checking out the next day anyway.

I struggled to get the guys up at 7 am on a day off after a long night of drinking, but we had a mountain to get to. We practically had to dress Roger and shove him in the cold car, where thankfully there was a bottle of Baileys waiting in the cup holder! Mr. Wee Wee didn't remember his nighttime urination. So off we went. Made it on the mountain and caught up with some of the crew who were already there.

We get a lot of people who can dramatically talk the talk and can't always walk the walk. Some of the crew on West Coast Underwater Fantasy on Ice were a bunch of these. They would talk snowboarding and then when it came time to show up, they had a million excuses. I was surprised some even showed up on the mountain.

Edward and I look at each other in excitement as the ski lift took us over an enclosed glade. Edward, Roger, and I make a bee line for the forest and Vince says, "You guys really going in there? I'm gonna take a warmup run first." We were already gone. The next time through the forest he came along but skirted all the trees on the edge, what's the point? I lost the group before lunch again and found the baby terrain park. I like little jumps and very short, wide rails. As I get older and without my liquid courage, I usually don't try any big jumps. I know how to fall in skating, I've been doing that for twenty some years, but when I go down on a board, which luckily isn't all too often, it's a giant snowball. So, my last lonely run before lunch I go into the baby terrain park and get a bit more speed than usual over the jump. As I'm sailing over what is supposed to be a little jump, I realize it has been dug away maybe ten feet under the take off ramp. I almost pissed myself and my legs became Jell-O. Lunch saw lots of extra liquid courage and recounting of my jump which Roger had witnessed. Several times over our weekend there I would go up to that jump but couldn't muster the courage to go back over it.

At the end of our first day, we met up with some of the skaters that had opted to sleep in and drive up. Our native skater had lent us his friends' cabin, so we went to the DAM Brewery for dinner and headed back to the cabin in what looked like a blizzard. Jeff had missed the day of snowboarding because of doing a publicity for the company but, he drove over two hours through a white out blizzard with two of his friends only to spend the evening and head back for another early morning publicity. Why would anyone brave driving in those conditions? Oh yeah, for a girl. We played drinking Jenga, one chick had food poisoning and as tradition demands we watched Out Cold, our favorite snowboard movie. Everyone else was tired and went to bed, Roger, Edward, and I went outside to make a snowman.

How do kids really build giant snowmen? It's hard work. I was tired and cold so I would just lay in the snow or throw snowballs occasionally. Roger is severely accident prone. He always said he hates, old, female drivers. One had hit him while he was crossing the road, breaking his arm in two places and he now has metal pins. Great for the metal detectors on every flight travel day. Roger was throwing his shovel on the roof to get fresh powder and it got stuck. So, Roger thought it would be a good idea to go on the roof, he slips and falls off the roof and luckily lands in a big snow drift. Meanwhile the rest of the house is fast asleep at this point. Mr. Snowman is bigger than six feet and almost done when his base gives way, and his top balls fall off. I said a lot of swear words and went to sleep for about four hours before it was snowboarding time again.

Tuesday snowed lightly all day, but the conditions were perfect, fresh powder everywhere. Toward the end of the day, I had a massive headache and all the lifts had stopped running. We were coming down the far-left side of the mountain and didn't want to walk back to our car, so we started cutting over to make it back to the lodge. I had voiced my opinion of not wanting to cut through the trees with deep powder, but Roger went through, Edward after him slowing down, and I was last, slowed to a stop. I lost it.

Edward said I was chest deep in powder strangling a little sapling of a tree. This poor Charlie Brown Christmas tree only had one little leaf on the top and I was wringing its neck and screaming at it. I wasn't even making words it was some high-pitched keening noise. I would get tired and pause giving the false allusion that my temper tantrum was over and then I was back at it killing that little stick of a tree. Edward and Roger were out of the woods watching this and Roger says, "Is she okay?" Edward's response was, "Shhh, don't distract her. If we let her take out her aggression on the tree, then she won't take it out on us." This went on for another five minutes until I took off my board and dug my way out. Roger feared me for the rest of the day, and I was nauseas with a killer headache, so while everyone else had the traditional end of day drinks, I laid in the cold car and took Advil.

That night we went to the local bar near our cabin and stayed up as late as our bodies would allow us. Wednesday half the group drove back and Roger, Edward, and I went back to the mountain. I had six layers on top, four on the bottom, two pairs of socks and mittens, plus four hand and foot warmers and I was still cold. It was a crisp, freezing, sunny day. Edward is never cold, and he was shivering. We did the bowls at the top where the wind froze tears to my face. I lost our little group and found a warming cabin that seemed abandoned. When my fingers had gone from white, to blue, and finally back to red I made my way back down. Despite the cold, we had to quit at half day and make our way back to Denver for an evening show.

We never do relax on our breaks.

Taos, NM

Snowboarding in New Mexico is an interesting art of mastering ice in the morning and by the sunny afternoon, you are surfing the slushy mountain waves as they melt. I'm not a fan of ice but I love the slow surf in the warm afternoon sun.

When I learned to snowboard, I had a tough time transitioning between skiing and boarding. I had always done sports requiring two feet. Ice skating, skiing, running, roller blading. My first attempt at snowboarding was in high school. Of course, it was to impress a boy. It did not go well, and I quickly resorted back to skiing. It was not until Edward took the time and patience to teach me that I finally began to master snowboarding. He took me on the bunny hill and had me follow his tracks. He could explain from one ice skater to another how to change edges.

Killington, VT

We had a week off over the Christmas holidays on one frozen forgotten tour. So, a few of us rented two cabins that were ski in at Killington. One cabin had the only person not participating in winter sports that got sick. She would shush the party people all night long and turn the cabin up to an unbearable 80 degrees. Ski in does not equate to snowboard in and out. It was about a mile of flat snow track so the skiers were just fine, but the boarders were pushing and cussing and exhausted by the time they reached the mountain. The boarders took the bus to the lodge every morning after that.

Our third day fell on a weekend and to avoid crowds we went to Pico. The fresh powder the night before made this smaller mountain perfect. My brother and the rest of the hangover bunch were in fine form that morning. My brother believing in his altered state that he was now the master of his snowboard, decided to try riding with the other foot forward. He would yell, "Switch!" every time he changed feet and promptly fall face first in the fresh snow. Travis was begging to be kicked off the mountain as he would yell on the ski lift, "I'm F-ing wasted!" and take a pull from his flask. All in all it was a good trip.

Steamboat, CO

Frozen forgotten tour saw twenty-two days of snowboarding. We traded up, getting my brother instead of Slapstick on our snowboarding trips. Steamboat remains to this day one of Edward and my favorite mountains. The conditions were perfect. We lost Adam a few runs in, and Edward and I accidentally went off the trail map. At first, it was exhilarating, we lost the crowds and were engulfed in powdery snow and ever green tees. Then we hit a large, flat field with snowy powder up to our necks. No way to walk out of this one. Edward and I lay down on our boards and paddled across the flats to safety and civilization. I later found out that not too much further off the map and we would have fallen off a cliff.

My brother was impatiently waiting for us at the bar. As luck would have it, it was St. Patrick's Day. We were feeling a little older and tired, so we had our token green beer and were ready for bed. My brother is annoyed and proclaims that he had heard so many stories about the party people we used to be. We agreed to stay out a little longer. And guess who falls asleep at the table before our next green beer arrives?

Snowshoe and the West Virginia Mountains

Never a dull moment with my brother Adam. We stopped on the drive to our next city in West Virginia to snowboard. We lost my camera while traversing the snowy woods of one mountain and my brother made friends with a deer as we were trying to pack up the car.

Adam was hung over and not in a mood to get out of bed, let alone help pack up the car and move on. Edward and I began the pack up routine and return to find Adam in his boxers enticing a deer with a large rack into the hotel room. He's saying, "Here puppy-puppy." While using meat lover's pizza as bait.

Edward scares off the deer before it goes buck wild in a confined space and makes a cheap hotel very costly. As we pull out of the hotel parking lot, we can't help but point out to Adam the abundance of signs that say, "Do not feed the deer. Wild animals."

Chapter 44
The Summer of Mishaps

Another four-month break between tours found me at my mom's house in the Ocala national forest of FL doing yoga for a month. I had bought two round-trip tickets for my brother and I to go to Moms. No sooner had I put a credit card down than Adam found out he had refurb for the company, and I decided to extend my time in FL. Refurb is another job the crew does either right after a tour season is finished or right before a new tour season.

The crew gets to work in a FL shop during the pinnacle of summer without air conditioning. They spend this wonderful two-week period working about ten hours a day, six days a week, fixing, renovating, and painting anything that goes above, below or backstage. Adam has some fuzzy memories of refub. One that Edward remembers was in the pool after a hard day. Adam enjoyed an entire bottle of Sailor Jerry and wanted to make sure everyone knew that Sailor Jerry was better than Captain Morgan because he was the subordinate and could do whatever he wanted! Adam finished the night passed out while the rest of the crew drew hinges on his joints and of course a penis on his face! This change of plans resulted in losing two airline tickets since I drove home in our Suburban with Edward after show refurb. With a four month break, you hoard your money closely and I had just squandered two airline tickets worth.

Our summer project was to refinish my dad's basement into a living area big enough for Edward and I to call our own little apartment. This turned into a major renovation project when an unused chimney had to be removed from four floors. Burning in the sun during a yard sale and forcing my dad to go through twenty years of boxes labeled with things like 1993 taxes, found a dusty house and finally an empty basement.

Edward made walls and floors and we painted as the plumbers laid the groundwork for a bathroom. The neighbors reported us for excessive junk on the front lawn, and the building inspector dropped in and said we needed a permit. The inspector was pompous and rude until he realized it was my dad; the Captain, who ran this ship. Then he helped us quickly get a permit. Two smelly days later the plumbers could come back and get our water working again.

That same summer Edward had just finished break work in Dubai, he received a call asking if he would be interested in more break work in Brazil. Of course, who wouldn't want to go to Brazil? I decided I would visit him while he was in Brazil and started researching an airline ticket for myself. The prices continued to skyrocket until a week before we left. I finally purchased a ticket to Rio with three days left and we drove to NYC for a tourist visa to Brazil. That was a nightmare driving a Suburban around NYC. We couldn't find large vehicle parking anywhere.

Edward and I had passports in hand, heading home, flying out in one day and I get an email to do break work in Mexico, with an offer for Edward as well. I told The Director of Talent, sure after the 9th, because I am visiting Edward in Brazil.

What we surmise happened next was the Director asked someone how Edward got a work visa for Brazil so quickly, it usually takes about four months. Then the truth came out that he would be working under a tourist visa and I think the company saw a legal nightmare culminating in if caught, the whole company might be banned from the country. They were in meetings all day and Edward was no longer going to Brazil. He would be compensated for all his expenses, but what about me? Luckily for a $250 change fee I could save the other thousand on the ticket, but I ate the cost of the visa, which at least is good for five years, but sadly I never got to use. My mother had also purchased a ticket for me to go to Ocean City and visit her family and that too went by the seaside because we accepted The Director of Talent's offer for break work. This offer meant Edward had to skate again.

Seven years in and I finally got my first break work assignment. This type of work happens when your show is between tours and another show needs someone your height and build. Insert skater A into slot B. As I've mentioned before male skaters are on high demand. Edward had not skated in shows for 5 years. He only agreed because I begged him, and they promised to give me break work too. I don't think they really needed another female, but I got to go because they needed Edward.

After swearing, never to return to Mexico, we were going back. It worked out to be about every three years we returned to Mexico. Third time is the charm, right? We got our flying orders three days before departure. Edward realized his skates were on a truck in FL with the rest of Under Water Fantasy's show. The Talent Coordinator was looking for boots his size and we happened to luck out. In Buffalo, we found an old, but unused pair of skates in his size. This meant they were also the right price for our dwindling budget. Edward started skating with me to get back into skating shape. He took off on an extra-large jump and something in his calf popped.

He called The Talent Director and said he couldn't walk let alone skate, what did she think? She said call her in a week with an update. I, however, flew to Mexico City by myself. A hectic week of learning shows numbers and a drinking social initiation where I was getting to know everyone. Of course, I became reacquainted with the Karisma Cantina and finally a week later, Edward was joining me on tour.

Monday as I've previously stated, is our only day off in Mexico, so you must make it count. Sunday night we all went to the Cantina and closed it down. The ugly lights had been on for an hour before they finally kicked us out. That did not slow us down, we stayed up drinking in Jeff's room, but at 5:30 am I told the diehards I was calling it quits. Not my compadres, they went to breakfast and racked up $250 worth of mimosas. I woke up at noon and went down to the pool to find them with orange juice and vodka and still no sleep. I jumped back on the drinking band wagon and spent my day off drinking by the pool. Ms. Professional did not even stumble when she turned in around 3 pm, she tricked the front desk into revealing her room because she could not remember it and slept the next twelve hours.

Break work for Edward and I was a great relief. We had no extra responsibilities like understudies, or coffee stand, life was nice and easy for one week together before the Mexico mishaps started. As I've implied before Mexico City is cursed for us, first time through Edward broke up with me, second time through I'm accused of breaking up another couple, but third time has to be better, right? With our second Monday off we went white water rafting. Something we have done every time in Mexico, thereby making it tradition. We left Sunday night in a van, drove six hours. I took a cat nap and the guys kept drinking, quick breakfast, safety meeting and then rafting. It was a great trip and the huts we stayed in had been upgraded with an inground pool, trampoline, and paintball field.

After rafting, we drank and swam all day, doing beer pairs, where Edward would hold me in various positions above his head while I drank a beer. We unsuccessfully attempted a three-person pyramid. I passed on paintball, and was ready to start round two or three of drinking as dusk settled in. Jeff talked one guy into wearing show laundry (tight skin colored spandex that is slightly see through when wet) with a bullseye drawn on his privates. He also convinced him to be our own private paintball piñata. Powerful powers of persuasion or just bad ideas turned good with alcohol? The chiggers were maddening, and we did not notice until it was too late, all of us itching and scratching, dehydrated and sunburned, this would be fun later in our costumes.

After this all-day drink fest, I think it is a clever idea to show off my back flip on a trampoline. Back flip score 1, Maddie score 0. I was completely upside down and landed on my head. If I had not been drunk, I might very well have broken my neck. I landed face first and rolled to one side where I lay crying. I tried to go sit with the group like nothing was wrong with my head cocked to one side and could not do it.

We are six hours from a major city, and middle of nowhere Mexico and my neck is killing me. I wake up Edward who had the good sense to pass out after dinner. We tell the host of this white-water rafting place and he makes a phone call. A questionable woman shows up who does not speak English and injects something into my butt. The whole drive home in the front of the van the next day is awful and I'm nauseated and in pain. The Mexico City hospital takes x-rays and gives me a C-collar and in broken English tells me to go to an American hospital. The company gets me on a flight home the next day and Edward is stuck ice skating in Mexico. Two of his least favorite things performing and Mexico City, now he must bear them without me.

I left with two other skaters who were going to rehearsals on the new show at 4:30 am. After sweating in line and fighting off nausea for half an hour, I am told that I am missing a piece of paper in my passport. When I arrived in the country, I entered on a tourist visa and then the company or its Mexican counterpart took the paper to change it to a work visa. I went to the immigration office which would not be open until 7. My flight was at 7:45.

I call our Tour Coordinator, who seemed irritated that I should be calling at that hour, but not surprised. He knew this might be a problem because he had given the other two skaters their papers the evening before. He said he would not be able to get my papers until the Mexican counterpart of our company opened at 8.

I laid on the floor to be first in line, for two hours, feeling ill. Even being first in line, I was not done until 7:15. I race to the front of the line to board, and security looks at my checked bags and says, "You and your bags will not make it." I do not care about my bags but in this suspicious, code orange, world, if I say put my bags on another flight, they think bomb. So, $185 later, there is a 1 pm flight to Atlanta. This is getting to be the most expensive summer to nowhere.

I spend the next six hours lying on the floor, since this is the only position that does not make me feel nauseated. I manage to get down some eggs and fruit and I used 15,000 frequent flier miles (which the ticket guy informed me they were not supposed to do but, he took pity on me), to upgrade to business class. Unless you are traveling overseas, business class is just a fatter chair, it does not lean back any further than economy.

I get on the plane and start vomiting, after the first time a prissy, flight attendant refuses to take my barf bag. Instead of asking if I am all right, he asks, "Are you sure you're well enough to travel?"

My response was, "I am trying to get to a NY hospital!" Instead of taking the vomit bag, he hands me a large shopping bag and several more barf bags. I threw up eight times, there was nothing left in my stomach by the end. I could not get comfortable, and I was ill. My neck brace never did smell right after that, even with a wash. There is a horrible sickly smell of sweat and vomit when someone is ill and heaven forbid you get it on anything, like the Velveteen rabbit, you might as well burn those cloths. Now imagine a neck brace that sits right under your nostrils smelling like that and wearing it for weeks.

I am eternally grateful to the Good Samaritan in the chair next to me, he was not disgusted (or if he was, he did not show it), he got me napkins and more vomit bags whenever I needed them, when I started crying by the end, he patted my back. I had asked for a wheelchair when I got off the plane which was nowhere to be found, so I dry heaved my way up the walkway, with everyone staring in horror at me and my vision more of a tunnel than full view.

When we were at the top of the exit ramp, we found my wheelchair but no attendant. My Good Samaritan from the neighboring seat started to push me along. We came across the wheelchair pusher and she took over, but he stayed with me. Then we came across an airport nurse who did not think I could make another flight despite my feeble arguments. Finally, I realized that she was right, I was not going to make another flight, so I asked for the paramedics as I threw my valuables on the floor and raced to a bathroom to throw up the bottom dregs of my stomach.

Good Samaritan left his card and said to call and let him know I made it because he had a daughter my age. The paramedics were nice guys who asked me questions and let me lay down, at this point anyone who let me lay down was my new best friend. The fastest way to get through customs is to lay down on a stretcher. My passport came back to me with a stamp, and I went for my third ambulance ride of the year, I guess when it rains, it pours.

The army guy in the ambulance told me I had good blood, like I cared about my blood at that point in time. He took a look at the monitors and asked if I was an athlete because otherwise, they might be alarmed at my low heartrate and blood pressure.

My nurse in the ER turned out to be from Rochester, NY, small world, and went on and on about abbot's frozen yogurt, which I would not have been able to keep down even if it had suddenly materialized. I am sure he meant well, but when someone repeatedly says, "I'm not asking because I'm interested," it starts to get a little creepy. Especially when you are green and smell of vomit, but whatever does it for you. I was given anti-nausea meds, fluids, and a CT scan. They think I caught a Mexican stomach bug. I was given a prescription for Zofran and released from the hospital.

I had five hours before my flight and the airport wasn't open. My taxi takes me on a goose chase to fill my prescription because most drug stores were closed. And then the taxi drops me at an airport hotel where I spend a few hours unable to sleep and still dry heaving. Fastest way to get abs of steel, ouch.

The next day without enough sleep and still experiencing dry heaves when in the upright position, I boarded the plane home. The flight attendants would not let me lay on the floor, so I stomached my self-pity and finally made it to Rochester. Dad bought me my favorite Arbys and I perfected the art of eating in the supine position for another three weeks before I could sit up without nausea. I got really lucky, I had irritated the C7 disc, maybe, a little bulge, but not herniated and nothing permanent. However, there was still, no clear ETA on full recovery.

Rather than call to see if I was okay, the company manager of my show called to tell me how irresponsible I was, and did I think I could start our tour on time, since I was the precious aerialist.

I spent that summer slowly getting better. So much for break work and my summer of mishaps.

Chapter 45
Sick as a Dog

Christmas in Europe was in Leiden the frozen Netherlands. Everyone pictures the Netherlands as windmills and tulips. Maybe one day I will see that Holland. Winter can be an attractive time in Europe with the Christmas markets and hot wine as it was in Paris before we moved on to the Netherlands. But by Christmas, the markets were packed up, it was dark and bitterly cold. The old Rhine River was frozen over, and you would see woolly bundles out skating. Apparently, this is where skating was invented as a means of transportation when an entrepreneurial soul strapped bones to their shoes and glided over the ice. The towns of Leiden and Den Bosch were cute but between the frozen tundra and the encroaching darkness of shorter days I began to get ill. Of course, working and partying all hours paved the path to sickness.

In our broken communication, the doctor I saw in Holland told me my 'lifestyle was not conducive to my health'. I received no medications just told to shoot salt water up my nose. I paid for internet and skyped my family for Christmas. My mom told me she would mail a package of cough and cold medications to me. Later, I learned they refused to mail drugs to other countries so that was a bust. Trying to read medications in other languages before the extensive accessibility of google meant I was out of luck.

The creeping cold did little to slow me down. I had a new dress from Edward to wear to New Years and as many reasons to gather and drink as days of the week. I even went on a snowboard trip to Engelberg Switzerland.

I could not believe that sixteen people traveled four hours by train and managed to make two transfers that were only five minutes apart from Den Bosche Holland to Engelberg Switzerland with snowboards and suitcases. We did not lose anyone or anything. One half of the group went to their hotel and the rest of us piled in a taxi and were dropped off in the dark in front of some apartments with no key and no working European cell phones.

I'm supposed to contact someone called the Key Master and like a ghost, he's nowhere to be found, the gaggle of skaters and crew that had followed me were quickly becoming grumpy and cold. Edward runs into some nice people that speak English, they invite all eight of us in and call the Key Master. Finally, he shows up and we all pile into our apartment for three days. We join the other half of our group after a few Baileys and hot chocolate for a Mexican dinner. We make it back to the apartment utilizing the only taxi in town and are ready to call it a night when we realize that Edwards backpack with our snowboarding lift tickets is in the taxi.

Up early and hung over the next morning I cannot wait for the lollygaggers to get going so, I hit the slopes alone pinning a note to Edward saying we'll meet at the main lodge for lunch at noon. We had bought two out of our three days of lift tickets so I purchased another one knowing we would utilize all the tickets if the backpack was ever returned. The scenery was majestic, tall peaks rising out of fog. As a snowboarder, I was not impressed with the lay out of the mountain. Too many flats for a board resulted in a lot of pushing and cussing. The downhill runs, when you could find them were great and the out of bounds was amazing, until I looked to my right and realized it was a shear drop off a cliff and there was not a lot of ski patrol or cell service. Since I was all alone, I decided to play it a little safer.

Toward the end of our first day Edward saw Declan being carried off the mountain on a stretcher. He had fallen and his hip had dislocated. He put that old injury back in its place, but that was the end of his skiing trip. Turns out the only taxi in town also acts as the ambulance. So as luck would have it for us, not for Declan, we retrieved Edward's backpack. Half of the group took the train back the next morning with Declan. The rest of us continued our snowboarding trip. We put the stove top in the apartment to good use with a home cooked meal of steak, played some drinking Jenga and were up with the sunrise for another day on the slopes.

This apartment was advertised as ski in. The mountain was divided into two peaks. One peak was across the village. Our half of the ridge was smaller and the snow conditions were not as good, but you could technically ski into our apartment, but not out. From the main mountain, you had to do a lot of walking to achieve the 'ski in'. We found an ice bar at the halfway point and literally froze our butts in icicle chairs with warm drinks. At the start of our second day, we met a group of British adults all dressed as superheroes! They meet every year at a different ski hill, and all dress up. That has been added to my retirement wish list.

Meanwhile that chest cold bid its time malingering and waiting. My dry hacking cough started during split weeks, when it was double the shows and double the cities per week. And continued for a month. The result was bronchitis and strained intercostal muscles. This might not have been a problem if I was only skating on small ice and changing costumes. I could not raise my right arm above my head.

The crux of the problem was I could not climb the silk and perform as the aerialist. I was out of my specialty role for a month while this one little muscle took its time to heal.

I called a doctor to be seen about my sprained intercostal muscles and he was late to show up to the hotel. Through a broken translation I was told no violent acts. Translation, no climbing. I was still able to perform the rest of the show so every day I would test those testy little muscles. The pain was excruciating, like paring knives under the ribs. And heaven forbid I had to cough; I dreaded any little coughs that still lingered from my bronchitis. Per my norm this did nothing to slow down my sightseeing or social activities. Which delayed my recovery from cold, cough, and intercostal muscles.

Eventually those little devilish muscles healed, I retrained to regain my strength and I was back in the air doing violent acts.

Chapter 46
Snail Mail

When I first joined tour, I had mail every week. My dad would write me little letters at work, and Mom sent boxes of candy and cards with money. The boxes of candy were twice the size of a shoebox and filled with the biggest bags of my favorite goodies, Twizzlers, mini Snickers, Twixs, and Whatchamacallits. After trying to eat as many as possible, with my teeth hurting from the chocolate and feeling rather sick to my stomach, I took them into the arena during Lakeland rehearsals, trying to buy my new friends.

The card with money came with instructions, I could use it to get a massage, get a pedicure, or take my roommate out to dinner. Under no circumstances was it to be used on my clothing addiction. So, in Orlando I started a ritual of going out to dinner with Jazmin, my first roommate. It was her first trip to Red Lobster, and her first experience with crab, which she deemed delicious, but not worth the work. It became one of our favorite restaurants when we could get to one.

We were friends for several years and many tours. Some people are emotional vampires. They take and take until they have sucked you dry. Like a puppy dog, happy to please, I gave, and I gave. I woke up one day years later and the realization dawned on me that the cost of that friendship was exhausting and not rewarding enough for the price. I separated myself and remained a friendly distance that was emotionally safe. Time marinated and matured both of us and we eventually rekindled the lost friendship.

My Dad would send little cards for any occasion, or cute ones he found whenever he was out shopping. He would also send postcards from all his travel trips, sometimes showing the hotel he stayed in. But any mail was appreciated. I even got compliments about always having mail. The first large bar of chocolate Dad sent was accompanied by a note informing me that he had hand-picked all the calories out with tiny tweezers. The perfect chocolate!

My brother never wrote, but that was his style. I know he loved me, but he was distracted by college and reading books about pickup lines to try at the bar. He tried to call, occasionally, and he grudgingly appreciated the mail I sent. My friends wrote emails.

As tour life got longer, the letters slowly stopped coming. I think my mom was the first to stop sending treats and cards. Then my dad only sent a letter about once a month. And the emails decreased in frequency about the second year.

Now the only time I get mail is when my dad must renew my birth control at home and mail it to me. And it's usually accompanied by a faithful post-it-note. The only faithful pen pals I have had this whole time were my Grannies. They wrote a reply letter without fail about every other week.

I collected new writers when they left tour for the real world, but they usually fizzled out as life pressed on and they were deterred by boy and girlfriends. Letter writing has become a lost art with the progress of technology.

How does mail work when you are in a different city every week? We had a Florida address that we give out to receive mail. Then the mail is forwarded on to us. This can take weeks. If it's something you need sooner, you can give the hotel address, however, hotels are not to be trusted with mail. Even though it might have been over-nighted, they won't have it the next day, or even the day after. You get a call right before you leave when it magically appears and has oops been sitting in the mail bin. The hoity toity hotel in Chicago, holds your mail in the mail room below the hotel and charges you a fee for getting mail, if they ever find it. It also had a charge for parking when, go figure you do not have a car on tour.

In Puerto Rico, we left our DVDs at the San Juan hotel. We did not realize our mistake until we were home. I called the three hotels we'd stayed at in a small hope that someone had found them, leaving contact info every time. And every time I was told 'nope, not found', but one hotel did find a PlayStation, that was not ours, but offered it to me to stop my harassment.

I received an email about a month and half later asking why we had not contacted the hotel? Said hotel had been contacted, called, and I'd been put on a do not answer list for heckling! They'd had our DVDs for several months.

There was clearly ineffective communication at that hotel. We were happy to get our precious DVD collection back. The same hotel, that inquired why I had not called about my mail, told me that my birth control had arrived. The birth control had been mailed as three-day air mail and was not there when we left nine days later. I didn't get my birth control until 18 days after a high-priced three-day delivery.

Still, I tried to be a faithful correspondent to my pen pals. I would send postcards out on a rotational basis. Mom and Dad received one every week. Then I would rotate through the other nine to twelve people. My Dad saved his postcards for me because eventually it is going in my trophy/travel room that Edward will build. When I return home, it is great to hear from the friends who enjoyed following the postcard touring adventure. Usually, it's followed by, "Sorry, I didn't write," but as Mom sagely says, "Either I enjoy sending snail mail without replies, or I don't." Besides, the Grannies are always my faithful pen pals.

I suppose life on the road begins with strangers and your family and friends are left behind. Long distance changes strangers to family and old friends become different people. Still, families are always there even as tour life takes you down different roads through ever-changing terrain and constantly morphing tour cliques.

Chapter 47
Escaping America

11/3/08
The UK

Liverpool, home of the Beatles! Walked to Albert Docks, went to the Beatles museum and the American cathedral. Had a huge turnout for my birthday, imagine trying to round up 30 some people to switch bars and cross the street. I am now a decade older than the youngest skater on tour, not something to celebrate! Liverpool is definitely a party, college town. I was still surprised that I could walk up to a packed bar and say, it's my birthday and all thirty of these people are with me and we would all get in, no questions asked. High lights included almost giving the old folks out at the bar a heart attack when twenty hot women walked into the first bar, a pub with retractable roofs that overlooked a bombed-out church, MIB chairs, and a wild Australian bar where two of our girls were selected to wax a man's privates!

I love the hop on hop off bus tours of the cities, it's an easy, relaxed way to see the city and I've turned it into some much-needed alone time. Took a short side trip to Crosby beach where an artist has made hundreds of life-size cast-iron statues at all different heights looking out to sea. It was eerie and beautiful. Some are buried waist deep in the sand and some are standing in the sea up to their shoulders. My travel companions were less impressed with the artwork and more impressed with the metallic dong that each statue had. Later in the week we went back to the bar with the retractable roof and met the owner who was intoxicated and proceeded to hit on me, "You're beautiful, don't thank me thank your parents, how would they feel about me joining the family?" He was old enough to be Dad's age and Edward was not impressed. When we walked to work on Sunday (it really was uphill both ways), the amount of litter covering the streets was unbelievable, and by the time we came home it was magically cleaned up.

We stayed at a historic hotel, The Adelphi where Dickens stayed, but you can give your historic hotels to the birds, I'd much rather stay in a normal, boring Holiday Inn. There was no AC so we left the windows open and would hear drunk Liverpool until five in the morning, half the time our power would blow so no lights, there was a tub, no shower, the mattress was from the same era as Dickens, and the last night we were there someone barfed outside our door, free of charge.

We got to Nottingham and the search for Robin Hood was on. Nottingham is cute, not a lot of sightseeing in the city itself. We went to the castle, which isn't worth the entrance fee, but the statue of Robin Hood was cool. There's a church that has been turned into a bar, expensive drinks but interesting atmosphere. Took the public bus to Sherwood Forest, nice weather and good company. The most we got out of it was being able to say we went to Sherwood Forest and saw a cool old tree.

The hidden gem turned out to be Newstead Abbey, home of Lord Byron who wrote Don Juan among other great works. We missed being able to go into the house by one day, it's only open through September, but the grounds were beautiful with many different gardens and what we could see of the house was interesting. If you find yourself in Nottingham, I would definitely recommend the abbey as a must see. We also found the oldest pub in England, or so they claimed, and it smelled of old men, pee and stale beer.

Tried to catch up on sleep in Newcastle. Took a rainy bus tour of the city and had my alone time. The highlights were the bridges. We took a train to Alnwick castle where the first two Harry Potters, Elizabeth, Black Adder, and Robin Hood Prince of Thieves was filmed. Beautiful castle with the family still in residence, we bought a little broom stick and took flying pictures. This was accomplished by repeatedly taking burst photos as we jumped up and down with a broom between our legs. The grounds also had a beautiful garden and a huge tree house where I took pictures doing upside down splits on a hanging bridge. We had a company bar-be-que and time ran out and sleep won so, I never made it to Hadrian's Wall.

From Manchester, we went to Blackpool, a seedy seaside town that has a year-round ice show called Hot Ice, good skating and scandalous costumes. Up early our next day off to go to York, which was attractive but, cold, and rainy. Walked the old city wall, went to a church, bombed-out abbey remains, and the ruins of a castle watch tower. Rushed home to make it to the musical Witches of Eastwick; I guess you can turn anything into a musical. Once a week if we have rehearsals, we have class, where we warm up practicing skating exercises to music and guide in a block of four. We decided to have an eighty's theme for class, so I put on blue eye shadow, four belts, funky tights and leg warmers. As I looked around, I realized there are very few of the cast who were actually alive in the 80s. Now who is old? Ended the week with a quick trip to Sheffield to see a Jr Grand Prix skating competition.

The bus tour of Manchester was pointless and from there my experience of Manchester preceded to go downhill. I walked through the makeup room curtain and banged heads with a new girl, of course she's fine, and I got a black eye. Same show I was performing as the understudy for the male fishy lead and the Whale literally ate me. I bumped my forehead and pulled off the top of my costume. Now I'm crying with hair sticking out of my costume around my face and smeared makeup. I'm sure I was a pretty, masculine, picture. I ended the week by spilling cider all over my new computer. Are you thirsty computer? Not just a little cider, it was dripping out the mother board. It's dead, I'll be shipping it to Best Buy in the near future. Needless to say, Manchester was not my favorite, but York was cool.

Finally, London, the city we've all been waiting for. Started with our good friends from another show coming to visit for a 30th birthday. Made a late night of it and was up early to go to Stonehenge the next morning and we all know how that sheep chase ended. We finished the Stonehenge excursion with dinner and an exhausted train ride home. I fell into bed and for once slept in the next day. After a nice, relaxed morning I set off and saw Big Ben, Westminster Abbey, walked along the river, went to the Globe theater, and danced and sang London Bridges on London Bridge while the locals rolled their eyes.

Then the massive amounts of shows started and the rest of our first week is a bit of a blur. We all went out for a friend's birthday on Sunday night, the party planner in charge walked us in circles for hours because he was dead set on this gay bar that was aptly named the Ghetto. We danced the night away and made the best of a crappy bar situation. Up early the next day and walked all over the city with Edward. We went to Buckingham palace, Whitehall, St. Paul's church, the Temple, walked around the river, went to the Tower and Tower Bridge but the lines just for tickets to see the crown jewels were impossible. The entire plaza was covered with people waiting for tickets. After our brief day off, it was back to shows, we finished up with a nine pack of shows, three shows times three days.

More later, Love, Maddie

Chapter 47.5
Across Europe

Europe was filled with exploration, shows and drinking I was barely able to see everything I wanted from city to city. Sleep was overrated and therefore often went by the wayside. I was upset with myself for missing any sights when I finally did succumb to sleep.

I had to pick and choose which sites I saved for Edward. The crew often only had one day off and when we had split weeks in France their only time off was when they traveled from one city to the next. Split weeks are performances in two cities in one week. We did this a lot in the smaller cities of France that were located close together. The crew does not have the magic of snapping their fingers and the set assembles on its own. Usually, the crew needs a half day for rigging the lights and the grid, which is then lifted above the ice. They also offload the trucks and do the initial set up.

A usual load-in during the second full day (before opening with an evening show), is spent building the set and putting props together. That is a great minimalization to what the crew does. If you play two cities in one week, how do you rig and load in? You would lose two performance days. The answer to this is a soul crushing load out, travel, and get up at 3 am to rig followed by loading in. Edward was understandably tired.

Added to his duties we were running the coffee stand together. As the name implied, we sold plenty of coffee, snacks, breakfast and lunches. The whole process of a coffee stand is made more difficult overseas. We would drag our giant suitcases on the trains or buses to the closest Costco and load up as much food for the week as possible. We would get strange looks as we were loaded down on the train with food spilling out of every pocket and bags. Four giant suitcases between the two of us and two backpacks. You notice little differences when you walk or take public transit in different countries. All the crosswalk characters are different and have different sound effects. I loved the autonomation for the train in England so much that I bought a shirt that says, 'Please mind the gap'. The little cross walk men in Germany had hats.

Not only was Edward exhausted but when you spend ten months in Europe, you get rather tired of cathedrals, seen one, seen them all was his motto. I was of a mindset to agree but that did not stop me from trying to go to as many as possible. I would save sites like Stonehenge, Notre Dame, and Versailles to take him to. Even still the response I often got was, "It looks just like the postcard."

Toward the end of Europe, we were both weary and really wanted to go home for our long summer break, but our travel to and from Europe had already been paid for courtesy of tour life. So, we decided to stay an extra 3 weeks. Our tour did not play Italy and Greece so that is where we decided to explore. I researched the most cost-efficient ways of lodging and travel. I purchased a euro rail pass and had it sent home to my dad's house since we were changing cities once or even twice a week and there was no telling when it would get to us. I dropped about $2000 on those passes, a fortune in tour wages. Dad mailed them to us, and go figure, they got lost in the mail.

We stayed an extra day in Rome hoping the passes would show up. Plus, there is so much to see in Rome that a fourth day was not wasted. Unfortunately, the euro rail passes never showed. We moved on saving our receipts. After our holiday was over, I mailed in mine and had forgotten all about the lost euro rails when two years later I received a refund check!

Other ways that I tried to reduce the cost of our holiday preceding a three-month break, with only unemployment to scrape by, was staying in hostels and we would only eat out for one meal. The Rome hostel was nice enough and had a shared bathroom for the floor we stayed on. We splurged for our own room which had two twin beds. We would come home exhausted from walking all over the city to eat PB &J in bed and pass out to do it all over again the next day.

This is not my husband's idea of a holiday or how to do sightseeing. I cram as much as possible into each day like a crazy woman with my check list and the thought that I may never come here again. His idea is to sit on a beach. He humors me, for a while. My compromise this trip was to do heavy sightseeing for the first half of the trip in Italy and Greece and finish with a week sitting on Greek beaches.

I have always kept a journal from the time I could write. I kept up this habit until after the Japan, Asia, Australia tour. I lapsed for most of the remaining tour years, especially with repeat state side tours except when we went to Europe. Even though I was not diligent with writing my experiences, I still dragged around that 1000 things to see before you die journal much to Edward's dismay. I have dragged Edward to a lot of expensive spots that he had no interest in seeing as I continued trying for my checklist and dopamine rushes.

Years later after my touring days I had forgotten about this journal and check list until I started going through photos for our photo frame in the living room. Out of curiosity I flipped to the check list to see if I had inadvertently done anything else on the list since 2008. We had climbed Kilimanjaro, so I happily checked that off. I told Edward it had been on the check list and his response was, "If I'd known it was on the list, I would have known it was a bad idea!" Then my journal mysteriously disappeared, again.

We finished our Europe tour in Dublin Ireland before we set out for our Roman Holiday. What do you do with four, 50-pound suitcases for three weeks? You can check them in for holding at the airport for a fee of course. This left us with two back packs for 3 weeks. There was a lot of washing and drying our cloths in the sink. We also packed all our oldest clothes and discarded these across Italy and Greece. I was tickled that I was leaving a trail of old undies across Europe.

Europe was a wonderful experience. It is all a bit of a blur and I'm glad I have the pictures and a journal to remember it by. As the Europe tour was coming to a close it was time to discuss what Edward and I were doing next in our tour careers. I was finishing eight years on tour, and he was finishing ten. We knew getting off the road was going to be in the semi-near future. We had finally made it overseas to Southeast Asia, Australia, and Europe. We decided to do the new show because that is where the crew makes the most money. Crew members are unionized but only when they work in the United States. If we were going to eventually start a new life, it was time to seriously start saving.

Having decided on the new show we were faced with the daunting task of getting all our stuff back to either home or the new show. As head carpenter and skate sharpener, Edward has two crates. I had been squirreling stuff away in his crates for years. Those crates would stay with the Underwater Fantasy show, and not go to the new show. So now we had two adult size crates to empty and mail home from Europe. Could we have planned this any better?

That was an expensive undertaking, and I could not throw out or let go of anything, I had to keep it all. Edward often exasperated would ask, what are you going to do with all these different collections? I collected dolls and masks from different countries, coasters, bottles, bottle caps, money from around the world, and shot glasses. Just to name a few. Many years later we bought a house and in the game room Edward has built the display wall to end all displays. This is where all the collections are housed!

Of everything we mailed home, only one box was completely lost, another showed up and was missing a few things after it had been 'inspected', like Edward's favorite snowboard jacket. When we finally did fly home after tour, Edward almost got detained. On our travels, we had gone to check point Charlie in Berlin. They offer stamps in your passport as a souvenir. Apparently, it's illegal to have anything stamped in an active passport except entry and exit stamps. They let me skate through security at the airport, but they took Edward into a private room, grilled him, and threatened full body searches. They berated his lack of judgement for the souvenir stamps and an hour later let him go! Eventually everything and everyone made it home and it was onto the new show for our final round of East and West Coast US.

Chapter 48
Backstabbing

Our comic relief, Slapstick, good natured cartoon Muppet grew a set of teeth after touring with us for five years. I do not know if he was tired of being the butt of everyone's jokes or maybe the stress of a hard won and harder to keep girlfriend that strung him along with boyfriends at home got to him. Perhaps since he was good friends with the company manager, he thought he finally wielded some power. Whatever minute bit of power he thought he had, he certainly lost our respect and friendship.

Birmingham, England. Another awesome Halloween party at an English pub. Edward had taken old spongy stretching matts, painted them black and attached dollar store lights. Instant robot from an imaginary, unnamed, awesome eighties type movie. I made a blue dress with wide hem line, painted my face green, wore a red cap with a giant toothpick going through my head and Edward affixed a giant sheet of plastic around my face making me an adult size martini with my face as the olive. Drinks required at least three connected straws to reach my mouth.

We were making our rounds and I left Edward talking to Slapstick's girlfriend. Slapstick was off talking to the company manager and with the addition of alcohol must have turned a paranoid, jealous shade of green. He marched over to Edward and accused him of smearing his name. Edward waved this off. Slapstick made more remarks and then left for the manager's table. Here he proceeded to hurl insults and slander. I overheard these remarks and reported back to Edward. The next time Slapstick came to harass Edward he saw red. Edward told him to leave him alone and when he gets that warning growl in his voice you do not mess with him.

Edward picked him up by the throat to make him shut up and be heard. He held him there. He later said that he knew this was inappropriate behavior but could not get Slapstick to see reason. Edward knew he was in control and had not completely lost his temper because he could have made it much worse. Edward put him down and we left. This was not the end of things.

Slapstick had the company manager's ear and concocted an elaborate story about trying to steal his girlfriend. In short, Slapstick tried to get Edward fired. There are always arguments and sometimes even fights when you live and work so closely with people. It never gets to the point of trying to get someone fired. That was a new low.

The boss took each of them into his office and asked for their stories. Edward was honest and admitted to what he had done. Several other people corroborated Edward's story including Slapstick's girlfriend. No one's story matched Slapstick. Edward's job was safe but Slapstick's friendship of five years with us, was over. As years rolled by social media connects us all. He kept in touch with my brother, and I see updates. He occasionally writes and sometimes I respond but it is like he doesn't understand why the friendship imploded.

Chapter 49
Mischief Unmanageable

At front of house (or audience side) the crew guys often got bored with the monotony of the show, but sometimes if they watched closely on three show day, they would get little, quirky treats as we changed things up to keep *ourselves* entertained. Occasionally my puffer fish would signal the guys running the motors upstage left with the help signals from Team America.

Eva loved to flirt with the dog's nose at the end of Beach Dolls, almost to the point of pornography. She was very possessive about her dog time. So, one Saturday three of us during free time, join hands around her and played ring around the Rosie. At first, she was mad at not being able to get to the dog, but finally she relented and laughed at our ploy. She would get her revenge.

For the last show of the season, there were extra special pranks. Edward wore a black cowboy hat in the traffic number instead of his fedora. In finale, instead of four cowboys and cowgirls, there were four car drivers minus their cars. Looking out of place like something from Men in Black. The toy soldiers would sometimes have war flashbacks and reenactment.

On some random occasions, Robots would fall over when vanquished by the space toy, but it was not a peaceful death as they would proceed to have dying convulsions while lying on the ice. These death spasms would continue well past the point of rigor mortis. We would drag out our death scenes for these lowly characters that the audience did not care about. This amused us to no end, and we might have done it on a more regular basis if one crew guy hadn't started whining about it being 'Costume abuse'. I don't know how it's any different than the four of us who lay dead on the ice for two and a half minutes while the remainder of the scene plays out. Isn't that also costume abuse? Or just part of the choreography?

In the second to last number in Toys on Ice, four of the beach dolls were back up dancers for a singing penguin toy. Sometimes the backup singers would have a staring match with the pyro guy. This would creep out the pyro guy who would double check to see if we had stopped with our Fem-bot stares.

Before the robots entrance they would perform different songs, works of art, or something new every day for the minions who exited the ice. The little change ups kill the monotony of three show day. By third year, I performed so many different understudies that I was hardly in my normal show for those five to six shows. My rock mate would ask, "So, how many shows you gonna be in the rock this weekend?"

I made the art of falling a new mission of mine in my big blow fish costume in Under Water Fantasy on Ice. Of course, we were not supposed to deliberately fall in costume, or ever. But on special occasions I had perfected the flying swan dive where I landed on the cushioned fish face in a belly flop and slid across the ice. It usually brought tears of laughter to my fellow tank fish and tears of frustration if the performance director caught me.

The albatross had a flying scene, and the carpenters would clip him into his harness, and he would get raised up backstage. The albatross gave big lip to the crew all the time. So, one day they strung him up, so he was only two feet off the ground and beat him back and forth like a piñata. His costume is very padded, he was fine, the only thing that suffered was his ego.

Edward referred to my characterization of the blow fish as a big shaggy dog and I would perform what he called the ooga booga dance. I asked him how he knew what my dance moves looked like, since he was the man behind the curtain. That's when I learned that he could see my shadow when dancing near his curtain. This delighted me and I would try to perform novel dance moves in my fat fish for his curtain preview. My blow fish antics certainly did not stop there. Given enough free time between dialogue anything can happen and usually did.

My favorite memory from the tank scene was when we took a small fish and stuffed it in the bubbling treasure chest. The performance director came backstage to the ladies' makeup room at intermission and was laughing so hard she was crying as she called me out. She said that was hysterical, but don't ever do it again! Got a freebie on that one.

Another scene saw the star fish faint. The blow fish comes knee sliding across the ice, collides with the star fish and rolls over her, after checking for a pulse the puffer fish performs CPR. This one they caught on tape and played it closing night when Edward and I were moving to another show.

On my final show Holiday Celebrations, Edward nicknamed me the 'bad zombie'. We had started watching Lost and at the end of each episode there is a little red robot and a bunch of children say, 'bad robot'. He took this and applied it to my zombie character that I had created for the Halloween number. My zombie was always playing pranks and tricks on the other zombies. But after a year of the same show track and the wish to leave the road, I did become a bit of a zombie. I was losing the joy of performing and wished for my next life.

This brings to light the dangers of staying on the same show or in the same show track for too long. It is easy to go through the motions on auto pilot. But it shows. There is an energy when a performer is really acting out the part. As my body hurt more often and the excitement of exiting the road grew closer, I was more and more a zombie doing a job, waiting for the next phase of life.

Chapter 50
Peru

6/7/10

After our final East coast show with Holiday Celebrations on a Sunday in Jacksonville, FL, Edward loaded out of the arena for three hours and then we were off to Miami, a four-hour drive and a cheap, flea bag motel by the airport. By the time we got in, Edward had about two hours before his plane left, he flew Miami, Bogotá, and Lima. I flew Miami, Atlanta, and Lima. I got in about 11 pm and neither of our airport pickups were where they said they'd be, so much for the best laid plans.

I started the trip off right by almost leaving my debit card in the ATM machine. The machine sucks the card in after giving you cash and does not beep impatiently for you to take your card. Luckily, the Good Samaritan behind me got my attention and gave me my card back. The taxi drivers get in your face and hound you until you finally submit to shut them up. I agreed to what I thought was 20 soles (conversion rate is three soles to one dollar), only to be swindled and informed no 20 dollars, 40 soles. I got in around midnight and slept for three hours.

Our first day started with a 3 am pickup. We drove through Lima to the bus station and got our bus tickets to Nazca, slept on the bus for seven hours only to wake to the horrifying sounds of Alvin and the chipmunks on the bus TV. When we got to the tiny bus station in Nazca, there was no pickup for us, again. Thankfully the information desk was extremely informative, they'd never heard of the tour group that was supposed to pick us up, but they called around until they found it.

Our package for Nazca included a day hotel, a beautiful little oasis from the dusty, desert town. We took a flight over the Nazca lines in a tiny plane.

There were all sorts of aerial drawings, a hummingbird, arrow, alien, and more. The little plane did fast circles to each side so that everyone got an equal look. Between the spinning and diesel smell I began to feel nauseated. By the end, I had to close my eyes and was happy to exit the plane upon landing.

We had a brief rest at our day hotel and then off to a tour of the burial grounds. The desert's dry wind preserved these bones so well, that the clothes and hair are still intact. This was followed by what is comparable to a high school presentation of how they used to mine for gold. It was complete with homemade sound affects as the guy pretends to crush rocks with a plastic hammer and encouraged us to buy his jewelry. Back to the day hotel for dinner and back on the bus. Lack of sleep, buses, constant on the go, after a long tour was adding up to the typical Maddie type vacation.

We spent the night on the bus, about an eight-hour trip to Arequipa. We were moving south through Peru. Arequipa is known as the white city. Our Incan trail hike date was pushed earlier due to the floods in Feb. So, with only one day in Arequipa, we didn't have enough time to visit the Colca Canyon. We did walk all over the city.

The Plaza de Armas, which is the central town square, was pretty with its white buildings and fountain in the middle. We visited some historic homes and churches, but my favorite was Santa Catarina. This used to be a convent that sits on five acres in the middle of the city and is considered its own city; like the Vatican. Once it housed 400 nuns now there are only about 30. It is brightly colored with fountains and gardens and the rooms have been left as the nuns would have lived in the past.

For lunch, we bravely tried ceviche. It looked like a giant fishing expedition in my bowl, each time the spoon came out there might be a tentacle or a fish. The fish is raw but the vinegar-citrus that it is marinated in seems to rubberize it. The dish is served cold. Edward liked it, I did not. I am all about raw and slimy sushi but not ceviche. That afternoon we took a bus tour of the surrounding areas. You could call this a tour of Peruvian buses.

We went to a place with a pleasant view of the valley and three mountains. One of which is still an active volcano that goes off every 300 years; apparently, it's due soon. At this house, they also showed us how some of the local fruit is grown and the guinea pig called cuy, which are a culinary delicacy in Peru. Another of our stops was to see lamas and alpacas. As soon as I was in spitting distance, the largest male lama took aim. We made it out to the water mill and then called it a night. After experimental food for lunch, we settle on pizza as a safe bet for dinner.

The next morning saw us on the bus to Puno. Now we were traveling east and north. Puno is 12,556 ft in elevation. I have never been affected by altitude like this, I took a few steps off the bus and my heart was double time. Only having one evening in Puno, we dropped our stuff at the hotel and took a boat tour on Lake Titicaca to the floating islands. These were quite different than the ones in Cambodia. They were clean and brightly dressed. Originally to avoid paying taxes, the people would take the reeds that grow long out of the water and anchor them, then they would pile layer after layer on top to create their floating islands.

Each island has a president and if there is a disagreement they just cut away and create their own island. They seemed like happy, carefree people. That high up we didn't have much energy, so we ate dinner and, in the rain, went to the main plaza when everyone lost power. While we looked for dinner, Edward and I both had crushing headaches, our legs were so heavy we could barely lift them and within minutes of sitting on the hotel bed we had both passed out. It was not until the next day we realized we had been experiencing altitude sickness.

Back on the bus the next morning headed to Cusco. The bus made a few sightseeing stops along the way. Our first stop was to Pukara a tiny town with a museum where we learned about Pre-Inca and Inca history. Edward was not feeling well for most of the day, the altitude sickness was still dogging us. Toward the end of the day, like a true couple we traded, and it was my turn to be plagued with lingering mountain sickness. Our next stop was a picture stop at La Raya, where we posed with an alpaca and purchased an alpaca rug. At the lunch buffet I tried purple potatoes and alpaca. Alpaca was okay, a bit tough, the purple potatoes had a different texture, denser and spongier but appetizing. We enjoyed a demonstration of local dancing, ruins in Raqchi, and a beautiful church in Andahauaglillas.

When we arrived in Cusco, we met up with Dad and his girlfriend at our Cusco hotel. We were all feeling sanctimonious since our hotel was in a convent. We had dinner at the Fallen Angel after escaping the nuns. The tables were bathtubs filled with fish and topped with glass. Both Dad and I started feeling altitude effects and hurried home to bed. Up early the next day, Edward and I were a little better, but Dad was worse for the wear and needed some supplemental oxygen. He decided to stay behind for the hike and meet us in Machu Picchu in four days. And so, we were off on our hike.

Chapter 51
Engagement or Bust

Our hike started with a three-hour drive to Kilometer 82. They said the first day was the easiest and flattest. I think the first day was just to break you in, and for the record it is not flat; undulating maybe. We saw the ruins of Llaytapa and the guard station of Wallabamba. The porters with their huge packs flew past us in their sandals, laughing and talking the whole way. The food was good, there was a lot of it, and more tea than a Boston tea party. At dinner, a tarantula joined us. Our tent was slightly down hill and all night our sleeping bags would slide down to the corner. That first night I had stomach cramps and Montezuma's revenge was not far behind. Montezuma is an old friend, but I did not expect to see him outside of Mexico. I can literally say I have now pooped all over the Inca trail; marked it and done.

Day two and I wanted to die. We hiked straight up for five hours. No switch backs like Fuji. It was straight up with giant uneven steps and that would have been doable, but we went up to 13,779 ft! Five steps stop and breathe, like I had been running a marathon. I saw a 60-year-old man pass me bye. Got to the top and heard his 60-year-old wife bragging. Both of which were great for my morale as I huffed and puffed. This was the highest point of the hike, the so-called dead woman's pass because a woman had actually died there! The next day our guide told us he didn't like to see my face, it's supposed to be vacation, Edward's response was "I see that face every morning!"

On the way down, no one could catch us. Guess that is where those skater thighs pay off, over developed quads, underdeveloped hamstrings. Edward calls them my Super Woman thighs. We collapsed by 3 pm! They woke us up for tea, which we did not want, but knew we couldn't sleep all afternoon. We were traveling with a nice group of two families from Argentina and one couple from Brazil. The youngest son would run around all day like a puppy not realizing the amount of energy that it expends; then he gets to the dinner table and looks as if he might collapse.

By day three, we were adjusting. We gave my pack to the porter for a fee and walked the ten hours. Our bodies were sore but managing better. In retrospect, I wish I had given up my pack at the beginning. Most of that day was up and down and the second half was all downhill. We saw many ruins that day: Runkuraquy, perhaps a resting place for the pilgrimage to Machu Piccu, Sayacmarca with balconies, and finally with our camp in sight a stop at Puyupatamarca with the best view of the valley and mountains. It was atop huge agricultural steps.

At this camp, there were hot showers! The showers were disgusting but still, a hot shower and no clean clothes in sight. The camp site also had a 'restaurant' which equated to beer, coke and water for purchase. One beer was all it took at this altitude. There were more ruins behind the camp that were believed to have the fountain of youth. Previous travelers used to bath in the waterfall that is now covered in lilies.

Finally, day four, the end is in sight. Up at 3 am this time because the porters needed to pack up and get to the 5 am train. At that hour in the morning, I can't think and they're banging on the tent telling me to hurry up. We waited to start until 5:30 and then the two-hour hike took us only an hour to reach the Sun Gate. And there below us was Machu Picchu. Another 45 minutes saw us in Machu Picchu and rounding a corner we ran into Dad and his girlfriend. Our guide for the whole trip took us on a two-hour tour of Machu Picchu. Dad and I compared bathroom tales because there is nothing like a cleanse for vacation. Edward found out there was a train and I continued to hear "There was a train? We could have taken a train!" For the duration of our lives.

During the whole tour I was looking for a good place to pop the question. Originally, I had wanted to do either of the two extra climbs. There is one that takes two hours and gives the best view of Machu Picchu and the other has more ruins to see. Both were long and straight up and thankfully Edward said he physically could not. Plan B was on the highest point in Machu Picchu, the sun dial, but at the end of our private tour the tourists were swarming in like ants and the sun dial was over run. Dad went for a bathroom break, and we left them for some privacy.

On the front side of Machu Picchu is a less walked trail and a splendid view of the valley below. Both Edward and I were exhausted by this point. I asked him to sit with me and he said no because his feet hurt. I asked him to please sit with me, he said that made his foot pain worse and proceeded to start pacing, I said you are being difficult, and he finally sat down. Then I cried, blubbered, and barely got out, "I want to spend the rest of my life with you, will you marry me?" He tried to give me the correct hand, but I put the ring on the wrong finger anyway and did not realize until hours later. He was a little annoyed and said, "The man is supposed to ask. I've been waiting six years to ask you, but you did not seem ready or interested in marriage." I told him this was my way of saying I was ready, and I had recently been acting uninterested so I could surprise him. The surprise attempt had failed as he had found the ring that morning when looking for my requested Imodium. I was getting upset and asked if this made him happy? He turned around and kissed me saying, "My little wife."

Then we told Dad, our guide, and anyone who spoke English or stopped to listen to me. By this time, we were tired and hungry, so we headed down to Aguas Calientes, the cute little town at the valley of Machu Picchu. At this point, I could have eaten anything, so I ate guinea pig! It tasted like roasted chicken. It was prepared by roasting the creature whole, it came out with eyes and teeth intact. With sauce and cuy (guinea pig) smeared on my face, I asked Edward if he wanted some and he replied, "I don't eat rodent!"

The train back to Cusco was not until evening so we walked around, had massages, dinner with a champagne toast and finally the train. Nothing is ever simple, the train track was not completely fixed from the floods, so it was a train, to a bus, to a van and finally at 2 am we took a hot shower and collapsed in a blissful hotel bed.

The next day we had brunch at our favorite restaurant so far. It was an all-day breakfast place called Jacks. Milkshakes and eggs, breakfast of champions. We went to the Inca Museum and walked all over the town of Cusco. We even hiked up and down Sacsayhuaman ruins (pronounced for the tourists as Sexy Woman) which had a splendid view of the city. There was a festival that went on all day, and we would repeatedly run into the small parade that circled the city. We finished the day with dinner overlooking the plaza and back to our sanctuary hotel at the convent.

Edward and I flew to Lima the next day and in true Maddie vacation style were exhausted. We took a trip to the central square and walked around for a bit. Edward noticed a guy following me, or more correctly my purse, and we called it a night. The buildings in Lima seemed more modern and it was a big, dirty city. Emissions codes were not the same and the smog became nauseating.

I had the midnight flight out and this time went through Mexico to Miami, got into Miami and I waited for Edward who arrived two hours later. Why did we fly separately? I used frequent flier miles and then found Edward a cheap flight, but from now on we will travel together. We drove six hours to my mom's house and were happy to be home.

Chapter 52
Making a Break for It

While in my master's program and traveling for clinicals, we had an old tour friend visit and stay in our trailer. The dog and cat took full advantage of him. He had to share the pull-out couch and they had their own personal snuggle buddy for the week. One morning he said, "It makes me so happy to see show people really make it after tour." Being very goal oriented I had not thought of it but there is a resounding truth to his words. When you become a lifer on tour, how do you switch tracks and move on or stand still? What is next when all you have ever known is skating?

For me, the name of the game has always been realizing the goal. This was a slow process for me. In 2004, on Underwater Fantasy on Ice, I started an online business class. I had a liberal arts associate degree prior to joining the company Family Fun on Ice and thought I could work toward a Bachelor's. I had a notion that I could have my own beach bar, I know how to drink so that translates right? Dad said he would put a down payment if I gave him grandkids so that was a dead end. He also left articles about freezing my eggs on the dining room table when I was home on breaks, and I had mentioned career first. I made it through one online course in 2004 and decided at 24 I would rather act 21 with the 18-year-olds so that was the end of school for a while. At that point, I was not ready to grow up. Five years later it was time.

I toyed with different career choices over the next few years. I was accepted into a PA program, but I was not ready to leave tour. My favorite physical therapist talked me out of that route. And finally, I had a conversation with my mom about her career. She said she could see me being a nurse anesthetist or a teacher. No contest there and so I had my goal.

Now how to make that happen? We left Underwater Fantasy after we finally traveled the European tour. We knew I needed online prerequisites and we needed to strategically save money to leave the road. The best place for Edward to maximize his earnings was a new show. Our plan was to join Holiday Celebration for two years and save money while I completed my prerequisites for nursing school online. This would get me to ten years on the road and leaving as I turned thirty, seemed like everything was falling into place.

I began taking online courses that I would need for a bachelor's in nursing. Taking one course at a time, each about five weeks, I calculated it would take me about a year and a half to complete the basics. Then I just had to find a school that would take my online credits and my associate degree. While I'm at it, a scholarship would be nice too. Edward and I began to act like real adults saving money and I would spend a majority of my time studying, doing homework and taking tests. Adulting at its finest, but did I really want to grow up?

Sounds so simple. Fighting for internet, noisy hotels, wishing I could go party rather than study. Let me tell you the issues that come from learning anatomy and physiology from a book and computer. My nursing friends still will not let me live down my pronunciation of petechiae, which I pronounced like a chia pet. I have the occasional candid picture of sitting at Edward's crate between shows in sweatpants, make up stains on my face, studying between shows.

The plan was in place, and I was putting in the demanding work, but the issue is in the details. I initially had my heart set on University of Buffalo. I could get my BA in nursing, work in Buffalo, and be a shoe in for the CRNA program there, right? So, I based my prerequisites on this plan. We even looked at houses in Buffalo between East and West coast tours. But this route was not meant to be. UB would not accept my associates as a whole degree which meant extra years and a wait list to get into their nursing program. I turned my eyes homeward to Rochester. We could live with my dad, save money while going to school, and work a few years before I went back for my masters in anesthesia.

There were two schools within walking distance to his house. One had so many extra prerequisites and would not accept half of my online classes. This would mean an extra year to my plans. The other accepted all my online classes and my associate degree. School number two offered me a scholarship and was a quarter mile from my dad's house. I was accepted into the program, and I was sold.

Toward the end of East Coast Holiday Celebrations, I began to get injured more often. I was out for a long stretch and frustrated. I cried and begged Edward to leave that year rather than tour one more year. My logical prince charming talked me into sticking to the plan. I could continue my online education while also making money. In the long run, this was the smart move, and I am glad he talked me out of leaving on a negative note.

In 2011, I ended my ten-year career with Family Fun on Ice. This was the end for me, but Edward stayed another year and a half to support me in nursing school. It was a hard first year apart with me studying and him working. Over the school's winter break I did work for his ice show and got a chance to put my skates and makeup on again. I loved playing an evil female villainess and it was a mental break from my studies.

It was so easy to slip back into the show routine. After learning new roles and new choreography, it was a no brainer. I missed the ease of this life and the comradery of a tour family. But when you live the life for two weeks you only remember the positives. I had, after all, acquired my spice rack, oven, and pets. Edward did not technically agree to the cat, but I knew the puppy and kitten needed to grow up together to get along. Edward still calls him my cat. Our sweet but hyper puppy was difficult to raise alone. The puppy loved to chew on everything including drywall. I sprayed it with dog repellent and he ate that too. I would often call Edward with tears of frustration about the newest member of the family.

The old skating life seemed so easy in the face of my nervous sweats while at clinicals. I would stand outside the patient's room, sweating and nauseous. I did not want to go in there. I did not want to talk to let alone assess the patient. I was so uncomfortable that I knew if something did not change, I would have to pick another career.

After break work with Edward's ice show, I took a part time job as a patient care tech at a local hospital. That cured me of my shyness in the clinical world. Edward was horrified with the stories I would bring home and once again I was not sure this was the path for me. I had to tell myself that this was a steppingstone to my ultimate goal and like time, I moved forward.

Edward's last year he got a gig flying in and out of Rochester every week. They would work him so hard that he would come home and sleep until he returned to tour. That job lasted three months and finally we were both done with tour life. Ten years on the road for me and twelve for him. At the ages of 30 and 34, we had finished our first careers.

Chapter 53
Mexico, the Final Round

7/10–8/30/2010

I've said it many times, I hate Mexico. To be more specific, I hate Mexico City; there are many other very nice areas in Mexico, such as Cancun, if memory serves from my childhood trip in the nineties, and Cabo San Lucas. My feelings toward Mexico City are due to the many times and many disasters that happen every time I'm down here. Luckily fourth time's the charm.

Travel day didn't start off well for me. I had three flights: Gainesville-Atlanta-Dallas-Mexico City, all 45 minutes apart. Due to the weather in FL and GA my first flight took off 35 minutes late. I ran to the gate and watched my second flight take off. The only flight in the whole Atlanta airport that did take off on time, go figure. I then played ping pong between Delta and American since my flights had been booked on two different airlines. After getting on a morning flight from Dallas to Mexico with American, Delta told me I was on standby for the evening flight to Dallas. They were fairly sure the connecting flights wouldn't make it. The flight out of GA was delayed so long that they were full and so being eighth in the standby line, I did not make the cut.

Then I stood in line for an hour and Delta gave me a little bag with travel deodorant, t-shirt, detergent, and the usual. They also kindly gave me a free night at the Crown Plaza. I got to the hotel and stood in line for another hour. After washing my only set of clothes in the sink and wondering where my luggage was, I got a short night's sleep. A seasoned traveler should know better and from that day forward I always traveled with extra undies in my carry on.

Day two of my travel day went off without a hitch. Somehow my luggage had made all its connecting flights even though it was physically impossible for me to make my flights. Our Mexican promoters were waiting for me, so I had an uneventful ride to the hotel. I relaxed the rest of the day and then the endless cycle of rehearsals and shows started. We had a long and grueling week of rehearsals (rehearsals are always long and grueling) and since we are without our line captains, who oversee the skaters, teaching, relaying notes, and generally keeping everyone mildly under control at work, I volunteered to be the fourth training line captain. A job I had done on past shows. This makes rehearsals even harder since you stay after and come in early to teach. Even if you are not in a show number, you still need to be on your feet and paying attention.

Edward and I were at that time thinking of buying a house in August on our next break. We were trying to save money. This kept both of us out of trouble since we have seen most of the city and do not feel the need to go out and party quite as much. There were also plenty of opportunities to pick up odd jobs at work. The ice in this arena is called tank ice because our company makes it. There are many arenas around the world that are not set up to have their own ice floors. No ice, no problem for us. One of the many things that keep our company's monopoly on the touring ice show is that we can make and travel our own ice equipment.

Ice watch is an extra odd job that paid $80 a night. If one were inclined after all day rehearsals or six days of shows, you could sign up to 'watch' the ice. Sounds boring, but every 2 hours you get up and check the controls and record all the numbers, while keeping a radio near your ear in case the alarms go off and the ice begins to melt. Perfect practice for future nights on call. I also signed up to count tickets because even though the arena has a ticket counting machine apparently, it's still about 2% or more off and so we count to double check, this pays a whopping $10.

Open ice for practice was also a hot commodity. Wrong time of year, ice time was in short supply. And if you were not walking distance from the hotel, it was a fight to get on the first practice sign-up list. One solution was to sign up for an ice watch. Besides the extra money you could get a load of laundry done without having to hound the people in front of you to move along and you could skate to your heart's content. I loved skating after hours with all the lights being out except the minimal sponsor lights that surround the arena floor. These lights cast a surreal shadow across the ice. I loved that no one else was in the arena except Edward and me.

On Toys on Ice, one entrepreneurial individual would stay late at the arena and had his own laundry service. He would do your laundry for a fee. With only one washer and dryer for the cast and crew to share, which was utilized during show hours for show laundry, there was not a lot of laundry opportunity. Rather than waste a precious day off sitting in a laundro-matt that may cost you a cab ride with a suitcase in tow. Paying someone else to do your laundry was fantastic.

There are several courtesies that were often overlooked when doing laundry. First of all keep it moving. A lot of people desire to do laundry. Second, if it is done maybe find the person who has the laundry and politely ask them to move their belongings along the line. Although why you need to hunt them down and baby sit, I don't know. Third, do not take other people's wet laundry out of the washer and place it on top of the dryer but not in the dryer to begin your own laundry.

These niceties were ignored, and one poor crew man lost his mind just a little. Milo came to move his laundry from the washer to the dryer only to find that the laundry businessman had taken his wet laundry and left it sitting on top of the dryer. He wrote an angry tirade in note form and pinned it to the board. The best part was the threat that Milo would 'wee all over the clean clothes' if this ever happened again. The letter was removed from the board before the skaters arrived but remains a giggle worthy memory of tour. Eventually Milo was able to get the crew their own washer and dryer for his show.

Often on our explorations of Mexico over the years, there was never a bathroom when you needed one. Since the need for me arose quite frequently it was a constant issue. I would try to perfect the art of holding it until movement was unbearable. This level of excruciating need became lovingly labeled 'Mexico pee-pee' by Edward. When you must go and are in so much pain that your eyes are tearing up and there is no restroom in sight, this is what it means to say Mexico pee-pee. I was not opposed to dropping a squat but, in the city, there are not a lot of trees or privacy.

We opened the show in Mexico and things seemed to be going off without a hitch. A friend of mine was out so I was enjoying playing two of my favorite roles the Big Bad Gal and the Cowgirl. Then one day old athletic age struck. My right hip seized up so bad I was in pain walking. Luckily, I did not have to deal with hospitals or language barrier. The promoter here took me to a doc who knew his stuff. I guess there was inflammation in my hip causing grinding and irritation. The doc said I need to warm up every time before I get on the ice. Well, my usual routine was come in as close to show time as possible and do a show. I had a mid-show 45-minute break, more breaks between shows, and a walk home. Apparently, I cannot do that anymore.

That means a lot of warmups on multiple show days. The doc gave me a shot in my hip and some pain meds along with four days off. After missing the end of show week two, I came in to do my last show as the Big Bad Gal and the Cowgirl. Then I taught my replacement those roles. I had politely begged to continue doing these roles until my friend was back, but I guess everyone has their lane to stay in.

Guadalajara happened so fast I wasn't sure we were even there. We closed Mexico City on a Wednesday and hopped a plane early Thursday morning. The crew got off the plane and went to load in. They continued to load in Friday and we opened Friday night. We preformed three shows Sat and Sun. During such a short-split week, all you want is to get in your room and relax, but good luck getting it. The hotel was beautiful with several pools, open, grassy lands, patios, and lots of mosquitoes.

The staff was another story. The key maker did not work, the backup key maker was broken, and this meant nobody could get a key. You could barely get them to give you your room number and if you were successful with that you went to your room and prayed there was a maid to let you in. Or in my case someone asks you to watch their suitcase and leaves you to go for a two-hour lunch.

The week did not progress well for me since I took my rings off on the 45 min bus ride from the arena to put lotion on my hands and then like a space cadet got up and left them on the bus. Or even better I put my passport in my backpack and then put my backpack on the luggage truck. You would never know I had been touring for nine years. One of the rings was my understudy engagement ring. While mine was being made and mailed to FL, Edward bought me a pretty amethyst to hold its place.

During our summer break before Mexico, Edward took me to look at engagement rings. I looked around and said diamonds are boring. Edward's response was, "Who says that?" And then he worriedly wondered what kind of ring I wanted. He saw a beautiful sapphire, my birth stone and asked, "What about that one?" It was perfectly me. The other ring, I tried to leave on the bus was a graduation gift from my mom's family. I lucked out both times, the promoter told me the luggage truck was coming to the arena later that day with my passport and she got my rings back. Goodbye Guadalajara and hello Monterey, finally a well-earned three days off for the skaters and two for the crew.

By the time we arrived in Monterey, there was a travelers warning, if you could possibly avoid going to Monterey, then do not go. All foreigners had a midnight curfew. We were in a suburban area and our stomachs had missed American food, so we ate at Carl's Jr, Chili's, or Subway for the entire week. It was extremely hot here, so we relaxed by the pool and had a luau for a friend's bachelorette party. After that, we did our shows and went home without any travel day hiccups, neck braces, or trips to the hospital. I would call this round a win.

Arriving to FL on break, Mom picked us up and we went for dinner. I had changed my home address to Mom's house in FL because there is no state tax! In a last-minute decision Edward decided to drive the truck to TX to pick up his stuff at his Dad's auto shop and meet me in NY. I hopped a plane the next morning home. Dad picked me up and our three-week break flew by. One of my best friends got married that weekend near Lake Champlain, beautiful, but it was the last straw in my decision to have an outdoor wedding. Both Edward and I came home bitten by mosquitos.

On our whirlwind time off, we looked at houses in Buffalo and were disappointed in what was available near the school in our price range. I had fallen in love with a house online while in Mexico, 4 bed, 2 bath, wood floors, brick, looked like a cross between my old Richmond house and Dad's current house. Well, we found out why it was only $98,000, it is dangerous to walk outside your door. Besides UB did not work out to be the nursing school for me.

Chapter 54
The Final Chapter

Planning a wedding is hard. Especially when you are in a different city every week, doing online school and are on a budget. Everything that needed to be done in person would have to be crammed into the first weeks home or have Dad signing paperwork for us. And considering our disagreement on simple colors this did not seem like a good idea. Trying to get an opinion from my groom was like pulling uninterested teeth. Can we agree you like blue? Okay then we have a color scheme. The harder I tried to keep it simple the faster that went out the window. My original plan was a simple outdoor wedding at a park in Rochester. The brides' maids would carry sunflowers instead of bouquets. Decorations could be cheap and easy.

Ten years on the road you make a lot of friends. You can't invite everyone from every tour to your wedding. I had narrowed the list down and sent out invites. I asked those invited on my current tour to keep their invitations to themselves. Most were willing to comply, but one went straight to the girl's make-up room and began braying, I mean bragging. Needless to say, there were some hurt feelings.

Over the Christmas holidays my last year on tour, I was injured, again. Rickety old ankles would not co-operate. I went to an orthopedic specialist that told me in a condescending voice that I was too young for this much ankle damage. I don't think he sees many ice skaters. I was back in my room over Christmas while everyone else was performing, feeling sorry for myself. I called my mom who was with her sisters for the holidays.

They put me on speaker phone and excitedly asked me my wedding plans. I told them, proudly, all the planning I had done, by myself, long distance. They quickly picked me and all my ideas apart and made me realize I was hopeless and nowhere near prepared. Merry Christmas! You can't please everyone, even though it's my wedding.

The combined bachelor and bachelorette party was a huge success. Our friends took us out of town to Savannah so we would not know what was brewing. The morning we were back in Columbia, SC we were ambushed and put on a bus with everyone in bathing suits with plenty of booze. I got a giant inflatable phallus I name Ricardo and Edward got Lucy, with a perpetual look of open-mouthed shock. We drank our way down a lazy river with water fights, sunburns, and libations. We ended the day like drunken, drowned rats making a mass exodus in a public park where horrified mothers and their children looked on as Ricardo and Lucy scarred their innocent eyes. The night was ended as always in a bar that was stumbling distance from our hotel home.

I continued with my planning, and schooling, and skating. When we arrived home, Dad said that he and Mom would like to pay for the wedding. I had been planning and budgeting to pay for my own wedding because I thought that's what a modern girl does. But I would be happy for their help.

"I know you have made plans for the park, but I want you to take a look at this venue I found." He took me to the Rochester Memorial Art Gallery. The idea had never even occurred to me. And suddenly I could see it, right in the atrium with the sky lights, just like the Galleria. Dad and I would walk down the wheelchair ramp. The gallery had a little room in the back where hor d'oeuvres could be served and a large ball room that looked like something out of Harry Potter. To make it complete were the wedding photos on the grounds with larger-than-life pieces of modern artwork.

The devil is in the details. My parents generously paid for our wedding and honeymoon, but you cannot believe what a money scam a wedding is. The gallery won't let you bring in your own food, that is okay since their catered food is good. But the cater does not have a cake only a cookie tray. I was not a stickler about many things, but wedding cake was a must for me. The gallery relented with a three-dollar cutting fee. Not only did we have to pay for our cake, but every piece sliced was another three dollars! I offered to cut it myself but that would not negate the cutting fee.

I found my wedding dress online for $200, from China of course. My brother's snide remark was how good could it be for that price. I put it on, and he said, "Wow!" I paid to have it fit to me and was quite happy with my find.

I still have dreams that I want to go snowboarding in my dress on one of our big wedding anniversaries.

No family occasion is complete without its awkward moments. In the congratulatory, handshake line instead of a 'congratulations', Edward got "You never came over and fixed my windows!"

Okay, can we do that after the wedding? Or my high school best friend's parents told Edward and I.

"We thought our son would always end up with Maddie, but you're a good choice too."

Thank you?

Now, a party is not a party unless my aunt's undies make an appearance. The tour guys threw her above their heads in pair lifts, one guy got kicked out for wheelchair races down the stairwell. Edward's brother burned holes in his pants from knee slides, and someone's mother peed outside the front door. It was a true to form, all out great party. We followed the night to a bar down the street and finally I told Edward's excitable partying brother that we had to say good night.

"But why must you leave?" I could not believe I had to explain why we would want to leave.

"There are things a bride and groom do on their wedding night..." By the gaping O his mouth made, he finally got it and then we received his blessing.

The next morning, we met our families for brunch and wished our out-of-town visitors farewell. On the road, there is an old superstition that you never say goodbye. Instead, you say, "I'll see you later."

And in true tour fashion, we got married and lived happily ever after.

The End...

For now...